The Making of Modern

L'invention de la France
(with Hervé Le Bras)

The Explanation of Ideology:
Family Structures and Social Systems

The Causes of Progress:
Culture, Authority and Change

L'invention de l'Europe

For David

The Making of Modern France

Ideology, Politics and Culture

Emmanuel Todd

Translated by
Anthony and Betty Forster

Basil Blackwell

Copyright © Éditions du Seuil 1987, 1990
English translation © Basil Blackwell 1991
La Nouvelle France first published in 1988 by Éditions du Seuil,
27, rue Jacob, 75261 Paris
First published in Great Britain 1991

Basil Blackwell Ltd
108 Cowley Road, Oxford, OX4 1JF, UK

Basil Blackwell Inc.
3 Cambridge Center
Cambridge, MA 02142, USA

British Library Cataloguing in Publication Data

A CIP catalogue record for this book is available
from the British Library

Library of Congress Cataloging in Publication Data

CIP data has been applied for
ISBN 0 631 16804 4
ISBN 0 631 17948 8 (Pbk.)

Typeset in Garamond on 10/12pt.
by Hope Services (Abingdon) Ltd.
Printed in Great Britain by
T. J. Press Ltd, Padstow, Cornwall

Contents

List of Maps

Explanation of Terms

Baccalauréat	General Certificate of Education (A level)
Agrégation	Competitive examination for posts on the teaching staff of *lycées* and universities
BEPC	Brevet d'études du premier cycle
CGT	Confédération générale du travail
EDF	Electricité de France
INSEE	Institute national de la statistique et des études conomiques
Lycée	Grammar school, secondary school
MRP	Mouvement républicain populaire
RATP	Régie autonome des transports parisiens
SNCF	Société nationale des chemins de fer français

Introduction

Between 1981 and 1986 the French political system imploded. Communism ceased to be an important force, and a party of the extreme Right made its appearance. The Socialist Party changed its nature, and so did the Right. This reorganization of the French political scene was not the result of conscious political action on the part of individuals. The electors, the political militants, the executives and leaders of parties have been the victims rather than the managers of French society's evolution. The arrival in power of François Mitterrand, the recovery of the Right, the conflict between Raymond Barre and Jacques Chirac, the emergence of Jean-Marie Le Pen, the eclipse of Georges Marchais epitomize historical changes whose meaning is not grasped by the actors themselves.

The factors that determine the political choices of individuals are complex and run deep. They should be looked for in man's subconscious and in the nation's past rather than in the current programmes of political parties. French political life, as it appeared around 1978 just before the implosion, was at the same time harmonious and contentious – with its two left wings, socialist and communist, and its two right wings, the classic and the Gaullist – and it was the culminating point of a very long history. The four great ideological forces making up the political system shared the French arena in stable fashion. The Socialist Party was powerful in the south-west and north. The classic Right was dominant in its frontier strongholds of Alsace, Franche-Comté, Savoie and the Basque country, to the south-east of the Massif Central, and in the west. Gaullism and communism faced each other at the heart of the national system, in the Paris basin. This regional distribution of political forces did not come about by chance, but to understand it one must go back a very long way in France's past. The Left–Right cleavage was only partly the result of class conflicts, as Marxist theory would have it. In France's case, the birth of regional Rights and Lefts represents above all the perpetuation of very ancient religious conflicts. The struggle between Church and Revolution was only the most recent of these wars of religion. The crises of the sixteenth century were in a sense still active around 1978. The established position of the traditional Socialist Party replicated that of Protestantism and of, further back, the medieval heresies, Waldensian or Cathar. A relative newcomer, the Communist Party, was simply heir to the revolutionary atheism of the years 1793–4.

However, the conflict of Left versus Right, which illuminates the political game in France so well (just as Australian tribes also have their totemic divisions), was only secondary, as everyone well knows or feels. The confrontation between communism and socialism, doctrines opposed to each other by their fundamental values, was unavoidable and indeed ended in the elimination of the feebler entity; communism. In order to understand the division of the Left, and at the same time the corresponding, less violent but finally more obstinate division of the Right, one must go back beyond the religious conflicts of the eighteenth or even the sixteenth century. One must look to factors in social life that are even more ancient, that have been stable for more than a thousand years, well anchored in space and capable of defying time. The family systems and agrarian structures of the various regions of France came into being and stabilized themselves probably in the Roman era. Family systems nurture and transmit from generation to generation the dominant values of liberty and equality and the minority values of authority and inequality which shape France, but divide both the Left and the Right. Certain demographic and cultural indicators drawn from the most recent 1982 census confirm that these family systems are still very active. Their enduring diversity helps to explain the inequality of birth-rates and academic performance in various *départements* and regions.

So this plunge into France's most remote past is no gratuitous intellectual exercise. By measuring the deep roots of the traditional French political system – visible for the last time in 1978 in all its perfection – one can also measure the scale of the transformation that occurred between 1981 and 1986. It had taken centuries to establish ideological structures that were liquidated in five years. It was a true crisis, a fundamental historical change that took place with astonishing speed. The emergence of the Front National – a shameful event in the land of liberty and equality – was the price that had to be paid for the violence of the shock; not too high a price finally because this movement, with its lack of any ideological substance, will soon disappear.

The political transformation of the years 1981–6 (which is indeed by no means over) has not been the result of chance, any more than was the traditional political set-up. It is the result of a social transformation which has been on the same scale as the political change. Most Frenchmen are consious of the economic mutations now in train. The mid-1970s saw the onset of a genuine industrial counter-revolution, with electronics fulfilling a dream which was also a nightmare – the physical disappearance of the working class. Automation, even more than immigration, disorganized the working class between 1975 and 1985. But these upsets are only the most visible part of the crisis. The cultural revolution of the years 1965–75, brought on by the expansion of secondary education and linked to the increase of the salaried middle class, predated the economic crisis by ten years. This revolution showed up spectacularly in the sexual and demographic fields – a falling birth-rate, an increase in the number of births outside marriage, and permissiveness. This cultural crisis has killed catholicism in those French provinces still controlled by the Church around 1965.

Industrial counter-revolution and cultural revolution together have led to a social transformation of a speed and violence unprecedented in the history of France. To gauge its effect, imagine the French Revolution and the Industrial Revolution taking place *simultaneously* within the space of twenty years.

Cultural revolution and industrial counter-revolution have destabilized the French political system because they have demolished the Left–Right structure. The physical and moral disappearance of the working class has smashed the Marxist mythology of the French Left. The collapse of catholicism has left the classic Right, whose backbone it was, deprived of a doctrine. From 1965 onwards, quite apart from global electoral results at the national level, disintegration of the regional Right and Left elements has proceeded steadily. The 'Right' invades the old 'Left' regions, and vice versa; but they are a new Left and a new Right.

An analysis in depth of the traditional French political system leads to the identification of those regional family systems which are stable factors in social life. The persistence of these factors allows us to fix the limits of the transformation now in progress. The Left–Right conflict changes in meaning. The joint decline of the working class and of catholicism is dragging the classic Right and communism to their extinction. The Socialist Party and the new Right are only accidental and illegitimate heirs to the doctrines and forces which still give them their titles. Yet France is not on the verge of escaping from the historical forces of gravity. Her family systems continue to define her fundamental ideological values – the happy predominance of the principles of liberty and equality inscribed on the pediments of her *mairies*, and the maintenance, on her outer limits, of contrary minority values of authority and inequality.

France existed before the Industrial Revolution and the 1789 Revolution. She will survive the disappearance of the working class and the terminal crisis of catholicism.

PART I

THE HIDDEN FORCES

The idea of nation is at the heart of the social and economic sciences. French society, French economy, French industry, French working class – the inability of intellectuals and politicians to use certain basic concepts without a national connotation is quite remarkable. This attitude is by no means peculiar to France. Elsewhere society, economy, industry, working class will be British, German, American, Japanese. But what is a society? An assemblage of human beings living together, whose aspirations and activities are complementary and interdependent. And what is an economy? A limited version of the preceding concept – an assemblage of human beings, whose activities in the production and exchange of goods and services are complementary and interdependent. At this stage of the analysis nothing justifies assigning a size or limited area to the human group, whether society or economy. The establishment of these parameters must depend on an examination of the facts. One has to observe the social and economic behaviour of the human beings in question and discover their scale in order to define closed and homogeneous groups which can then be called society X or economy Y. Such a study has never been made, for ideology and habit have decided that the right scale is the nation. The choice was made long ago, for the book which launched political economy, Adam Smith's *The Wealth of Nations*, has an unambiguous title.[1] The date of publication was 1776. Its sociological equivalent, Émile Durkheim's *Le Suicide*, published in 1897, goes so far as to confuse nation and society almost systematically. The rate of suicide given is primarily national – French, English, Italian or Danish. Its area of definition hardly differs from that of national product per head, the indicator most used today to characterize and classify the different countries of the world.

This initial choice can be explained. It is not the result of an inevitable logic, but of a coincidence in time. The social and economic sciences on the one hand, and the modern ideal of nationhood on the other, were born in the same era, the years 1750–1900. It was therefore natural that the ideological effort involved in constructing patriotic feeling and the State should influence the first halting steps at concept-formation in sociology and economics.

Unfortunately, this initial hypothesis is often very largely wrong. The real scale of development in social, economic or even political phenomena is not always national. The nation is rarely a homogeneous and enclosed human ensemble. This discrepancy between ideal and reality is particularly clear in the case of France. Notions of 'French society', 'French economy', 'French industry', 'French working class' are to some extent myths – myths that nevertheless have their uses.

It would be unreasonable to deny the existence of national processes of political and economic regulation. There exist without doubt in France a state, a taxation system, a currency. There even exists, obviously, a government. However, one can demonstrate that social, economic and political forces, spontaneous and creative, do not have the *nation* as their natural area, as do the central systems of regulation. One can represent France as a heterogeneous and open area in which social, economic and political forces emerge, spread and establish themselves quite independently of the central power and of the overall national structure. To destroy the old model of 'national sociology' and 'national economy', one has to climb down one step in the geographical scale to observe the phenomena that show up in the *départements*. At that reduced, infra-national level, one can witness in unexpected places – often on the borders, or even outside France – the birth of social, economic, cultural and political forces. These economic forces do not have as their natural framework the 'national society', but regional, provincial, and in certain cases even foreign societies.

AN UNDERDEVELOPED CENTRE

Administrative and political centralization is a fundamental French value. It is an ideology, an essential component of the republican and Jacobin system. It is also a methodology, with a very concrete realization in a network of railways and roads radiating from Paris. The uniform administrative division of the country into *départements* has proclaimed the homogeneity of the national territory ever since the Revolution. Yet when one looks at the historical development of cultural and economic forces in the country between the Middle Ages and the last census (1982), one is struck by the social passivity of the political centre. The capital and its region never appear as the starting-point of any important cultural or economic mutation.

The literacy movement, which took the country from an oral to a written culture between the eleventh and nineteenth centuries, did not start in Paris. Nor did industrialization, a parallel but separate element in the modernization process, have the capital or its region as its point of departure. The two real poles for cultural or industrial take-off were situated elsewhere.

The first pole was within France. It was the South, to which should be added a few fringe elements to be found in the north of the country. This internal polarity gave rise to a south–north axis.

The second pole, of equal importance, was external. It was the Germanic cultural conglomerate situated to the east of France. From the medieval period onwards this exerted a ceaseless influence across vague and shifting frontiers on the whole process of French development, placing the country on an east–west axis.

So neither cultural nor economic forces have operated from Paris. But, as one would expect, the directing role of the capital manifests itself in the political sphere. The ideological divisions of French territory, which took their final form during the Revolution, have given the Paris basin a special position.

1

South and North: Two Systems

The first great cultural crises of Christianity affected France in her southern half. The religious heresies and dissents of the Middle Ages stirred up the people of the south, who at that time did not speak French. The Waldensian dissent and the Cathar heresy in the twelfth century, and the protestant reformation from the sixteenth century onwards, seem to have had little difficulty in destabilizing the provinces in the south of the country. They did not find an equivalent welcome in the north, particularly in the Paris basin. The South's special aptitude for protest must be regarded as a proof of cultural superiority.

Ideological agitation among the masses, which took a religious form at the dawn of modernity, supposes a certain level of intellectual development. The diffusion in society of theological concepts, whether simple or complex, implies an initial intellectual apprenticeship among large sections of the population. The most important element was the capacity to read and write. This essential prerequisite for ideological activity applies as much to the medieval heresies as it does to the protestant Reformation, which succeeded them on a much larger scale after a gap of three centuries.

The right to read and comment on the Scriptures in the vernacular was one of the basic demands of the Waldensians, and then of the Protestants.[1] The Cathars for their part rejected the Bible, which they considered to be the work of the Devil, like other earthly things. Yet this condemnation was also the result of reading. In Occitania, before 1300, those who could read were automatically considered by the common people to be Cathars.[2] The link between the diffusion of written culture and the progress of religious dissent is certainly very strong.

At this stage of our analysis the theological content of the doctrines is relatively unimportant. It is the simple existence of dissent, an expression of progress and cultural crisis, which matters.

Waldensian doctrine and protestantism are very close and represent two successive branches of the same current of reform, which does not break with the basic principles of Christianity. The Waldensians, having taken refuge in the Alpine valleys after the medieval persecutions, managed to survive in certain places until the sixteenth century. They then rallied to the Protestant reform movement at the synod of Chanforan in 1532.

The Cathar religion, on the other hand, was Manichean and rejected basic Christian dogmas, in particular the principle of God's unity. But these theological systems, in whatever respects they differed or resembled each other, had one element in common – the rejection of an authority and tradition, namely that of Rome.

The geography of these revolts, massive and diverse in their natures, was remarkably clear and stable in France (see map 1). The South of the country, between the Alps and the Garonne, always revealed itself as a pole of heresy, ready to question the dogma and organization of traditional catholicism. The province of Languedoc, between Toulouse and Montpellier, was always an epicentre of crisis. The geographical proximity of doctrines so metaphysically different as the Waldensian dissent and the Cathar religion, and so widely separated in time as the medieval heresies and the Protestant Reformation, is a puzzling phenomenon. An unknown factor at work in the southern part of France seems to have created a predisposition to religious activism.

Between the twelfth and seventeenth centuries northern France asserted at once her doctrinal passivity and her military power. On two occasions the Paris basin became the champion of orthodoxy.

Between 1209 and 1229 the crusade against the Albigensians brought Occitania to heel. Officially directed against the Cathars, in passing it settled accounts with the Waldensians in the region.

In the sixteenth and seventeenth centuries, the Paris basin was again the centre of support for Catholic orthodoxy. But protestantism was more powerful than the medieval heresies. Its defeat in France took a century and a half, from the Wars of Religion to the revocation of the Edict of Nantes in 1685. Once again, however, the liquidation of religious dissent was in practice a calling to heel of the South. As the dominant majority religion of the area, protestantism was suppressed in Occitania. Yet it was there, long after the persecutions of Louis XIV's reign, that Protestant groups survived, clinging to their faith. The disappearance of protestantism as the majority religion did not imply its complete elimination as an ideology. From the Reformation and the various heresies, the South retained a cultural imprint which was not wiped out by the official return of Roman catholicism. In the twentieth century the Occitanian tendency to heterodoxy remains evident in fields no longer religious, but political.

The revocation of the Edict of Nantes was both the expression and the symbol of the North's belated achievement of cultural superiority over the South, of Occitania's being overtaken by the Paris basin. The literacy rate of the North probably exceeded that of the South by about the middle of the seventeenth century. The growth of the North's cultural strength, however, was not the effect of any endogenous mechanism. It was the result of a wave of influence coming from the north-east, from the Germanic world. From the end of the sixteenth century the Paris basin benefited from its proximity to the principal centres of European development, which were situated in Germany and Flanders. The reversal

Map 1
The first crisis of catholicism:
Cathars, Waldensians and Protestants

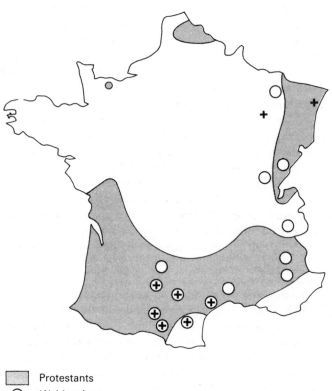

▨ Protestants
◯ Waldensians
✚ Cathars

Based on data drawn from several works. For protestantism: Mours, S. 1966: *Essai sommaire de géographie du protestantisme réformé français*. Paris: Librairie protestante; *Annuaire statistique de la France*, 1879; Deyon, S. and Lottin, A. 1981: *Les Casseurs de l'été 1566. L'iconoclasme dans le Nord de la France*. Paris. For the Waldensians: Gonnet, J. and Molnar, A. 1974: *Les Vaudois au Moyen Age*. Turin; Tourn, G. 1984: *Les Vaudois*. Turin. For the Cathars: Borst, A. 1974: *Les Cathares*. Paris.

of the cultural balance of power between the French North and South was a local expression of the general change in the European equilibrium. The continent's cultural centre of gravity passed from the South (Italy) to the North (Germany) at the time of the Protestant Reformation. The paradox of the French situation is that the Paris basin, which unlike Occitania rejected and crushed protestantism, then profited from the cultural and economic dynamism stimulated by the Reformation, simply because it was situated in the northern half of Europe.

THE FRONTIERS OF THE NORTH

The Paris basin, the historical and political heart of the nation, today no longer stands for the whole of northern France. To the north and east, provinces have been annexed which did not belong to the kingdom in the Middle Ages or the Renaissance. Flanders and Artois, Alsace and Lorraine, and Franche-Comté were all later acquisitions, made after the Wars of Religion. Most of them, bordering or even within the Germanic world, produced more or less powerful Protestant movements, which was the opposite of what happened in the Paris basin itself. So these regions constituted, from a French point of view, minority poles of cultural development, quite as dynamic as the Midi but much less large. The two most notable centres of protestantism were the Strasbourg region and the triangle Arras–Lille–Laon.

Strasbourg, an Imperial Free City and entirely German-speaking when Luther provoked the crisis in the Church, moved smoothly through a Reformation which was kept well in control by the traditional city authorities. From the German point of view it was one of the great centres of the religious upheaval in the sixteenth century.[3]

The reforming zeal of Artois and the part of Flanders annexed by France came rather late; it was distinctly more undisciplined, and Calvinist rather than Lutheran. It started noisily in 1566 with a wave of iconoclasm. Columns of reformers went about the villages destroying the images, the 'idols' of Roman catholicism. This aggressive protestantism of the north was not checked by France, but by Spain, which then controlled the Low Countries. Philip II, however, did not manage to prevent the secession of the United Provinces, i.e. the Dutch Calvinists. In the extreme north of France, as in Occitania, the official return to catholicism did not preclude the survival of a Protestant cultural imprint.

FROM THE MIDDLE AGES TO THE YEAR 2000

The cultural dynamism of the southern part of France should not be looked upon as a thing of the past. Many conclusions drawn from the census of 1982 emphasize the reappearance, at the approach of the third millenium, not only of the North–South divide, but also of the South's ascendancy.

Analysis of the most recent data highlights the re-emergence of the South as the leading region at the strictly cultural level. In 1982, it had the highest proportion of men and women with the *baccalauréat* (see map 2).

The geography of the present situation recalls at once that of the heresies and the Protestant Reformation. The only notable differences are the increasing strength of the Breton peninsula and the decline of Flanders-Artois, and in the South a slight shift in the cultural centre of gravity towards the east, from the valley of the Garonne to the valley of the Rhône. This slide to the east is not the result of any special provençal

Map 2
The *baccalauréat* in 1982

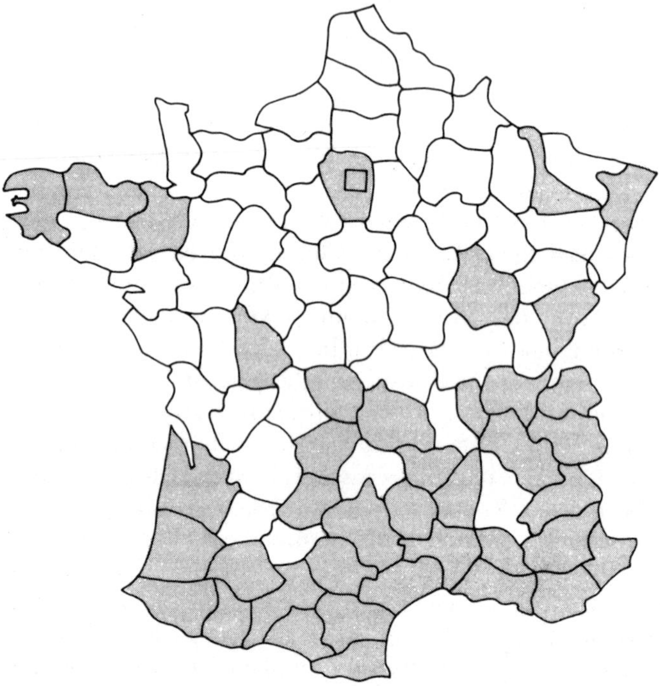

More than 26 per cent of women aged 15–34 hold a diploma equal or superior to the *baccalauréat*

Based on data from the 1982 census (INSEE).

dynamism, but of a recent influx of highly qualified personnel into the South-east. The cyclical occurrence of cultural thrusts, affecting primary education towards 1150 or 1550, and secondary education between 1970 and 1980, hints at the existence of a hidden but stable factor, capable of resisting northern pressure over long periods.

The search for this hidden factor leads us to anthropology, which defines local cultures as behaviour systems, or coherent wholes embracing the different elements of existence. Behind the differing cultural performances of the North and the South, one may detect and scrutinize two major anthropological systems, two concepts of life that divide France.

One system dominates the South and also certain outlying areas of the East (Alsace, Lorraine, the Jura Mountains), of the extreme North (Flanders and Artois) and of the West (lower Brittany, i.e. the part of Brittany that spoke the Breton language until the end of the nineteenth century). The other system is characteristic of the Paris basin, taking that term in its widest sense.

TWO ANTHROPOLOGICAL SYSTEMS

Description of family systems offers a first approach to the contrast between the northern and southern systems within France. In the northern part of the country *nuclear* (i.e. individualistic) family systems predominate, in which interaction between adult generations is weak. The marriage of children constitute a break, a real acquisition by the children of autonomy *vis-à-vis* the older generation. In the southern part of the country, on the other hand, interdependence of parents and children remains strong after the children's marriages, a trait that sums up, all by itself, a *complex* (i.e. close-knit) family system.

In traditional rural circles, the existence of one or other *family system* has direct implications for the formation and structure of the *households*, or domestic groups.[4] In a complex system, interdependence of generations fosters a tendency for parents and children to live together. So three-generation households are formed – children, parents, grandparents. In the nuclear system, however, families are inclined consciously to avoid these forms of cohabitation. Being adult means ceasing to live with your parents: not only forming a new partnership, but also a new domestic unit, a quite independent household.

A direct description of family systems, in the sense of sets of values structuring the affective relations between individuals, is unfortunately not possible. Sentiments do not lend themselves to exhaustive statistical inquiry, nor are they very responsive to opinion polls. Households, on the other hand, are visible social and economic entities, and one can, with the aid of census returns, describe their organization. Their structure then reveals the existence of typical regional forms of behaviour, visible reflections of that crucial but hidden variable – the family system. The behaviour of individuals reveals their implicit conception of life.

The *typology* of households laid down in the 1975 census points up a division of France into two zones, by major family type (see map 3). One is nuclear and the other is complex. One can calculate, especially in rural and agricultural circles, *the proportion of households containing more than a conjugal family unit*, i.e. in which the parents-children group is augmented by grandparents or, less often, by uncles or cousins. The map obtained by means of this simple indicator could hardly be clearer, despite the residual character of the complex household at the end of the twentieth century. Households with three resident generations are

Map 3
Complex households

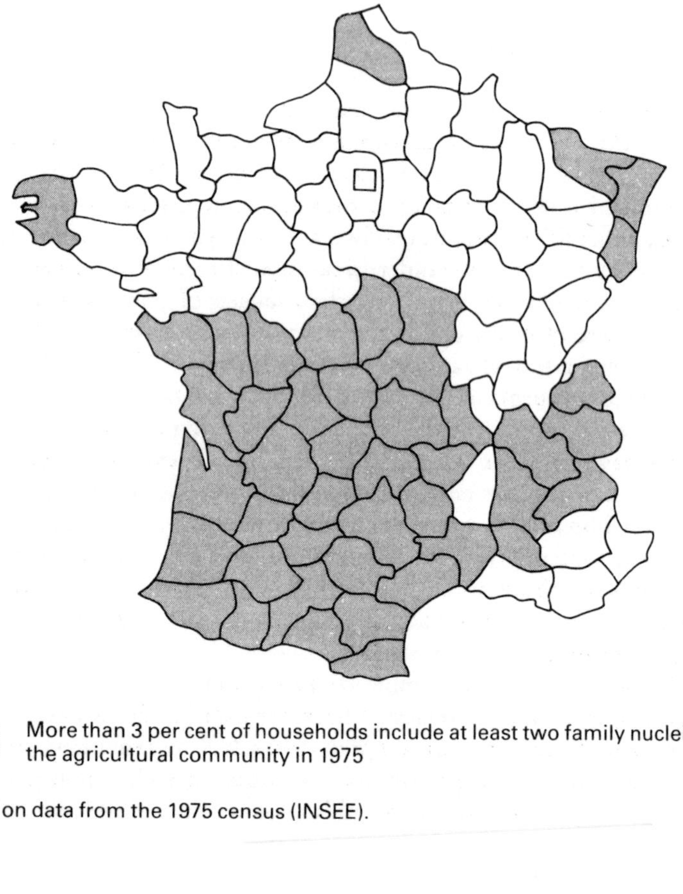

More than 3 per cent of households include at least two family nuclei in the agricultural community in 1975

Based on data from the 1975 census (INSEE).

numerous south of the Loire, in Breton-speaking Brittany, in Alsace and in the extreme north of France.

Contrariwise, in the northern part of the country, which here includes the whole Paris basin and the non-maritime zones of the West ('the western interior'), nuclear households dominate absolutely.

This clear-cut map, describing *household structure*, allows us to posit the existence of two major *family systems*, one corresponding to the 'southern anthropological system', the other to the 'northern anthropological system'. This map, however, cannot be taken as an absolutely faithful representation of the family systems, which are complex wholes imperfectly defined by a simple inspection of the structure of households. Other descriptive details – age at marriage, systems of inheritance – must be included in an exact description of these elementary social forms.

Integration of these new elements, particularly inheritance customs, necessitates a typological refinement, amounting to a subdivision of the two major types and revealing other systems, not predominant indeed but significant, in the western interior, on the north-west edge of the Massif Central and on the Mediterranean littoral.

The contrast between a South dominated by complex family systems and a Paris basin pervaded by nuclear family systems does, however, sum up fairly accurately the general anthropological organization of the French nation. As a first step, it explains the tendency of the southern system to achieve, in cyclical fashion, cultural thrusts that are stronger than those of the northern system. The educational performance and family systems of the southern world are merely two aspects of the same reality. The low cultural pressure and the nuclear family systems of the Paris basin are also merely two distinct and visible expressions of the same reality, diametrically opposed to that of the South.

One must at this stage concede the existence in northern and southern France of two conceptions of life, regulating, from the cradle to the grave, the choices of individuals in their family, educational and professional spheres. In order to analyse this North–South duality, it will be simpler to describe first the fundamental aspects of the southern system; the Midi is more conscious of family values than the North, so it applies precise standards, often codified. The North defines itself negatively, by an absence of equivalent standards, at least at the conscious level.

A REGION OF FEW CHILDREN

The southern part of France has very precise demographic characteristics (see map 4). The fertility index is low compared with the national average, and the latter itself is not very high in the world ratings. Most of the

Map 4
Low fertility

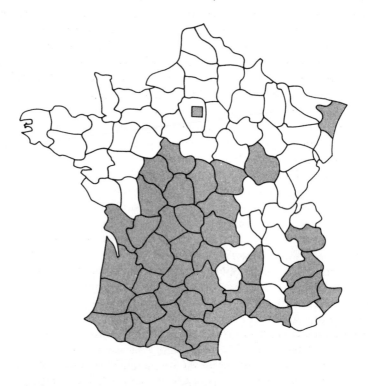

Fertility rate less than 1.85 between 1981 and 1983

Based on data contained in Sautory, O. 1986: *Données de démographie régionale,*
1982. Paris: INSEE, series D, 115.

départements south of the Loire had, between 1980 and 1987, a fertility
index of between 1.45 and 1.85 children per woman, a very low level
which recalls that of the most Malthusian countries of present-day
Europe – Germany, Switzerland, Scandinavia and northern Italy. On the
other hand, the *départements* to the north of the Loire, to which should
be added an appendix going south towards Lyons and the valley of the
Rhône, have a fertility index superior to 1.85 children per woman, in fact
very close to 2.1 which, at the present mortality rate, is the figure
theoretically ensuring the replacement of one generation by the next.
Below that level the population is thought to diminish in the long run.
Above that level it grows, but these movements are very long-term, and
the model entirely ignores the migration factor.

The fertility map of France is a classic mystery of demography, well known but unexplained. If one integrates it into an overall anthropological model, it loses some of its mystery. The map of household structures taken from the data of the 1975 census is in fact very similar. The regions of low fertility are generally those where the household structures are complex and where, very often, several adult generations are living together in a rural district. The correlation coefficient linking fertility in 1982–3 to the complexity of rural households in 1975 is strong – 0.62 at the level of the *département*. Curiously enough, the regions where few children are produced remain those where the relationship between parents and children remains very strong throughout life.

STEM FAMILY, NUCLEAR FAMILY

So the very low fertility of the South of France proves the existence, in a significant proportion of families, of the ideal of an only child. This conclusion, drawn from an examination of the most recent demographic data, reveals, on the threshold of the third millennium, the persistence of a very ancient local idea that one can easily date back to the *ancien régime*. Occitania was at that time dominated by a peasant family system that favoured a single heir. The average couple generally produced several children, in the absence of contraceptive methods, but only one of them inherited the family farm, where he continued to live with his parents after his marriage. The other children were condemned either to celibacy, or to marriage with the heir or heiress to another family farm. The heir was generally the eldest son. Yet he could, as in Lozère, be freely chosen by his parents for his supposed talents. The heir could also, as in the Basque country, be a first-born, but without distinction of sex, an eldest daughter always being preferred to a younger son. In every case the daughters were heirs in the absence of male children. In the north of France, on the contrary, there prevailed a strictly egalitarian system, the children sharing the parental assets in equal portions. This difference in customs was abruptly highlighted by the 1789 Revolution. The egalitarian North, in its quest for justice and national uniformity, wanted to impose its ideas on the South. In spite of the introduction of the egalitarian Code Civil, the South was not brought to heel. So for southern peasants, the nineteenth century simply became a long struggle to get round the law, with younger sons enthusiastically helping their elders to dispossess them. Thus in 1897–8, when the German Alexander de Brandt carried out a rapid but systematic inquiry into peasant inheritance systems in France, the traditional map was still more or less intact.[5] On the simplified map derived by de Brandt himself from his data by districts (see map 5),

Map 5
Peasant inheritance customs *c.*1900

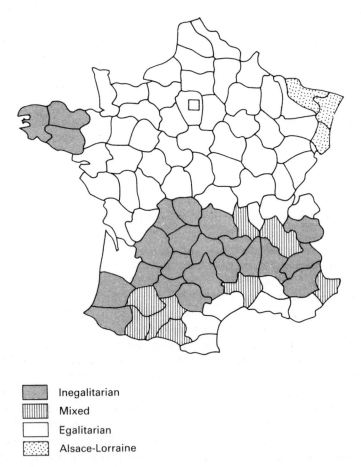

- ▨ Inegalitarian
- ▥ Mixed
- ☐ Egalitarian
- ▦ Alsace-Lorraine

Based on map supplied in Brandt, A. de 1901: *Droit et Coutumes de la France en matière successorale*. Paris.

around 1900 the whole of Occitania, except the Mediterranean littoral, remained faithful to the traditional practice of a single heir. The Breton peninsula followed the same model. Alsace-Lorraine, excluded from the study at that time because the territory belonged to the German Empire, did likewise. The correspondence with contemporary maps illustrating the structure of households and fertility, without being perfect, is still striking. It would be still better if de Brandt had not schematized the results of his inquiry and overestimated the extent of the national, i.e. egalitarian, norm.

The family type most common in Occitania, the Basque country, Brittany and Alsace, combining the single heir and cohabitation of generations, was named the *famille souche* or stem family by the sociologist Frédéric le Play around the middle of the nineteenth century. Its presence in a region reveals the existence, more or less conscious, of a plan to found a line. The family aspires to perpetuate itself through a line represented by a single heir in each generation. This system tends to create a structural imbalance in demographic terms, for whereas the family needs only one heir to perpetuate itself, society needs two to sustain itself quantitatively.

EDUCATION AND AMBITION

The only child in the South is cherished by its parents, who take a special interest in its education, whether the child is a boy or a girl. It embodies the hope of a line of descent, and they expect it to get on, for the school system is the simplest and most direct road to social advancement.

The break-up of peasant society would seem to nullify the advantage of different generations associating on a single farm. But it releases the potential for progress in the stem family. In the context of a rural economy the social ascent of a peasant family is limited to the purchase of parcels of land, to a microscopic local strategy of accumulating real estate. Educational achievement, in theory, has no limits.

It is because of this parental concern that the South of France has constantly outstripped the North within the educational system (which is both national and uniform), producing year after year more successes in the *baccalauréat* and more university degrees per inhabitant. This superior performance by the South can be grasped negatively. The proportion of men and men between fifteen and thirty-four with no academic qualifications, i.e. without even the *certificat d'études*, is much smaller in the South than the North (see map 6). As on the map of inheritance systems produced by de Brandt, the Mediterranean littoral differs from the rest of the Midi, in this case by reason of a high proportion of individuals without academic qualifications. In the North, as on the map of inheritance customs, Brittany is distinguished by a very small proportion of people without academic qualifications. Alsace, the other 'Nordic' region of the stem family, also follows the South in the race for educational qualifications. As for the Paris basin, it seems to be distinctly underdeveloped from the cultural point of view.

The South is, however, the victim of an insoluble contradiction which has prevented it from attaining a dominant position at the national level. It is strong educationally but weak demographically. Its highly educated

Map 6
Ignorance

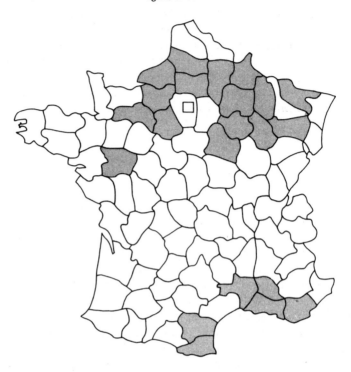

More than 30 per cent of men aged 15–34 had no diploma in 1982

Based on data from the 1982 census.

children are too few in number to swamp the national system. The North, which is less effective educationally, turns out numerically more *bacheliers* simply because it produces more children.

Curiously enough, the overall national balance is nowadays not very different from what it was at the time of the Albigensian Crusade. At the beginning of the thirteenth century a North, culturally retarded but powerful in numbers, attacked a South that was demographically weak. Forgetting crusades and massacres, the relative positions of the North and South have not changed.

TRADES AND PROFESSIONS

Without at this stage describing the whole economic and socio-professional structure of the South, one can highlight certain aspects that

distinguish it from the structure of the North, and which result from the
South's ideas about family and education. The Midi's particular affection
for the direct line of descent shows up in professional life in an over-
representation of certain specialized trades, followed by skilled, self-
employed workers and often handed on from father to son. The liberal
professions and craft enterprises answer perfectly to this definition. The
1982 census shows up their unusual strength in the southern half of
France (see map 7). A superficial interpretation of this phenomenon
would stress the archaic and rather undynamic nature of such a
preference: crafts are an old-fashioned mode of production, the urban
equivalent of the family farm. Ten years ago no one would have cast
doubt on the validity of this interpretation. But nowadays the collapse of

Map 7
Craftsmen

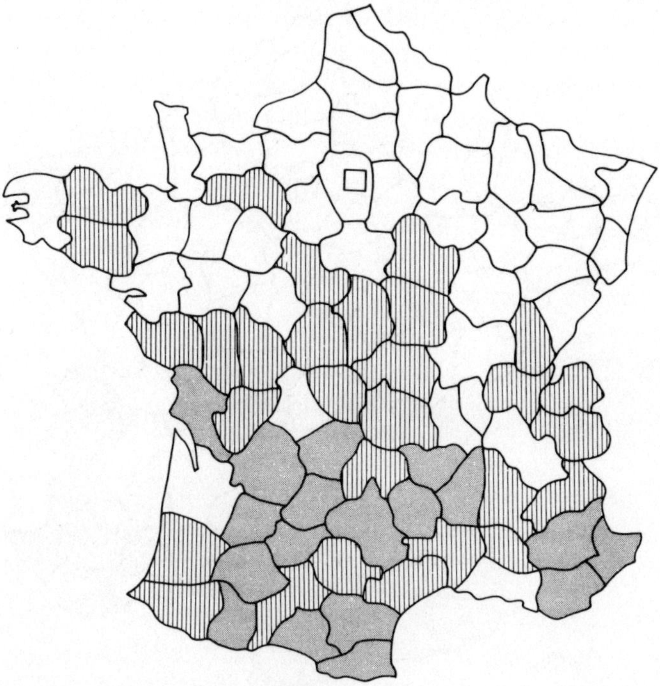

Craftsmen in the working population in 1982

More than 6 per cent

Between 5 and 6 per cent

Based on data from the 1982 census.

heavy industry and the return to a preference for small units serve to modify this attitude. Craft and professional jobs call for qualifications far superior to those required for most industrial employments. The medical profession is a case in point. It involves self-employed work which assumes a high level of education and the mastery of advanced techniques which are in a constant state of change. In this sector the South enjoys a significant surplus in all branches of medicine – general practitioners, specialists and related professions such as dentists (see map 8).

The South's lead in this field is probably very old; in any case it dates from well before the 1982 census. There is firm evidence of a medical tradition in the South in medieval times. It is indeed disconcerting to discover doctors in the twelfth century playing a leading role in the Cathar movement.[6]

Map 8
Doctors

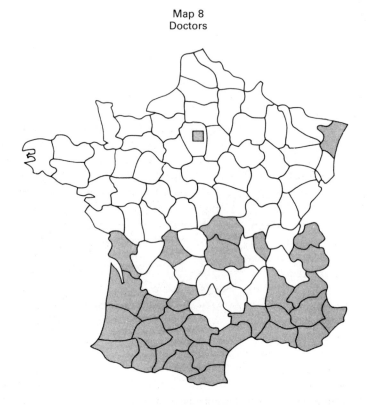

■ More than 15 qualified doctors per 100,000 inhabitants in 1983

Based on data supplied by the Caisse Nationale de l'Assurance Maladie des Travailleurs Salariés: *Carnets statistiques*, 10, June 1984.

THE NEGATIVE NORTH

Thus a wealth of anthropological, economic and demographic evidence shows that the usual idea of French society is largely a myth. The reality inclines towards a duality of systems. In the realm of morality and behaviour there coexist two societies – *northern* and *southern*.

The internal boundary between these two universes varies according to the parameters used. At its maximum extent, southern society stretches to the Loire. In its most reduced form it is limited to a narrow strip running from Bordeaux to Nice via Toulouse and Marseille. Sometimes it swells towards the east and contracts in the west, and vice versa. These fluctuations reveal slow interactions between northern and southern societies, now integrated into a single political unit and, since about a hundred years ago, into a unified linguistic system.

Southern society, therefore, seems to be dynamic on the cultural plane. However, individual lives seem to be firmly governed by a system of family, educational and professional norms. The Midi is constantly threatened by its slow metabolism: because it produces few children (even though it promotes their intellectual training), it inclines inevitably towards demographic ageing.

Northern society can be described negatively, feature by feature. It is more static on the cultural plane, but more mobile in other ways. The lives of individuals are not normally limited by family, educational or professional norms. Behind this social universe (anthropologically speaking) lies the nuclear family, which favours early independence for children, and a certain geographical and social fluidity. The North produces more children, but educates them less; and it is not really threatened, as is much of Europe, by a serious population imbalance. However, in the context of economic crisis and unemployment, the North, more than the South, tends to produce marginal characters, candidates for what is nowadays called the 'new poverty', i.e. drifters without job or family, disengaged from all coherent social solidarity.

Two small regions in the North seem to combine the advantages of both systems, northern and southern. Lower Brittany and Alsace have close family systems and strong cultural dynamism while maintaining a high level of fertility and, in consequence, a young age-structure in their population. The existence of these provinces usefully recalls the fact that the North–South divide is the dominant aspect of a more general opposition of centre to periphery. The northern system is centred on Paris. It does not influence Brittany to the west or Alsace to the east, which are both as far from the capital as is Occitania.

The extreme North, limited to the *départements* of Nord and Pas-de-

Calais, recalls Alsace and Brittany in certain aspects of its family organization and its fertility. It has the characteristics of peripheral systems. But the early appearance and high level of industrialization in the locality, because of the coal deposits, make it a case apart. Rapid industrialization on a massive scale can in fact partly destroy a local anthropological system.

Southern society also has its exception – the Mediterranean littoral. This area, between Perpignan and Nice, differs from the rest of the region in various respects. Its traditions of inheritance are egalitarian and the proportion of people without academic qualifications is high. Yet this coastal strip belongs to the South by reason of its low fertility and by the large presence of liberal and craft professions. Its existence has a theoretical interest in that it justifies the assertion that southern society is not the French version of a Mediterranean model, similar to the Italian or Spanish types. This Mediterranean model does exist, but is restricted to the narrow strip consisting of the coastal parts of six *départements* – Pyrénées-Orientales, Aude, Hérault, Bouches-du-Rhône, Var and Alpes-Maritimes. Beyond this seaboard strip, southern society can be seen as an autonomous type, becoming even more clearly defined as one leaves the Mediterranean for Aquitaine, the interior of the Alps and the Massif Central.

2

The Influence of Europe

The splitting of western Christendom by the Protestant Reformation was probably the result of the North of Europe's overtaking the South in the cultural sphere. This historical turning-point marks the close of ancient history, which had been dominated by Mediterranean societies.

The North of Europe, converted to Christianity by the South between the fifth and eleventh centuries, thus rejected in the sixteenth century the cultural tutelage of the Mediterranean world. Christianization, and the rejection of the South by the North a few centuries later, were two crucial episodes which were both linked to the progress of literacy. Christianization allowed the transmission of the Latin alphabetic script, derived from the Greek, to the North of Europe. Ecclesiastics were then, in fact, the only people who could read and write. In accepting the religious pre-eminence of Rome, the peoples of the North admitted their cultural backwardness. The schism of western Christianity occurred at the very moment when the North–South balance of power tipped in the opposite direction, i.e. when the literacy rate of the North overtook that of the South, and when Germany outstripped Italy in the race for cultural development.

It is not necessary to bring forward new hypotheses in order to understand this reversal of the balance of power. The dynamism of northern Europe, like that of Occitania, rested on family structures of the stem type, demanding vigorous interaction between parents and children, and very favourable to the full transmission of cultural and technical gains. In the north of Europe, within the German world, structures of the stem type were in a majority. They shaped the destiny of the whole area. In the Latin world they were enclaves in a universe dominated by family systems of the nuclear type. Occitania occupied a minority position within the French whole. The northern provinces of Spain and Portugal, where stem-type structures dominated, represented only a third and a quarter respectively of their national areas. In Italy the disproportion was even greater, for the stem structures were concentrated in the Alps and their foothills. In these regions heresy, possible in theory and widespread in practice, was overcome by the forces of the Catholic Church.

The schism within Christian Europe led to an acceleration of cultural and economic progress in the mainly Protestant northern parts of the continent, and to a slowdown in the Catholic south. The German world, the Low Countries, Scotland, Denmark, Sweden and (to a lesser extent) England were from the beginning of the seventeenth century making fast progress towards mass literacy. Protestantism based religion on the reading of the Bible, and demanded that the Word of God should be accessible to all. Italy, Spain and Portugal chose the opposite way – i.e. restriction of access to Holy Scripture, which remained the preserve of an ecclesiastical élite. This choice entailed cultural torpor for the nations in question.

France became a victim of this reversal in the North–South balance of power, and accepted it passively. She had difficulty in crushing her own Protestants, the Huguenots. However, being more Nordic in a geographical sense than Spain or Italy, she then underwent cultural and economic pressure from the North of Europe. From the sixteenth to the twentieth century, the main influence on the development of France no longer came from within the national system. It no longer originated on the fringes, but was actually external. So for five centuries cultural and economic waves washed over a frontier which shifted but was at all times only political. Once again the Paris basin was not the driving force of progress. It was simply the beneficiary of developments which penetrated it from the north and east. Southern society, between the revocation of the Edict of Nantes and its recovery in the years 1950–80, was not in a strong position and lost its cultural lead. By the end of the seventeenth century at the latest, the North had even outstripped the South in its rate of literacy.

The pre-eminence of the Paris basin endured until the first half of the twentieth century, but was probably at its zenith in the eighteenth and nineteenth centuries. It was discernible at that time through the existence of a dividing line along the Saint-Malo–Geneva axis (see map 9). To the north of this line the country appears developed, to the south backward. Yet the literacy movement did not spring from the capital but from the eastern frontier. Strasbourg rather than Paris was at the heart of French literacy, a mark of the East that was still noticeable around 1930. On the eve of the Depression and the Front Populaire, the residual pockets of illiteracy were still all situated in the western half of the country. The educationally most advanced regions clung to the eastern frontier – Alsace, Lorraine, Franche-Comté and Savoie, all provinces where literacy exceeded 97 per cent.

Literacy is only one element in the modernizing process. Industrialization is another, considered, probably wrongly, as more important by many historians and sociologists belonging to the 'economic' tradition. But this raises no problems, as the maps for industrialization only confirm those

Map 9
Literacy *c.*1930

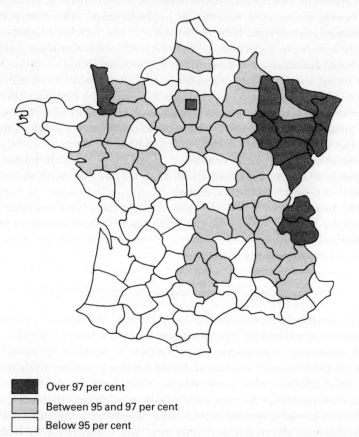

■ Over 97 per cent

░ Between 95 and 97 per cent

□ Below 95 per cent

Based on data from the 1931 census.

for literacy. Once again they prove the preponderance of Europe, and the unimportance of Paris, in the development process. A map of European industry on the eve of the Depression makes French industry the south-western appendix of a vast continental industrial zone centred on Germany and Switzerland. Workers employed in the secondary sector are numerous in the *départements* situated to the north-east of an axis running from Caen to Valence.

An historical analysis of the geographical distribution of French industry shows that this frontier effect is not just recent. It appears in diverse forms even before the Reformation. The commercial and industrial economy of medieval France had already ceased to be an autonomous economy, and was largely governed by outside influences. The importance of the East in the industrial and commercial development of France is common knowledge to medievalists. The first poles of European growth were Italy and Flanders in the thirteenth century, then south and west Germany in the fifteenth. The Capetian kingdom expanded politically, but it experienced European economic development as a thrust moving along an imaginary line from Bruges to Florence. An automatic consequence was that the East of the kingdom underwent growth by a classic process of diffusion. A characteristic symptom was the great size of the fairs in Champagne in the thirteenth century, then of the fair of the important commercial and financial centre of Lyon in the fourteenth and fifteenth centuries. These facts are well known and undisputed; before France officially assumed her final rigid shape, they raised no problems of national pride.

The map of French industry has not, however, been static for long. From the Middle Ages to the twentieth century, there have been strong variations. After the Reformation the fundamental changes concerned only the North and the East.

THE HISTORICAL GEOGRAPHY OF FRENCH INDUSTRY

Even in the Middle Ages the geographical distribution of 'French' industry was peripheral. The secondary sector was then principally textile and developed autonomously in Occitania, between Toulouse and Nîmes. In the northern sector of the Paris basin it grew by diffusion from the great Flemish centres of industrial development. In the sixteenth century the map for the iron and steel industry, on the other hand, shows diffusion from the eastern frontier. This is natural, as the main centre of iron and steel development at that time was Germany. One finds this North–East–North oscillation throughout the industrial history of France. It did not arise out of variations in internal forces on the national level, but out of successive changes in the industrial leadership of Europe, as follows:

Thirteenth century – the textile industry is predominant and Flemish.
Fifteenth century – the iron and steel industry is predominant and German.
Nineteenth century – the supremacy is British and covers all sectors.
Twentieth century – a return to German dominance in iron and steel is evident.

The Flemish and British advances favoured the North. The German phases, on the other hand, favoured the East. Paris was content to umpire a contest which took place entirely outside the national frontiers.

From the middle of the nineteenth century the censuses allow one to follow more accurately the distribution of the working population employed in industry (see maps 10, 11, 12). Mining, building and transport are excluded from the statistics presented.

First stage, 1856

This was the great period of English supremacy. French industry, especially textiles, inclined towards the North-west. Artois, Flanders, Picardy and Normandy were to the forefront. The East (Alsace and Lorraine) was nevertheless quite prominent. Paris and Lyon were small isolated centres, and did not take their respective regions with them.

Second stage, 1921

Great Britain was replaced by Germany as industrial leader. The North-west remained in the game, but the main zone for the diffusion of industrial techniques was from now onwards the East. On the edge of the developing area, Paris and Lyon began to involve their respective regions.

Third stage, 1975

The whole of France north-east of a line from Caen to Valence is significantly industrialized. The map highlights the general influence of Europe. The expansion of the years 1945–75, which took place within the framework of the Common Market, extended and gave free rein to the tendencies of the preceding centuries. However, the Common Market simply took over the constraints which weighed on the French economy in the Middle Ages and under the *ancien régime*, and even operated during protectionist phases.

ARCHEOLOGY OF THE SECTORS

A description of French industry by sectors in 1982 also reveals the existence of a very tidy model of spread from east to west. Each industrial sector – textiles, engineering, light chemicals, automobiles, electrical household goods – is in fact the product of particular period; and a sector has its geographical base further west according to the recentness of its emergence (see maps 13a–d).

Engineering, the solid core of industrial expansion between 1860 and 1914, covers the whole of the north-east. Highly significant in terms of volume, the engineering sector reflects, all on its own, the geographical

Map 10
Industry in 1856

☐   Over 25 per cent of population living off industry
     (excluding building, mining and transport)
+   No data

Based on data from the 1856 census.

arrangement of French industry as a whole, particularly the great
industrial zone lying to the north-east of the Caen–Valence axis.
However, the geographical disposition of the sectors born or reaching
maturity between 1950 and 1970 is just as clear.

The light chemical industry is stretched out along the Dijon–Rouen
axis, roughly following the line of the Seine valley and the western
frontier of the great 'engineering' zone.

Automobiles push one stage further, to the west of the Paris region.
The establishment of Peugeot in the East has hardly affected the general
structure of the map.

With electrical household goods, an industry born after the Second
World War, we really reach the western limit of industry's expansion. A

product of the growth of the sixties, this branch has expanded most in the Caen–Orléans–Angers triangle.

Two industrial sectors do not conform to the general model (see maps 14a and b). One is the most ancient and the other the most recent in its technology.

The textile industry has partly retained its medieval geography, being quite widely dispersed over the whole country, with establishments in the North, in the Lyon region and in Occitania.

The electronics industry is situated in the centre of the national territory, between Paris, Orléans and Rouen. It is probably the first time in the economic history of France that the nation's capital has achieved an absolute ascendancy in an advanced industrial activity.

Map 11
Industry in 1921

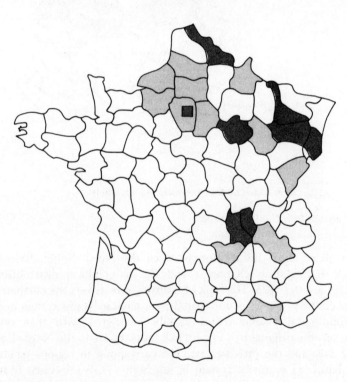

 Over 35 per cent of the active population

 Between 25 and 35 per cent

Based on data from the 1921 census.

Map 12
Industry in 1975

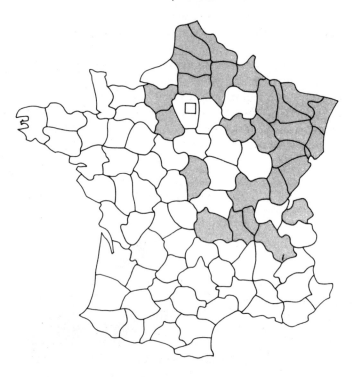

☐   Over 35 per cent of the working population

Based on data from the 1975 census.

The maps show no relation between the North–South division of
France described in chapter 1 and the geographical distribution of
industry around 1975. The bulk of industry now covers the northern half
of the country, which is dominated by a nuclear family system and the
anthropological characteristics usually associated with that system.
However, the original bases of French industry are in the Nord–Pas-de-
Calais area and the extreme east, and correspond to regions where the
stem family (a minority system in northern society) prevails. Industry
penetrates a corner of the south along an axis traced out by the Rhône
valley as far as Ardèche and Drôme.

   Yet there is no sign of southern society attracting industry as it had
attracted literacy in the mid-nineteenth century. Literacy originated in
the north-east but was very soon drawn to the south. By 1900 the

Map 13a
Engineering in 1982

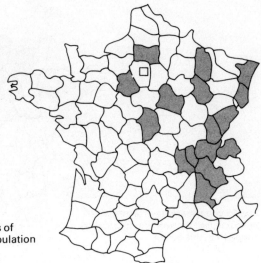

Top 16 *départements* in terms of
proportion of the working population
engaged in this sector

Based on data from the 1982 census.

Map 13b
Light chemicals in 1982

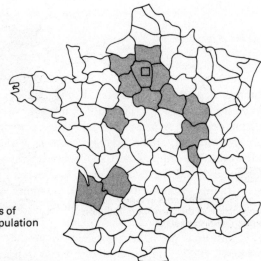

Top 14 *départements* in terms of
proportion of the working population
engaged in this sector

Based on data from the 1982 census.

Map 13c
Automobile industry in 1982

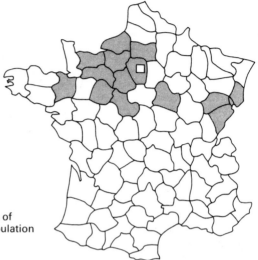

Top 15 *départements* in terms of
proportion of the working population
engaged in this sector

Based on data from the 1982 census.

Map 13d
Household electrical industry in 1982

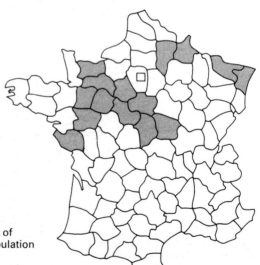

Top 15 *départements* in terms of
proportion of the working population
engaged in this sector

Based on data from the 1982 census.

Map 14a
Textile industry in 1982

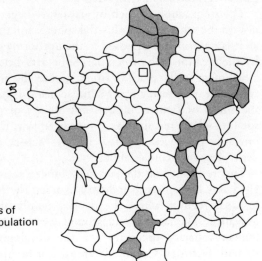

Top 15 *départements* in terms of
proportion of the working population
engaged in this sector

Based on data from the 1982 census.

Map 14b
Electronics industry in 1982

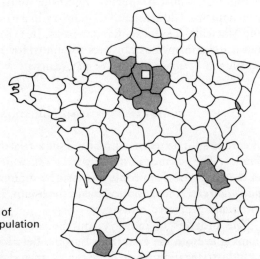

Top 9 *départements* in terms of
proportion of the working population
engaged in this sector

Based on data from the 1982 census.

Toulouse region had clearly joined the zone of total literacy, but around 1975 it remained largely outside the industrial zone. This was particularly true as regards engineering, that key sector of traditional industrialization.

The stem family, which by its nature begets cultural dynamism, does not do the same in the industrial sphere, and this for two reasons. First of all it is on principle opposed to the uprooting of people, which is implied by the creation of a proletariat. Solidarity between generations supposes attachment to the place of origin and to the home. The second source of resistance to industry was Malthusianism, a characteristic of family life in the south of France, though not always of the stem family. Southern society, whose fertility has always been low, from the nineteenth century onwards produced too few men to satisfy the needs of an industry dependent on manual labour.

This resistance on the part of southern society explains why, between 1945 and 1975, French industry avoided the Midi and headed due west, towards regions where the nuclear family and demographic surpluses prevailed. The rural world around Rennes and Le Mans had the spare human capacity necessary for the development of the Citroën and Renault factories. Coming from nuclear family systems little attached to tradition, these men could easily be uprooted and turned into semi-skilled workers.

Although industry in the south is insignificant in terms of sheer volume, it should not be underestimated. It concentrates on key sectors like aeronautics and the space industry. It often uses highly qualified manpower, whose production figures prominently in the French balance of payments. The aeronautical industry in particular is concentrated along the Marseille–Toulouse–Bayonne axis. In 1983, for example, the aircraft, naval and armaments industries accounted for 30 per cent of the industrial surplus in France's balance of payments.[1]

CULTURAL DYNAMISM, INDUSTRIAL DYNAMISM

A certain split between cultural and industrial dynamism is now typical of France. The advance in the cultural level, which is shown by an increase in the proportion of people possessing a diploma equal or superior to the *baccalauréat*, is most noticeable in the South. It has come to look like an internally generated movement.

The progress of industry, on the other hand, appears like a wave coming in from the east, from Europe. Between 1945 and 1975 the wave of industrialization reached the centre, then the west of the Paris basin. It was during this period, 'the Thirty Glorious Years', that France became a real industrial power.

The divorce of *industrial* from *cultural* dynamism, which is particularly evident in the case of France, is to a certain extent typical of all European history. The stem family embodies an ideal of lineal continuity. Its high potential in culture does not preclude a tendency to reject uprooting. In the early stages, it always seems to resist the upheavals of industrial revolution. A typical example was Germany, which was well in advance of England from the cultural standpoint, whether in terms of her high overall rate of literacy or for the expansion of her universities; but she lagged behind in the development of mass industry. Between 1750 and 1850 it was England that took off, and not Germany. The dominant family system in the British Isles did not insist on the continuity of peasant lineage. It was a nuclear system, encouraging an early separation of parents from adult children. It favoured uprooting and the formation of an industrial proletariat.[2] Cultural and industrial dynamism go fully hand in hand in only one region of France, a situation dictated by geographical chance. At the meeting-point of East and South, the Rhône–Alpes region, to which can be added Alsace, combines the indices of both cultural and industrial development. Taking advantage of the South's ability to produce educationally well-qualified people, and of the industrial movement originating in the east, the Lyon region (using the expression in a broad sense) has asserted itself as an impressive centre of development. The outstanding economic energy of this region of France has turned it into one of the great centres of resistance to the dominance of Paris.

We have not yet mentioned in this book the dominance of Paris. She does not make herself felt in the cultural or the industrial sphere. The forces of development at work on the French scene seem in fact, rather mischievously, to have avoided Paris, the political centre of the nation. The Paris basin even seems to be a sluggish enclave in the history of development. For the geographical heart of the national unit only serves as theoretical centre in the *political* history of the nation.

3

The Church and the Revolution

In Occitania in the years 1150–1600, in Artois, Flanders and Alsace in the sixteenth century, cultural progress, internally generated and connected with specific anthropological structures, released activity in the ideological field. The rise in the literacy rate brought in its train an ever-increasing participation of the masses in political and religious life. Heresy, dissent and the Reformation grew out of this progress. The Paris basin, being less advanced, was then reduced to the role of watchdog for orthodoxy. But the eventual cultural take-off of the Paris basin, which was a much later phenomenon originating in the East, likewise gave rise to ideological activity. In the North of France in the eighteenth century, an advance in culture brought on a second crisis for catholicism, which was faced this time not by protestantism but by another enemy, the Revolution. The programme of the Revolution, which was political before it was religious, was not that of the Reformation, which was religious before it was political. However, the ideological crisis was determined in both cases by the same factor. The rise in the literacy rate introduced a large sector of the population to the written word, so allowing the expression of other ideological values than those of the clergy.

Like protestantism, the French Revolution attacked the Church. Like protestantism, it secularized a large amount of the Church's possessions. Like protestantism, it challenged the authority of the pope and of priests. Here the resemblance ceased. Protestantism went with an increase in religious faith, a raising of the level of spirituality, and a strengthened belief in God's action in the affairs of the world. The God of the Protestants was hardly less powerful than the God of the Catholics, and probably more severe.

The French Revolution very rapidly developed into a negation of Christianity and its basic beliefs. It opted for agnosticism and sometimes for atheism. It did not limit itself to rejecting the authority of the pope and Catholic priests: it rejected the authority of God. The fundamental hostility of the French Revolution to religion itself cannot be denied, even if in practice the political chiefs went less far than the crowd in expressing this fundamental tendency.

In revolutionary writings, which had their origins in eighteenth-century thought, the Church appears above all as retrograde and as a champion of negative moral values. *L'Esquisse d'un tableau historique des progrès de l'esprit humain*, written by Condorcet shortly before his arrest and suicide, is a document that is both fundamental and typical. *L'Esquisse* is fundamental because of its historical breadth, and almost religious in its presentation of a rapid but complete vision of human destiny. It is typical in its portrayal of progress as an unceasing struggle, from Antiquity to the Enlightenment, against the obscurantism of priests and religion.

The Revolution, unlike protestantism, wanted the destruction of the Catholic Church and not simply its reform. At the end of 1790 the Assembly passed the civil constitution of the clergy: war had been officially declared between Church and Revolution. The civil constitution enforced the election of parish priests and bishops by assemblies of citizens. This amounted to destroying the very notion of the Church, in the Catholic sense of the term. For one of the fundamental tenets of catholicism after the Council of Trent was absolute obedience to the Pope and the bishops, whose authority derived, according to Roman principles, by legitimate succession and personal transmission from the authority of the Apostles. The Revolution was opposed to all idea of authority, in the name of a fully conscious egalitarian individualism. In the minds of the men and the thinkers of the Revolution, liberty and equality were two principles that were complementary and inseparable. Equality before the law was a condition of political liberty.

The Church was not hostile to the principle of equality. Mankind as universal, the same everywhere and in every social condition, is one of the basic tenets of primitive Christianity. Yet catholicism energetically refuses to accept the principle of liberty; it sees submission to earthly and divine authority as a necessity. It is a religion of obedience – to God, to the Pope, to the bishops and the priests. It offers a vertical vision of the universe and society, according to which human beings are on this earth not to understand but to believe. The short Catholic catechisms of the first half of the twentieth century are quite unambiguous on this point. One of them, for example, published in 1947, lays down, like others, the basic principles of the believer's submission to the Church's bureaucracy, in a time-honoured game of questions and answers.[1]

Who are called the Church's faithful?
The faithful of the Church are the Christians who are obedient to the Pope and the bishops. To be truly one of the Church's faithful, you must believe

what she teaches, do what she commands, and receive her sacraments. (Question 134.)

What are the duties of the priests and the believers in regard to the Pope?
The duties of the priests and the believers to the Pope are to love him as a father, and obey him in everything he commands in the name of Jesus Christ. (Question 120.)

What are the duties of believers to their bishops and priests?
The duties of believers to their bishops and priests are to respect them, to obey them, and to help them in their pastoral work. (Question 124.)

It would be unfair to take a purely political view of this teaching. The subservience in question is not chiefly material. It is intended as a guarantee of obedience to metaphysical and moral laws as laid down in the Bible and the Gospels. It implies a certain intellectual passivity, but also a certain moral discipline.

It was this acceptance of the principle of authority which finally brought together catholicism and counter-revolutionary aristocratic thought. The ideal of nobility also, of course, required the submission of the humble to the leaders of society. Yet the nobility went much further than the Church. They declared the necessity of inequality among men, the existence of two distinct humanities, nobles and commoners. The association of Church and counter-revolution was not complete, at least on the theoretical level. In practice, however, a symbiotic relationship did come into being in France, and the Church adjusted herself to the principle of inequality. Counter-revolutionary thought regarded itself officially as Catholic in essence. Yet the works of a theoretician like Joseph de Maistre evoke a rather strange form of catholicism – vindictive, rejecting the notion of pardon, contrary in its very spirit to the Gospels, and rejecting the idea of universal mankind.

De Maistre writes in *Considérations sur la France*:

The Constitution of 1795, like all its predecessors, was made for Man. Yet there is no such thing as Man in the world. I have seen in my life French, Italians, Russians, etc. I know, thanks to Montesquieu, that one can be Persian; but as for Man, I declare that I have never met him in my life. If he exists, I don't know him!

From the Vatican's point of view, one could hardly be more heretical. In the same book, de Maistre rightly notes the anti-Christian character of the Revolution; but he manufactures an *ad hoc* Christianity, more social and political than metaphysical and moral.

SCHISM

So the civil constitution of the clergy marked a turning-point. It sealed the alliance of the Church and the counter-revolution, but it divided France. From now onwards two pairs of opposing principles confronted each other. On the Catholic and counter-revolutionary side, with splendid unanimity, the necessity of the authority principle was affirmed; and likewise the importance of the idea of inequality, albeit with some reservations on the Catholic side. On the revolutionary side the values of both equality and liberty were defended without misgivings.

France was cleft in two. In fact the Church herself, which until 1789 identified with French society, was also cleft in two. Some priests accepted the civil constitution, which destroyed the Church, while others rejected it. In 1791 a little more than half of the parish priests consented to swear an oath of loyalty to the constitution. A minority refused. It would be wrong to think of these choices as randomly distributed and solely dictated by doubt-stricken consciences. Geography was a potent factor in these choices, which were only superficially individual. Certain regions seem to have opted for the constitution and the Revolution, while others rejected them both. There now appeared for the first time a map which was an almost perfect reflection of 'Catholic survival', and whose characteristics will be seen as still operative in the most recent developments of French society (see map 15). This geographical evidence ought in fact to be called a 'map of secularity' or a 'map of dechristianization', the Revolution rather than the church being the active principle, modernizing or destructive according to one's point of view.

The American historian Timothy Tackett, professor at the Catholic University of Washington, has shown graphically the appearance of this fundamental cleavage. He has measured at the district level the proportion of 'sworn' priests, i.e. those who accepted the civil constitution in the spring and summer of 1791.[2]

CENTRE AND PERIPHERY

This time Paris was at the centre of French history. It was in the Paris basin that the priests of the *ancien régime* accepted revolutionary principles. The Church's resistance was strong in the fringe areas: the West, the South-West, the extreme North. Savoie, Joseph de Maistre's native province, was not then part of France and does not appear on the map, but would later join the group of Catholic regions.

The position of the capital is so central on the map, and its historic role

Map 15
The second crisis of catholicism:
acceptance and rejection of the *serment constitutionnel* in 1791

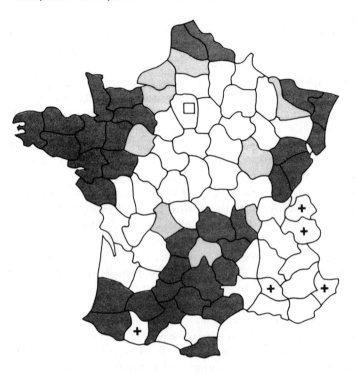

Proportion of priests accepting the *serment*:

Under 50 per cent
Between 50 and 60 per cent
Over 60 per cent
+   No data

Based on data assembled in Tackett, T. 1986: *La Révolution, l'Eglise, la France.*
Paris, 344–430.

has been so much emphasized by historians of the French Revolution, that one is almost tempted to interpret the ideological division of France into two halves as the effect of a wave of influence emanating from the political centre of the country. The outlying regions, situated far from the main centre of anti-royalist and anti-religious activity, would have resisted most effectively. They would have had time to develop a resistance that was appropriate to the events. This would no doubt be the explanation given by historians of the Revolution who believed in stable structures being brought into existence by the violent and decisive accidents of history.

However, the existence of a secondary centre of dechristianization, right on the periphery of the country, puts this theory out of court. The Mediterranean *départements* of Aude and Var, with fingers going out to Ariège on the one hand and Isère on the other, can be seen to constitute an independent centre of dechristianization. In 1791 its proportion of 'juring' priests, i.e. those who accepted the egalitarian and anti-authority principles of the French Revolution, was high and even preponderant. This impression is confirmed by the recent maps of religious practice drawn up during the 1960s. These show up the secularist tendencies of the Mediterranean littoral, especially in Aude, Pyrénées-Orientales, Bouches-du-Rhône, Var and Alpes-Maritimes.

The Mediterranean is peripheral to France, and one cannot quite see how a wave of secularism originating in Paris could have reached Carcassonne and Draguignan without touching Rennes, Besançon or Arras, which are physically much closer to the capital. So it is not possible to consider dechristianization as the product of diffusion, a change brought about by a mysterious Parisian alchemy and spreading across the country from a central starting-point.

STABILITY

The geographical regularity of the dechristianizing process is very striking: if we exclude Provence and Aude, there is a fine balance between centre and periphery. Its stability is no less remarkable. Canon Boulard's research into religious geography has furnished material for various maps illustrating religious practice towards the middle of the 1960s (frequency of attendance at Sunday mass, participation at Easter communion, church weddings, christenings, numbers of priests per canton, etc.). All these maps, which closely resemble one another, reveal with some variations the same structure – the one which appeared dramatically in 1791. A hundred and seventy-five years of history and of conflict, both physical and political, have not fundamentally altered the geographical profile revealed by the Revolution. In the mid-1960s, active catholicism remained a fringe phenomenon, peculiar to the Basque country, Brittany, Vendée, Anjou, Rouergue, Gévaudan, Savoie, Franche-Comté, Alsace, Lorraine, Artois and Flanders (see map 16). The Paris basin and most of the Mediterranean littoral remained the hard centres of dechristianization, which yields nothing to catholicism in terms of geographical stability.

Under the Third Republic the conflict between radicalism and

Map 16
Catholic religious practice *c.*1965

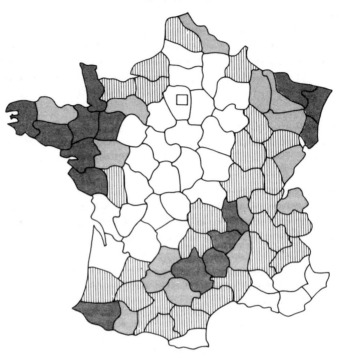

Proportion of adults attending Sunday mass:

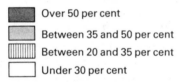 Over 50 per cent

Between 35 and 50 per cent

Between 20 and 35 per cent

Under 30 per cent

Based on detailed data presented in Le Bras, H. and Todd, E. 1981: *L'Invention de la France*. Paris: Livre de poche, 'Pluriel' series.

catholicism revived the religious confrontations of the Revolution, but in a more civilized form. Arguments in the local café replaced the Terror and the guillotine. This renewal of an old conflict roused ideologies and ordinary people everywhere, and ended in the legal separation of Church and State. But to a large extent it was an illusion. There was no really substantial modification in France's religious geography. Above all, although catholicism was a minority force in the country as a whole (being truly preponderant only in some thirty *départements*, out of ninety), it was neither broken nor weakened. In fact the few noticeable swings during the years 1791–1965 indicate a return to the original balance, confirming catholicism in its strongholds and dechristianization in its regions.

Over a longer period it is the number of religious vocations, i.e. ordinations of secular priests or entries into monasteries or convents, that is the most effective statistical index of the relative vitality of catholicism. Research by Claude Langlois into female communities in the nineteenth century suggests that the post-revolutionary period was a phase of recovery and re-establishment in catholicism's traditionally strong areas. In view of the really spectacular increase in the number of religious vocations, one may even wonder whether catholicism's hold on the border provinces under its sway did not become stronger than in the pre-revolutionary period.[3]

Julien Potel's statistical studies of the secular clergy in France, which deal mostly with the twentieth century, show a return to stability in the strongly Catholic areas, and a distinct weakening of residual catholicism in the dechristianized regions. Between 1904 and 1960, the number of secular clergy per inhabitant is just about stable in the dioceses of the traditionally Catholic regions, with a very slight diminution. However, there was a substantial fall in clerical manpower in the Paris basin and on the Mediterranean littoral.[4]

Generally speaking, all these movements indicate a slight gain in Catholic power in the nineteenth century, and a slight loss in the first half of the twentieth. Taken as a whole, the position was remarkably stable.

A SECONDARY MODIFICATION – THE WIND FROM THE EAST

Nevertheless, between 1791 and 1965 a significant change in the map of catholicism is noticeable – even if comparison between two indices as unlike as 'the proportion of priests accepting the constitutional oath in 1791' and 'the percentage of individuals attending mass around 1965' entails some methodological ingenuity and a certain wariness of the reliability of the results obtained.

The maps showing secularization in 1791 (taken from an analysis of the constitutional oath) and around 1965 (taken from the proportion of individuals attending mass) are strongly correlated – +0.67. They do, however, show up certain differences. The parameters measured are not the same, making a direct comparison difficult. In particular, from the two indices used, it is impossible to measure the strength of religiosity or secularization in absolute terms. How could one have an equation of this sort: *The percentage of priests refusing the constitutional oath is equivalent to such and such a percentage of individuals attending mass?*

For each of the two maps one can list the various French *départements* according to strength and identify those whose place in the classification has moved between 1791 and 1965. For argument's sake let first place be given to the most secular *département* and ninetieth to the least secular, i.e. the most Catholic. If a *département* holds the same position in 1965 as in 1791, one can certainly not assert that the strength of catholicism (or secularity) has remained constant there, but one can say that it has not varied in relation to the current national average. If a *département* slips from third place to thirty-fifth in secularity, one can say that this represents a rise in catholicism relative to the national average. If another one slips from fortieth place to fifteenth for catholicism, a relative advance in secularity is evident.

Map 17 shows the *départements* where secularity has progressed or dropped by more than twenty places. Their distribution is not haphazard. Secularity seems to have gained ground in Limousin (Haute-Vienne, Creuze, Corrèze) and in the Nord–Pas-de-Calais region. Secularity seems to have lost ground in most of the eastern part of the country, especially in Lorraine and the Rhône–Alpes region. The *relative* gain of secularity in the extreme North and in the Limousin probably arises from internally generated ideological diffusion effect. The relative rise of catholicism in the East is even more interesting. It takes us back to the analysis of cultural and economic movement set out in chapter 2.

In Lorraine and the Rhône–Alpes area, one finds the opposite of what happens in Limousin and Nord–Pas-de-Calais. Homogenization has taken the form of a *relative* weakening of secularity and a revival of catholicism. Why? No doubt because cultural and economic forces travel from east to west. In the nineteenth century mass literacy was finally attained and industrialization began. These movements came from the east – from Germany and Switzerland. They probably brought in their wake the solid and durable catholicism of south Germany, non-Protestant Switzerland and northern Italy. The foreign lands to the east of France are in fact staunchly Catholic (except for a few Swiss cantons), from the German Rhineland all the way to Italian Piedmont.

These adjustments to the map of Catholicism, or of its opposite, secularity, ought, however, to be regarded as minor. They do not affect the general structure of the map, in particular the geographical centrality of secularization and the peripheral position of catholicism.

CATHOLICISM, THE LAST OF THE HERESIES

The final configuration of French catholicism, as it emerged in 1791 and still survived around 1960, seems surprising to the historian of religion and heresies. It is difficult not to notice the structural analogy between maps of post-revolutionary catholicism on the one hand and of protestantism, Waldensianism and Catharism on the other. They all occupied the outer regions of France, avoiding the Paris basin. Competing and at the same time complementary, these diverse expressions of religious faith formed geographically an almost perfect circle, leaving an extensive gap in the middle. Waldensians and Cathars, Protestants and Catholics seem to have joined hands to form a ring round the Paris basin and the French Revolution.

Map 17
The movement of catholicism betwen 1791 and 1965

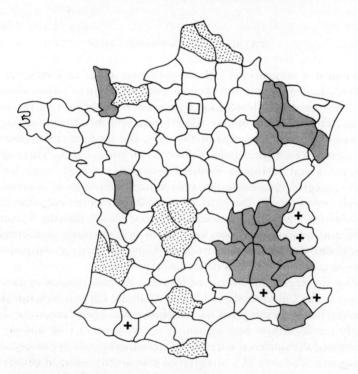

In terms of the relative strength of catholicism (see text),
départements which have:

 Risen more than 20 places

 Dropped more than 20 places

+   No data

Derived from maps 15 and 16.

Protestantism, in particular, was insignificant throughout the revolutionary and anti-catholic zone. Indeed it only survived in regions where catholicism had managed to endure. Residual in the Garonne valley, it was still widespread in Lozère, Ardèche, Jura and Alsace until about 1960. The protestantism of the extreme North of France did not survive.

This strange conjuncture of religious forces which opposed each other over the centuries was no accident. The Waldensians, Protestants, Catholics and even Cathars all had something in common which the French Revolution rejected: quite simply, God. Anthropological factors corroborate this theological evidence. Nor is it an accident that belief in God survived or increased only in certain regions. An analysis of profound and lasting factors will explain the geographical constancy of the religious phenomenon and its persistence over time.

CATHOLICISM AND REVOLUTION

Continuity of nomenclature should not, however, be allowed to obscure a certain discontinuity in the religious phenomenon itself. The catholicism which survived the Revolution was not the catholicism of the *ancien régime*. The pre-revolutionary Church was probably already stronger in the outlying bastions revealed by the crisis. But the Church's organization and ideas covered the whole of Paris basin equally well. There indeed occurred a real schism in French Christianity in 1791, since half the priests accepted the Revolution. One would be justified in asserting that French catholicism in the years 1791–1960 represented only one-half of pre-1791 catholicism. Conversely one wonders whether the Revolution itself, anti-religious but operating in an area formerly dominated by catholicism, did not assume part of the Christian heritage. An analysis of doctrine confirms the hints of historical geography.

What the Revolution borrowed from the Roman tradition in its widest sense, i.e. the Empire followed by the Catholic Church, was the idea of universal man. On this point the Revolution was not an innovator. It was simply the legitimate heir of Saint Paul who, more than anyone else, determined the universal vocation of Christianity, which had begun as a Jewish sect. The very idea of universal man is only a sort of ethnological application of the principle of equality. Men are equal within society, and likewise outside. The equality before the law of the noble and the bourgeois becomes a moral equality of the Frenchman and the foreigner.

The Revolution's gain was to a certain extent Christianity's loss. The universalist ideas of the Catholic Church lived on but lost their vigour. Their survival was inevitable, for the edifice of religious organization, which covered a large part of Europe, was centred on Rome and was inevitably multinational. But the universalist message languished; more generally, the ideal of equality, so important in the history of Christianity, faded away. The fact that a thinker like Joseph de Maistre could profess to be a Christian was a sign that the universalist conceptions of Christianity had gone into cold storage.

PROTESTANTISM, INEQUALITY AND AUTHORITY

Protestantism moved away from universalism even more than did post-revolutionary catholicism; it rejected far more firmly the ideal of equality among men. In certain respects it was a doctrine that was consciously inegalitarian. It is true that it sought access for everyone to the Scriptures and the word of God, but it demanded neither a levelling of social conditions nor equality amongst the peoples of the world.

It was hostile to the redistributive agencies of traditional Catholic charity, to alms and begging, which had been promoted in theory and practice by the medieval Church. It was also essentially indifferent to the idea of a communion of peoples within a universal Church. One of the characteristics of the German Reformation was a virulent nationalism. The separation from Rome was everywhere accompanied by the establishment of national churches, and by the introduction of beliefs and dogmas within limited ethnological boundaries. Reading of the Bible, especially in Calvinist countries, led to the idea of a chosen people, so that in Holland, England and Scotland people imagined themselves to belong to the nation chosen of God.

The concepts of faith, grace and predestination were the logical and indispensable mainsprings of Protestant élitism. With Luther the Reformation laid down a fundamental distinction between the elect and the damned, between an élite of true Christians and the mass of humanity that would not escape from original sin. Within the Protestant world the French reformers following Calvin and Théodore de Bèze, were extreme hard-liners. According to them, election and damnation were equally the effect of a decree, positive or negative, handed down by the Lord: 'We call Predestination the eternal counsel of God whereby He has determined what He wishes to make of each man. For He does not create everyone in like condition, but destines some to eternal life and others to eternal damnation. So, according to the end for which man has been created, we say that he is predestined to death or to life.'[5]

This vision of 'double predestination' certainly represents a radicalization of the Lutheran concept of grace, which saves certain souls without explicitly adding to the miseries of others. From its beginnings protestantism was denounced for its inegalitarian principles, and Calvin was perfectly conscious of this. He writes in the *Institution de la religion chrétienne*: 'It is therefore falsely and mischievously that some accuse God of inequality in justice, because in his Predestination he does not treat all men equally.'[6] His justification of God's attitude is not convincing. Logically it cannot be, for the doctrine of predestination presupposes inequality.

Among the Calvinists of Europe, the French Huguenots were certainly considered among the most loyal to this orthodoxy of inequality. It was in Holland that Arminianism was born, and in England that it triumphed. Arminian theology softened the principle of predestination, but the French Calvinists of the seventeeth century were less affected by it than their English or Dutch contemporaries. More explicitly inegalitarian than catholicism, protestantism was no less authoritarian, but in a different way.

The Reformation fully accepted a vertical vision of the universe and society. The theoretical summit of this pyramid was, as in catholicism, God. Protestantism, however, demands direct access to his Creator for each individual, short-circuiting the fixed hierarchies of catholicism, i.e. the parish priests, the bishops and the Pope. Before the Arminians, no Reformation thinkers were liberals, opposed to the very notion of authority. The God of Luther and Calvin, who saved and damned, was indeed the expression of an authoritarianism against which there was no appeal. But protestantism was haunted by a fundamental problem, for it refused to allow that the Pope and the Church were the visible incarnation of God's authority on earth. So who is to be credited with this transcendental authority? For, whether one is a believer or not, one has to admit that the direct manifestations of the divine will do not have the clarity, precision and bureaucratic substance of those of the Holy See. In fact the Protestant conception of authority created and kept unhealed an open wound: humanity is entirely subjected to a being whose existence cannot be demonstrated. Here lie the beauty and power of Protestant doctrine, which automatically induces individual anxiety, and consequently cultural dynamism.

Protestantism combines an abstract desire for submission with a refusal of all visible authority in the religious sphere. This basic ambivalence, albeit hesitant and formless, was certainly present at the very outset of the Reformation. In 1520, Luther wrote in *Concerning Christian Liberty*: 'A Christian is a free lord in all things, and subject to no one,' and 'A Christian is a serf liable to forced labour in all things, and subject to everyone.'[7] The Lutheran solution, which cannot logically be gainsaid, implies a dualist conception of the human personality. The person within is absolutely free and in contact with God, while the person without is absolutely the servant of the authorities of his time. Protestant Man, from his birth in the sixteenth century, divided his basic acceptance of authority. The internal person was nourished spiritually by the Scriptures; the external person rejected the Church but accepted without reservation the civil authority, whether a king, a prince or a town magistrate.

The authority of Scripture, a fundamental characteristic of protestantism, only shifts the problem of the actual transmission of divine authority to a different level. Neither the Old Testament nor the Gospels set forth a message that is absolutely clear. This is very plainly shown by the variety of answers found in them by the various Protestant churches and sects. Holy Writ clearly lays down a few great moral concepts, but intensive reading of it also permits psychological projection, the texts being scanned for examples and interpretations that suit the reader. Study of the Bible stimulates moral reflection, but it also acts like a psychological test, a Rorschach diagram of the soul. The individual does not see in it lamps or dogs or women dancing, but practical, ethical choices. The authority of Scripture is also, perhaps principally, a liberation of the spirit, a mechanism by which the conscience becomes autonomous.

So the Protestant personality is marked by a polarization: the internal man is the vassal of his conscience, the external man of his state. Luther's thought provides from the start a model for all late pietistic ideas of inner liberty and outer resignation. Because it is dualist, the Lutheran solution is not stable: a Protestant can only seesaw between respect for his conscience and respect for the state.

PROTESTANTISM AND REVOLUTION

As the French Revolution attacked the French Church, which had persecuted the reform movement, it might seem the natural ally of protestantism. Indeed, there was some confusion from 1789 onwards. The ideologists of the Revolution, like Condorcet, could not hide a certain affection for the protestantism of the South, which had anticipated their resistance to the dogma that the Pope and the bishops were all-powerful. So the Protestants remaining in France forged a sort of tactical alliance with the Revolution. Under the Third Republic the Protestants took part in the establishment of the secular and republican educational system, which guaranteed their independence. This alliance stemmed from the unequal balance of power between catholicism and a protestantism that had, between 1685 and 1880, become very much a minority, not to say a remnant. For on the level of basic values, protestantism subscribed to principles that were violently opposed to those of the Revolution.

The Revolution, egalitarian and liberal, clashed head-on with a protestantism that was inegalitarian and a supporter of authority.

Nothing was more contrary to the ideal of universal mankind as preached by the Enlightenment than the Calvinist notion of double predestination. Passing from the realm of ideological coherence to that of geographical continuity, one can see that the anti-Protestant regions at the time of the Wars of Religion, held by the League and centred on the Paris basin, were the very ones that in the eighteenth and nineteenth centuries proclaimed themselves champions of dechristianization as well as of a liberal and egalitarian ideal. Paris was the great anti-Protestant city of the League before being at the centre of the dechristianizing process.

THE MYSTERY OF RELIGIONS AND IDEOLOGIES

Our main object, of course, remains: to understand the regular and stable geographical distribution of religion and secularity in French territory. The very stability of the structures under analysis suggests the existence of profound determinants in the anthropological sphere. The stability of catholicism between 1791 and 1960 provides *a priori* proof that the traditional economic hypotheses are incapable of resolving the problem. Between 1791 and 1960 France experienced a total economic and social upheaval. She passed from the rural stage to the urban stage, from agriculture to industry. So the historical and geographical examination of religious systems proves by itself that religion was very largely independent of the processes of the Industrial Revolution.

4

The Peasants

The division of French territory into Protestant, Catholic and dechristianized zones occurred between the sixteenth and eighteenth centuries, at a time when France was still a great rural nation. In 1789 the proportion of peasants in the working population was still over 75 per cent. So it seems logical to look among the structures of French rural society for features that can help us to understand and explain the religious and ideological geography which emerged from the *ancien régime*.

One must examine the organization of French peasant societies between 1500 and 1800 for differential factors favouring the appearance of protestantism in one place, the survival of catholicism in another, and elsewhere the disintegration of all religious belief. So a comparative study of different French peasantries under the *ancien régime* is necessary. Strangely enough, the remarkable progress of French historiography in agrarian history does not provide us with such comparative data.

Les Paysans du Nord pendant la Révolution française by Georges Lefebvre (1929, Lille), *Beauvais et le Beauvaisis au XVIIᵉ siècle* by Pierre Goubert (1960. Paris: SEVPEN) and *Les Paysans de Languedoc* by Emmanuel Le Roy Ladurie (1966. Paris: SEVPEN) contain some of the most meticulous studies of the *ancien régime* peasantries ever carried out. These books undoubtedly analyse with very great precision the structures and conditions of certain provincial and rural societies. But it is difficult to extract from a few regional surveys a general picture of French agrarian systems that can be reduced to map form. These accounts describe the reality of rural life in depth. What we need, on the other hand, is a simplifying, even superficial synthesis covering the whole territory of France.

The poor state of documentation for the eighteenth century prevents us from carrying out such a study. One can only attempt a general description of French agrarian systems from the mid-nineteenth century onwards. At that date the first censuses provide researchers with statistical data that can be processed uniformly for all *départements*.

The date is late. The use of the 1851 census for analysing agrarian structures before the French Revolution seems *a priori* inappropriate, particularly if one looks upon agrarian systems as essentially fluid phenomena which are affected by demography, economics and politics. The *continuity* of rural societies has to be assumed if one wants to use the first censuses of the nineteenth century to analyse certain aspects of rural France under the *ancien régime*. There are several justifications for this approach.

THE STABILITY OVER TIME OF AGRARIAN SYSTEMS

The universally applicable hypothesis of a continuous and rapid development of agrarian systems, much loved of Marx, is absurd. No evolutionary model, showing growth by concentration of capital from the family farm to the large estate dependent on hired labour, can be observed either historically or geographically. For example, the large estate is not a product of the modern world. In Europe it makes its appearance in Roman or medieval times. Nowadays we find it both in industrially advanced countries like England, and in notoriously backward regions like southern Italy and southern Spain. Nor can the family farm be associated with a specific level of industrial development, for it is typical not only of the agriculture of western Germany, Japan and Sweden (hardly backward countries), but also of northern India, Africa and northern Portugal.

Credit is due to Kautsky – Lenin called him the 'renegade' – for being the first to question, and in the clearest terms, Marxist models of the mechanism of agricultural concentration. In his later works he hypothe- sizes the long-term stability of agrarian systems, thereby reconciling agrarian history and social anthropology. In France the results obtained from the 1851 census generally coincide with the soundings taken by historians working in a more distant past, e.g. by those working on the sixteenth to eighteenth centuries, and even by medievalists studying earlier periods. The great domains described by Georges Duby in *L'Économie rurale et la Vie des campagnes dans l'Occident médiéval* were situated in the very regions where large estates were dominant in 1851, i.e. in the Paris basin. In the Middle Ages peasant *alleux* (freeholds), suggesting the existence of independent family farms, were more numerous in the southern part of the country. In 1851 Occitania remained the leading region for peasant proprietorship.

On the other hand, few facts support the opposite hypothesis – that agrarian systems in France were essentially unstable between the Middle Ages and the nineteenth century, in spite of the sale of certain Church properties during the Revolution.

After 1851 the hypothesis of a fundamental stability of agrarian systems is confirmed in a most remarkable manner, despite the economic turmoil occasioned by the Industrial Revolution. The areas of France occupied by family farms on the one hand, and by great estates using hired labour on the other, have varied very little in the last century in spite of the mechanization of agriculture. This stability between 1850 and 1980, in a period of intense technological upheaval, allows us to postulate a corresponding stability between 1750 and 1850. These stable agrarian systems can then be set alongside the stable ideologies, religious or secular, that were described in the last chapter. The description of French agrarian systems based on the 1851 census justifies a division of the rural territory coinciding fairly closely with the religious division that became apparent during the course of the *ancien régime*, between the sixteenth and eighteenth centuries.

THE TYPOLOGY OF FRENCH AGRARIAN SYSTEMS

Two major types of agrarian system can be distinguished on French territory, of which one must in its turn be subdivided into three separate categories:

First category: the large estate dependent on hired labour, unlike the family holding.
Second category: the family holding, itself subdivided into three categories – proprietorship, tenancy, share-cropping.

To take the first contrast, the basic criterion separating a large estate from a family holding is that of concentration. In the case of large estates, a handful of rural entrepreneurs control most of the land in each village and employ an agricultural proletariat to cultivate it. In the case of family holdings, the land is more or less equally divided up among the people of the village, and the main input of labour comes from the farmers' families. This system reduces wage-earners to secondary and often marginal importance.

The subdivision of the family holding into three sub-categories is a question of the ownership of the land:

● In a regime of *peasant proprietorship*, the land cultivated by a family belongs to it absolutely.
● In a regime of *tenant farming*, the land belongs to others, and a variable rent is paid in money.
● In a regime of *share-cropping*, the farming family does not enjoy ownership of the land, but the rent is paid in kind and is assessed as a fixed proportion of the crops.

In practice, share-cropping weighs heavily on the peasant family, who own neither the land nor the equipment. In the case of tenancy, on the other hand, the family owns the tools, the seeds and the fertilizers. It is in a far stronger position contractually in its relations with the landowner. The 'big farmers' using much hired labour are moreover often tenants themselves, treating with their landlords on equal terms. The 'family' tenant farmers enjoy a certain security of tenure, in which they differ from the share-croppers, who are often turned out.

The chief characteristics of each of these four categories can be summarized as in table 4.1.

Table 4.1

	Size of holding	Security of tenure
Large estate	large	good
Family holding 1: owned	moderate ($-$)	good
Family holding 2: rented	moderate ($+$)	fairly good
Family holding 3: share-cropped	moderate ($+$)	poor

For each of the four agrarian systems there is a corresponding distribution of the agricultural working population. In a region of large estates, the agricultural labourers – the 'journeymen' or 'day-labourers', to use the old terms – make up the majority of the population. In a system of family ownership, the peasant proprietors make up the largest group in the working population. In a system of tenancy or share-cropping, where the holdings are generally rather larger than under peasant proprietorship, the tenant farmers and share-croppers represent 15–30 per cent of the agricultural working population, the rest consisting of house servants, relations (these categories can often be confused), and a certain number of agricultural labourers.

The systems which have just been described are of course ideal models. Various mixes are possible, as few French regions exhibit absolutely pure types.

The large estate attains its most perfect realization in the centre of the Paris basin. In 1851, more than 70 per cent of agricultural workers were day-labourers in the *départements* of Aisne, Eure-et-Loir, Seine-et-Marne and Seine-Maritime.

The family farm is particularly dominant in the South where, in the 1851 census, more than 60 per cent of agricultural workers were proprietors in Alpes-de-Haute-Provence, Hautes-Alpes, Ardèche, Creuse, Drôme, Lot, Puy-de-Dôme and Hautes-Pyrénées.

Share-cropping is characteristic of the agrarian structure of the Centre-West. In Allier, Corrèze, Dordogne and Haute-Vienne, share-croppers made up more than 25 per cent of all farmers.

In each type of agriculture a social category dominates the local culture by its numbers, by its control of the actual cultivation of the soil, or by a mixture of these two factors. In a regime of large estates, the people who own and run them, being few in number, are economically all-powerful but culturally marginal. A village in the Paris basin in the eighteenth and nineteenth centuries consisted mainly of farm labourers and their families. The day-labourers dictated the behaviour, tastes and opinions of the local population. In a system of family ownership, the peasant proprietors, who formed a majority of the population and were masters of the land, determined almost entirely the local life-style. The situation for tenant farming and share-cropping was a little more complicated. The tenant farmers and share-croppers were numerous without being in a majority, and in addition they were the actual exploiters of the soil. Without dictating the local life-style, they gave it its dominant flavour.

So on consideration of the social functioning of villages and local communities, it is not absurd to describe the Paris basin as a country of day-labourers, the South as a country of proprietors, the Centre as a country of share-croppers and the West as a country of tenant farmers. Each of these social categories characterizes the psychological patterns of the regions under scrutiny. Their existence depends, however, on a whole anthropological fabric which we shall have to analyse. Day-labourers, proprietors, tenant farmers and share-croppers do not appear by accident in such and such a region.

One can apply the typology distinguishing societies of day-labourers, proprietors, tenant farmers and share-croppers to the whole French territory. On map 18 special symbols indicate the *départements* which in 1851 boasted more than 17.5 per cent tenant farmers, more than 38.5 per cent proprietors and more than 14 per cent share-croppers. The regions remaining blank indicate a majority of hired hands, of day-labourers. This classification is somewhat arbitrary, but it does show up, on a single map, types of local society without much overlap of dominant agrarian types.

Peasant proprietors dominated the whole of southern society below a line from La Rochelle to Bourg-en-Bresse. The only exceptions were the *départements* of the Mediterranean littoral. The region of peasant proprietors also included a strip stretching east towards Alsace across Jura and Doubs.

Day-labourers held sway in the central area of the greater Paris basin, which extended as far as Poitiers to the south and Nancy to the east.

Map 18
Agrarian systems in the mid-nineteenth century

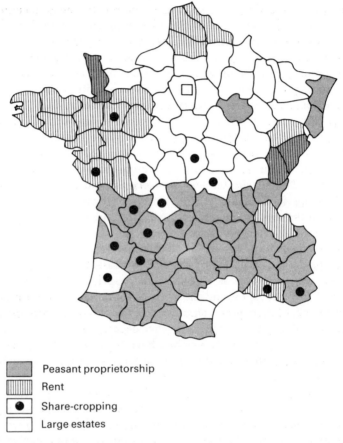

Peasant proprietorship
Rent
Share-cropping
Large estates

Based on data from the 1851 census.

Aube, where there were many small proprietors, can be regarded as an exception, the result perhaps of mistakes made by the census officials.

Tenant farmers constituted the typical element of rural society in the West, in the extreme North, and to a lesser extent in the Haute-Saône–Doubs–Jura area where they shared the land with small proprietors.

Share-croppers were at the centre of rural life along the western edge of the Massif Central and, less obviously, in Var and Bouches-du-Rhône. The share-croppers of Vendée and Mayenne were more a misnomer than an economic reality. The security of their tenure related them more closely to the tenant farmers of the West than to pure share-croppers.

Generally speaking, it would be absurd to look upon the data of the 1851 census as wholly reliable and sacrosanct. The description of occupations is a perpetual headache in agricultural history. In the middle of the nineteenth century the names of trades were not yet fully standardized at the national level. So the more or less coherent map based on 1851 classifications must be regarded as a quite unexpected achievement.

This map of agrarian systems probably changed little between 1789 and 1851, in spite of the disturbances and rural reforms of the revolutionary years. Recent historical writing, obsessed by the idea of agrarian concentration of capital, derived from Marxism, has mainly looked for transformation and change. However, for the most part, the results of detailed historical soundings are actually in perfect agreement with the map drawn for the year 1851.

In the Middle Ages the great feudal domain flourished in the same regions. Even in the Roman era the favourite settlement zone of the *villae*, large agricultural estates based on slavery, was the region between the Loire and the north-east of France. From earliest times, the South appears on the contrary to have been a territory of *alleux*, i.e. small peasant properties.[1]

It is therefore perfectly reasonable to assume a *continuity* of agrarian systems, and to regard the map obtained for 1851 (which moreover matches the one drawn from the 1982 census) as the expression of a structure which remained stable over centuries.

AGRICULTURAL WORKERS AND DECHRISTIANIZATION

It was within this stable, age-old structure that the French Revolution developed, with its aspirations, its dogmas and its obsessions. Whereas it is difficult to establish by maps a relationship between secularity and industrialization, it is easy to superimpose the map of dechristianization, in 1791 or 1965, on that of the agrarian systems. Dechristianization overran the territory occupied by a numerically preponderant agricultural proletariat, i.e. the centre of the Paris basin. In the north, the west and the east it ran up against tenant farming regions. It pushed out further south-west into the share-cropping regions, but was halted everywhere to the south by family proprietorship.

On the Mediterranean littoral, dechristianization flourished among the share-croppers of Var and Bouches-du-Rhône, and among the agricultural proletariat of lower Languedoc. In this region, however, the correspondence between agrarian systems and dechristianization was weakened by the narrowness of the coastal strip.

Overall, one would be tempted to propose the two following entailments:

Day-labourers + share-croppers → dechristianization
Proprietors + tenant farmers → survival of catholicism

The correspondence between agrarian systems and dechristianization is far from perfect. The East of France appears 'too Catholic' for its high proportion of day-labourers around 1965, but not around 1791. Haute-Provence, both in 1965 and 1791, seems 'too secular' for its large number of proprietors. Of course one cannot exclude the possibility of local aberrations in 1965 caused by secondary movements of autonomous ideological diffusion; as it happens, the main anomalies affect the East of the country, where the relative strength of catholicism increased between 1791 and 1965.[2]

Once this correspondence has been established, it is very difficult to resist a last temptation to interpret in a Marxian manner. How can one avoid seeing in the dechristianization of the agricultural proletariat a healthy and logical reaction to wage-exploitation of a capitalist type – a rural exploitation certainly, but no less intolerable for that? The basic problem is that the equally unbearable capitalist exploitation in the towns never produced such radical effects. The *agricultural wage-earners* of the years 1790–1960 abandoned God. The industrial wage-earners of the years 1920–65, when they lived in the extreme North or in the East of France, remained loyal to him. So an alternative non-economic interpretation of this correspondence between agrarian and religious maps must be found.

AGRARIAN SYSTEMS AND FAMILY TYPES

When one analyses the life of a rural community, there is no concrete distinction that can be made between economic and family life. If one identifies an agrarian system, one also implicitly characterizes the form of family life that underpins it. The terminology employed, which contrasts 'large estate' with 'family holding', reveals this same confusion of the economic and the anthropological in a peasant setting. Yet it would be wrong to draw a general contrast between 'agricultural wage-earners' and 'peasant families'. In fact an ideal family type goes with each agrarian system, as much in the case of wage-earners as in the case of different types of family farm (see map 19).

It is difficult to imagine *peasant proprietorship* without the support of a stem family to ensure a continuous lineage on the farm. In such a system one of the heirs is privileged, for he inherits the whole farm. So the rules

Map 19
Family types

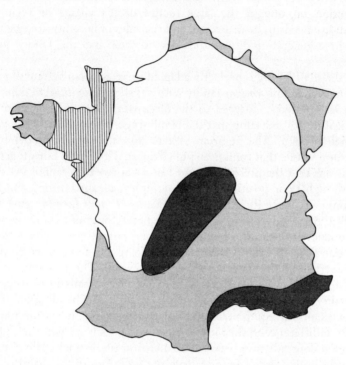

	Relations between parents and children	Relations between brothers
Egalitarian nuclear	liberal	egalitarian
Stem	authoritarian	inegalitarian
Community	authoritarian	egalitarian
Absolute nuclear	liberal	non-egalitarian

Based on the map provided in Todd, E. 1985: *The Explanation of Ideology. Family structures and social systems.* Oxford: Basil Blackwell.

of succession are inegalitarian. Relations between generations are close, and even authoritarian, because the married son remains under the sway of his father in a three-generation household.[3]

Agricultural wage-earners display the opposite family archetype. No land is transmitted from one generation to another, so no continuity is necessary. Relations, therefore, between generations are not close, for a child can very soon earn his living independently from parental protection on one of the large estates of his village or region. No patrimony needs to be protected, and the rules of heredity are egalitarian. No three-generation households are formed and the family ideal is nuclear.

So the *stem family* is perfectly adapted to an agrarian system of *peasant proprietorship*. The *nuclear* family with a system of *egalitarian* inheritance is no less perfectly adapted to the *large-estate* system. But there is no justification for asserting that the family type is a product of the type of agrarian system. The agrarian system and the family model form a structural whole that cannot be pulled apart. They were born together in conditions that the present state of historical research cannot yet define.

Although their position is more complex, tenant farming and share-cropping also have their family equivalents. *Tenant farming* goes with a family type of agriculture in which the family does not enjoy ownership of the land. It does not therefore call for a continuity of generations on the same farm. It can go with a *nuclear* family system, in which parents and married children are not closely associated. The existence of stable farming units, not owned by peasant families, entails in practice some inequality among the children when it comes to the handing on of farms and agricultural equipment. Refusal to divide up the farms implies a certain indifference to the ideal of equality. In such systems there appears a general contradiction between a collection of abstract egalitarian rules (derived, in the case of France, from the traditions of the majority of the nation) and a flexible practice in the actual handing on of inheritances. This contradiction is evident in the work of Alexandre de Brandt, cited earlier. His *map* of inheritance systems shows the West as a region of egalitarian division while his *text*, which is much more precise, describes in detail the extensive use of wills in the West, the habit of not dividing up the farm but buying out some of the children by cash payments.[4] A family system of the nuclear type, but without strictly egalitarian inheritance rules, is perfectly suited to the workings of the tenant system.[5]

Share-cropping in practice coincides with family groups which, unlike stem families, do not follow inegalitarian rules of inheritance. There are no possessions to transfer because the property does not belong to the farmer. Share-cropping is a system that is harsher and more unstable than tenant farming, and it functions in the context of an economy where money plays a smaller part. It frequently inspires horizontal family co-operation, particularly among brothers, so as to make up work groups of sufficient size. It often corresponds to a *community family model*, bringing together parents and married children without any brother being favoured above the rest. It coincides with a family structure that is complex but egalitarian, unlike the stem system.[6]

The existence of these family communities is very well attested for Provence and the region immediately to the north of the Massif Central – Berry, the Nivernais and the Bourbonnais. They were identified in the mid-nineteenth century by Le Play[7] and his school. They are cited by de Brandt.[8] They have been re-examined in Allier, the west of Saône-et-Loire, the south of Nièvre and the north of Puy-de-Dôme by Henriette Dussourd.[9] The situation is less clear in the south-west part of the vast share-cropping area extending from the river Allier to the Dordogne. The *départements* of Creuse, Haute-Vienne, Corrèze and Dordogne are linguistically part and parcel of Occitania, and many studies on inheritance customs ascribe to them inegalitarian habits typical of the South-west; de Brandt is a case in point.[10]

The stem family, however, seems to be quite incompatible with the insecure share-cropping tenure typical of some farms of the region. It seems that in Limousin and Périgord two agrarian and family types are superimposed locally one upon the other. The peasant proprietors live in a stem-family system and the share-croppers in community families. The whole zone between Dordogne and Saône-et-Loire should be regarded as a point of contact between the stem system of the South and the egalitarian nuclear family structures of the North. The presence of intermediary agrarian and family types, which combine certain northern and southern features, is here the result of centuries-old interaction between northern and southern systems.

These logical connections between economic and family variables explain why the map of agrarian systems based on the 1851 census and the map of family systems based on the analysis of household structures and inheritance rules fit quite well together. If we take the categories used in *The Explanation of Ideology* (op. cit.), we arrive at table 4.2.

An examination of agrarian and family maps reveals certain discrepancies. The area of tenant farming is more extensive than that of the absolute nuclear family. Tenant farming occupies too large an area in the West, to which we must add bastions in the North and in the Jura. The link between share-cropping and community families is equally imperfect, particularly along the Mediterranean littoral.

Nevertheless the link between family structure and agrarian system is very close. So it is possible that the geographical distribution of agrarian systems, based on exhaustive statistical data, in certain places describes the real family structure better than the distribution of family types shown in *The Explanation of Ideology*. The map of family types uses disparate and discontinuous data: inheritance rules, monographs on villages, and structure of households at a late date (1975).

The map of agrarian systems does, however, contain an important inaccuracy. It concerns Brittany and results from the use by census officials of inadequate analytical categories. The rarity of peasant proprietorship in the area seems to exclude the stem family from lower Brittany. In actual fact the 1851 census did not take account of the existence in this region of France of a special type of farming, half-way between ownership and tenancy. Under this system the buildings belonged to the peasant and the land to the landowner. This was the *domaine congéable*, nearer to true ownership than to tenancy in many respects, which allowed the stem family, with its classic single heir, to exist in lower Brittany.

Table 4.2

	Links between generations	Inheritance type	Agrarian system
Stem or authoritarian family	strong	inegalitarian	peasant proprietorship
Egalitarian nuclear family	weak	egalitarian	large estate
Absolute nuclear family	weak	not egalitarian	tenancy
Community family	strong	egalitarian	share-cropping

An ideal geographical distribution of family systems would no doubt consist of a subtle and intricate blend of the agrarian systems map and the family systems map shown in *The Explanation of Ideology*.

A CONCEPTUAL REARRANGEMENT

The link between family and agrarian system will help us to understand why dechristianization gained ground, from 1791 onwards, in regions of large farms and share-cropping, and met with resistance in provinces where tenant farming and peasant proprietorship were predominant. This proposition can, moreover, be reformulated thanks to equivalences between family types and agrarian systems. Dechristianization spread in regions where the family structure was *egalitarian nuclear* or *community*, but failed in provinces where the family was *stem* or *absolute nuclear*.

However, at this stage, it is not enough to make the maps fit. We must understand the logical necessity that links certain family types to certain ideological types.

5

Family and Ideology

When you admit that there is a necessary relationship between family structure and ideology, you can understand the special affection that certain regions felt for the principles of the French Revolution, and the no less strong love of others for counter-revolutionary principles.[1]

Modern ideologies, whether political or religious, can be regarded as abstract, depersonalized reflections of ideas that are latent in family life. Notions of equality and inequality, authority and liberty, so fundamental in political life, do in fact structure family life itself. They are particularly visible and identifiable in the traditional world of the peasant, for connection with the land reveals affective models with great clarity.

Relations between brothers can be egalitarian or inegalitarian, as is shown by an analysis of inheritance customs. These divide up the land or do not do so; they often proclaim the equality of the children, but they can sometimes assert their inequality by favouring a single heir, who will deprive his brothers of the parents' estate. Relations between parents and children can be authoritarian or liberal, according to whether or not a grown-up son must continue to live with his parents after marriage, subject to their authority in a three-generation household.

These relationships between brothers and between parents and children, repeated from one generation to another by imitation and upbringing, act as models for political ideologies, which in their turn concern themselves with abstract equality among all men, or with the abstract authority of the State over all men.

TWO MAJOR TYPES

It is not really surprising, therefore, to see the ideology of the French Revolution, summed up by its motto 'Liberty, equality', spreading with ease in a vast central area like the Paris basin, where family ideas were indeed *liberal* and *egalitarian*. Children there left their parents to get married, and brothers divided up the smallest piece of land handed on by their parents.

Nor is it surprising to note that rejection of the Revolution is loud and clear in the provinces where the dominant family structure proclaims at once the authority of the father and the inequality of brothers, in a world where adult children remain subjected to the father's control and only one of the children inherits the parents' estate. It is the stem (or authoritarian) family which resists the revolutionary principle of liberty and equality.

To get an idea of the regional strength of revolutionary feeling, we must here use a tool that is statistically imperfect, the map of dechristianization. However, abandoning the Church, the Pope, the bishops and the priests is not strictly a political choice, but mostly a religious one. So we have to be satisfied with an approximation, justified simultaneously by the antireligious fury of the revolutionaries and the claims in support of catholicism of the counter-revolutionaries.

LUCIDITY AND ILLUSIONS OF THE EIGHTEENTH CENTURY

The men of the eighteenth century were largely aware of the connection between family and ideology, whether they supported the authority of God and the king, or republican liberty.

Catholicism is explicitly a support of the family, and God is 'Our Father'. As for the monarchists, they clearly identified the king's authority with that of a father. But, characteristically, revolutionary thought also accepted the principle of family–ideology interaction. Rousseau makes this perfectly clear in his *Social Contract*:

> The most ancient of all societies, and the only natural one, is that of the family. Even then the children only remain tied to their father for as long as they need him for their security. As soon as this need ceases, the natural link is severed. The children, freed from the obedience due to their father, and the father freed from the care which he owed to his children, all enter equally into a state of independence . . . So the family, if you like, is the first model of a political society. The leader is the image of the father, the people are an image of the children, and they all, being born equal and free, only surrender their freedom for practical reasons.[2]

It is the egalitarian nuclear family that Rousseau is describing, and he puts it forward as an ideal. So the Church and the Revolution could agree on one proposition that was both abstract and precise – the world of family and of politics show certain analogies of a structural type.

What made Catholic and revolutionary thought both incompatible and false was the notion that there existed only one form of family life, the stem family according to the Church and the egalitarian nuclear family according to the Revolution. Moreover, the desire of each side was to adapt the anthropological reality to their ideological concepts. The Church through all her institutions set herself up as the protector of the stem family, so she fought for the respect of parents, which is a striking detail of all Catholic catechisms in every epoch. Conversely, the Revolution wanted to break up the stem family. The Code Civil is always at pains, with certain exceptions, to impose the egalitarian division of estates.

The actors in this ideological war of family types were in fact the playthings of regional anthropological systems. For, of course, the Paris basin was in the Rousseau camp and the outer regions of France were pro-Catholic. Rousseau wanted to create the egalitarian nuclear family type, but in the event it was that family, where it existed, which took over Rousseau. The Church thought it was defending the stem family, but it was really the stem family, where it was predominant, that permitted the survival of the Church. The egalitarian nuclear family at the centre and the stem family in the outer regions occupied between them about three-quarters of all French territory. So it is not surprising to observe that their respective zones of influence lead to an effective and lasting confrontation of French ideologies. The egalitarian nuclear family won the day in terms of numbers, but not by an excessive amount. It was forty-two *départements* against thirty-three – an estimate that carries a certain element of simplification. The dominance, at the national level, of the republican ideal (liberty, equality) also sprang from the fact that the anthropological forces behind it occupied the centre of the country.

However, 20 per cent of the national territory was not held by these two major types, one of them linking the ideals of liberty and equality, and the other the ideals of authority and inequality. The first deviant group was the inland West where the dominant family type, absolute nuclear, combined liberty and inequality, or at least non-equality. The second deviant group was the western border of the Massif Central between Dordogne and Allier, and a part of the Mediterranean littoral, where the community type of family had authority and equality existing side by side. In all these cases the nationally dominant group of ideas did not fit properly. The participation of the regions in question in the national debate presupposed certain limitations and choices.

THE INLAND WEST AND THE CHURCH

The family system of the inland West, a large, compact region including French-speaking Brittany, Maine, Anjou and the western part of

Normandy, is dominated by family systems of the *absolute nuclear* type. Relations here between parents and children are not authoritarian. The family households described in the 1975 census even show up a particularly small proportion of three-generation examples. The inheritance customs are egalitarian in theory, but flexible in practice; and the land is not divided up among the children. This system, though less violently inegalitarian than the stem family, can certainly be described as non-egalitarian. On this point the regions of the West are clearly the opposite of the egalitarian inheritance zones of the Paris basin. The break between the two territories is physically marked by the change in the countryside from the *open fields* of the Paris basin, combining hedgeless fields with grouped housing, to the *bocage* of the West, combining enclosure of the fields by hedges with dispersed housing.

In theory, the absolute nuclear family could not be entirely favourable either to the egalitarian individualism of the Paris basin or to the inegalitarian authoritarianism of the outer lands. Its liberal side, which came from its nuclear structure, could make it lean towards the Revolution. Its non-egalitarian side, which appeared in its flexible inheritance customs, could, on the contrary, make it side with counter-revolutionary thought. It was this second logic which prevailed, for reasons which were not simply historical and accidental. The choice of this ambivalent type, not well adapted to the major French debate, shows perhaps that the ideological principle dominating the whole revolutionary process, and which dominated the attitudes of the regions, was equality rather than liberty.

However, certain historical conditions would have led the West to join the counter-revolution – in a situation where the pairs liberty-authority and equality-inequality were in strict equilibrium. At the time of the French Revolution, and throughout the nineteenth century, the inland West was one of the most backward areas on the cultural plane. The literacy rate there was particularly low, and the popular masses were quite incapable of expressing their own ideals either in politics or religion. The landed power of the nobility there was probably more crushing than elsewhere in France, as was observed by André Siegfried.[3] The strength of the aristocracy there was in any case much greater than in the stem family regions, where the typical peasant was a proprietor. The peasant of the inland West was, by contrast, a dependent tenant. Tocqueville was thinking of this nobility of the West when he opined that the aristocrat's residence on his estates, rather than at Versailles or Paris, was one of the strong points of the counter-revolution in certain provinces. In addition, the personal family system of this ruling aristocracy was by definition the stem type, for it is primogeniture that founds an aristocratic line.

At the moment when the choice between Revolution and counter-revolution, dechristianization and catholicity had to be made, i.e. between 1785 and 1850, the population of the West was an inert mass, well kept in hand by the *seigneurs*. The implicit liberal aspirations of the family system were restrained, and indifference to the equality principle, an innate trait of the anthropological system, was encouraged. The West became one of the most important bastions of reaction in the country. Superficially it took on all the characteristics of the anti-republican regions, and notably their catholicism. But this membership of the Church was less natural and spontaneous than it was in Savoie, Lower Brittany, Alsace, the Basque country, Rouergue and all the other regions of the stem family where catholicism gained support from a conception of authority engendered by the very structure of the family. Liberal and non-egalitarian, the family system of the peasants of the West is in fact far removed from the fundamental concepts of catholicism. It is not authoritarian, but its absence of egalitarianism, although it accords with aristocratic convictions, is nevertheless not a trait that is officially approved by the Church.

One can agree with Siegfried that it was the political power of the nobility in these regions of the inland West which enabled the organization of the Church to impose itself. Around 1900 the château carried more influence than the presbytery in the nuclear family regions of the West.[4] In other Catholic regions where the stem family predominated, the parish priest was on the whole the more powerful. The establishment of the Church in the inland West required political and institutional effort, simply because it did not flow from direct anthropological determination. This catholicism was to a certain extent imported, for it relied less on families and more on specific organizations, notably of an educational kind. For the period 1850–1960 the map of 'free' (i.e.: Church) primary education (see map 20) shows that the weight of the private school was much greater in the inland West than in the other regions of Catholic tradition. In 1959 the proportion of pupils taught in private education exceeded 50 per cent in only five *départements*, all of them in the west – Maine-et-Loire, Ille-et-Vilaine, Morbihan, Loire-Atlantique and Vendée. Of all organizations that can influence ideas, primary education, which moulds children from six to eleven years, is certainly the one that is most capable of replacing the family. It is difficult, therefore, to regard the special efforts of the Church as the result of chance. Priests taught the majority of children only in the one Catholic region where the stem (or authoritarian) family was not dominant and was not in a position to inculcate directly respect for God and the principle of authority.

You have then the economic and political weight of the nobility and the

Map 20
'Free' primary education *c.*1960

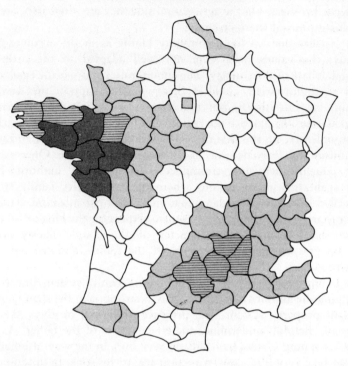

Proportion of primary pupils outside the State system:

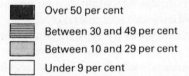

■ Over 50 per cent

▦ Between 30 and 49 per cent

▨ Between 10 and 29 per cent

□ Under 9 per cent

Based on the map provided in Coutrot, A. and Dreyfus, G. 1965: *Les Forces religieuses dans la société française.* Paris, 328.

establishment of the Church's organization. So it came about that, for the inland West, the pair equality-inequality defined the political alignment of the region rather than the pair liberty-authority.

THE COMMUNITY FAMILY AND DECHRISTIANIZATION

To the west and north of the Massif Central, between the *départements* of Dordogne and Allier, and in certain regions of Provence, community family types were in the majority. These are authoritarian as regards relations between parents and children and egalitarian as regards relations between brothers. On the agricultural side they are often associated with the institution of share-cropping.

It is clear that, in the community family as in the absolute nuclear family, the values held were not well adapted to the main ideological debate of the country. The community family, being egalitarian as well as authoritarian, could in theory neither support the Revolution (egalitarian but liberal) nor the counter-revolution (authoritarian but inegalitarian). In practice the regions in question came down clearly, and even violently, on the side of the Revolution. The dechristianization of Limousin and Provence was as thorough as anywhere. Once again the pair equality-inequality triumphed over the pair authority-liberty. The egalitarianism of regions where the community family structure prevailed led them towards revolutionary dechristianization, while their authoritarianism did not breed in them respect for the king or for priests. Here the less important character of the couple liberty-authority can be grasped at the very level of the family and the agricultural structure.

It is improbable that in the community family system and in share-cropping the authority of the father is as strong as in the stem family and peasant property system. The presence of several brothers, equal and mutually helpful, undermines the effectiveness of the father. As in the share-cropping system he hands on very little in the way of inheritance; he can take very little concrete action against his sons. In the community family system the solidarity of brothers seems to be the central axis of the family organization. What differentiates it from the egalitarian nuclear family is the fact that fraternal solidarity survives marriage.

In the case of France, studies of this minority type of family are too lacking in detail for us to arrive at any certainty. But we have clear data for central Italy and notably Tuscany, which is a large region of community family living and share-cropping (*mezzadria*). The striking feature there is indeed a lateral organization of households, association between married brothers being much more frequent than between father and married sons. There were 75 per cent lateral links in households consisting of several married couples against 25 per cent vertical links in a Tuscan community of the eighteenth century.[5]

The authoritarianism of the community family is therefore more spread out than vertical. The individual is taken in hand by the family, but not especially by his parents. This form of authoritarianism does not suit the Church, which fights for a purely vertical submission of the son to the father, of man to God and the priest. In the regions of community families, as of absolute nuclear families, it is in the end the pair equality-inequality which proves stronger than the pair liberty-authority in the determination of the region's ideological destiny.

However, the ideological ambivalence of the community family regions is not cancelled out by the choice of the principle of equality. Between 1789 and 1850 the authoritarian element was only hidden. This was perfectly natural, for the regions concerned were in a minority and situated in the part of the country that was least advanced culturally. The family system of these regions got its chance in the twentieth century with the world-wide emergence of communism, a doctrine that is egalitarian and authoritarian, which gave the French regions with a community family system a chance, though a late one, to express themselves fully. The west and north borders of the Massif Central, as well as part of the Mediterranean littoral, then saw the birth of a powerful rural communism. In these regions the shift from traditional French revolutionary feeling towards Bolshevik attitudes, from 1921 onwards, was painless. It resolved a basic contradiction, a structural incompatibility of the local anthropological systems with the main ideological debate which divided France.

THE PROTESTANTS

At this stage one can understand the coming together (geographically speaking) of protestantism and catholicism, which ended by their occupying much the same fringe positions on French territory.

Protestantism and catholicism were in fact helped at this late stage by occupying the same anthropological ground – the stem family, which, in the Judeo-Christian context, always seems to have been the vital prop for strong religious belief. The stem family is also typical of the Jewish tradition. Interaction between religion and the stem family is certainly one of the easiest to establish and explain. Religious doctrines place the family at the front of the stage, and they use its symbolism directly in their dogma and ritual. God is inevitably a father, an explicit and systematic representation in the Catholic, and even in the Protestant, tradition. Judaism tries not to give the Godhead too anthropomorphic an image, but the Bible leaves us in no doubt – in His relations with the Jewish people, God is a father, and rather a severe one, who gives His children orders and punishments. This interpretation is not novel. It is even commonplace, since Freud himself in *Totem and Taboo*, and then in *The Future of an Illusion*, gives God the image of a father. But frankly the reading of a Catholic catechism will spare us the trouble of too deep or time-consuming a plunge into the classics of psychoanalysis. God is generally given the name of father ('Our Father, which art in heaven').

One can, however, criticize Freud for not having used a variable family model which would take account of the diversity of family structures in the Judeo-Christian world. The identification of God with the father only achieves stability where the family structure lays down a strong paternal authority, i.e. in the regions of the stem family. The father in the Paris basin who is liberal or absent cannot imprint on his children's minds unconscious images that are clear enough to act as support for strong religious manifestations. Freud, on the other hand, functioned with a varying *religious* model. Only monotheistic religions, that concentrate divine qualities in one being, can rely effectively on a family where after all there is only one father.[6]

Protestantism and catholicism are equally monotheistic and equally supported by the stem family. But an important difference must be underlined – the coincidence of ideology and family values is stronger in the case of protestantism than of catholicism. The authoritarianism latent in the stem family poses no problems for catholicism or protestantism, two doctrines which fully accept, though in different ways, the principle of submission of the individual to a superior authority. Protestantism, however, reflects better the inegalitarian values of the stem family, which excludes all children from the father's estate except one. The Protestant concept of divine grace falling on the elected one reveals a striking structural analogy with the fundamental mechanism of the chosen son succeeding his father on the farm. In the stem family system the father predestines the children to election as heir, or to exclusion.

The chapter of the *Institutes of the Christian Religion* devoted by Calvin to predestination opens in a very classic manner with a discussion of Esau's right of primogeniture transferred 'by God's will' to his younger brother Jacob. Jacob is the chosen one, while Esau is rejected. Furthermore, Calvin in this passage has to state his position on a popular idea which equated divine election with primogeniture on earth. Calvin argues at great length to demonstrate the symbolic importance of primogeniture. He attacks the writers who profess 'that we must not pronounce on the eternal life in treating of these trivial and inferior matters and that it is a mockery to write that the man who has been raised to honour through primogeniture should be heir to the same rank in heaven.'[7] He continues: 'For if we do not relegate Jacob's primogeniture to a future life, the blessing conferred on him would be plainly ridiculous seeing that he would get out of it nothing but misery and calamity.' Calvin defends an abstract version of predestination, but one feels that, in the stem family regions that rallied to the Reformation, the identification of the inegalitarian ideology with the inegalitarian family was almost conscious.

Catholicism on this point seems rather lame by comparison. It persists in preaching the equality of men, and a bastard doctrine seems to be the result, typical of a stem family which has not fully developed its potential on the ideological plane. However, as always, the Church showed a capacity for practical adaptation which was lacking in the reformed Church. Catholicism needed a large number of parish priests, much more than protestantism with its suggestion that 'we are all priests'. Catholicism had to reproduce a mystic bureaucracy which, being unmarried, did not produce children and successors.

Catholicism thus grafts itself in a way on the stem family. The younger sons, generally excluded from any inheritance, are all possible candidates for the priesthood, individuals who respect authority but have no connection with any domesticity. The stem family produces bachelors who are employed by the Church.

According to this description, the stem family fits in with two distinct religious systems. There is no basic anthropological difference to be seen between Catholic and Protestant zones. The division of the territory has in this case followed a historical rather than an anthropological logic. The Protestant regions were often situated along communication routes, near to the largest centres of civilization of their time, whether it was in the Nord–Pas-de-Calais area or in the valley of the Garonne. The Catholic bastions were often isolated provinces, lost in the mountains like Rouergue or in the mists of the Atlantic like the Basque country and Brittany. We are here talking simply of tendencies, for very Catholic Alsace was at the heart of the European system. An examination of French ideological territories suggests that an element of chance came into play in the division of stem family regions into Protestant and Catholic zones. Anthropological analysis, however, suggests that the natural ideological form for the stem family to take was protestantism rather than catholicism, an impression that is reinforced by a historical examination of the differentiation process.

An analysis of the cultural thrusts in France between the twelfth and sixteenth centuries reveals an independent tendency of stem family regions in Occitania, in the East and in the North to breed cultural dynamism and religious dissent. Between 1550 and 1700 this potential in France was resisted by forces centred on the Paris basin, i.e. by regions whose family structure was egalitarian nuclear. So France remained Catholic in name. But within Catholic France the stem family regions which had not had time to go over to protestantism took up a dominant position in the Catholic world itself. The reason for this was very simple. Being authoritarian in their concept of the family, they were more able than nuclear family regions to engender strong religious temperaments and a clear vision of a transcendent God. The stem family, which had already supported protestantism, then took control of the Counter-reformation in places where the political and cultural balance had prevented a slide across to the Protestant camp. The Catholic Counter-reformation, which was so powerful in the middle of the seventeenth century, made use of this diversion of the strong religious temperament of the stem family regions, which were a minority in France, Spain and Italy, but a majority in southern Germany, Austria and Belgium.

At this stage, the regions of the egalitarian nuclear family, which were a majority in the Latin world and unsuited to religious transcendence, had so far played only one role – that of acting as a brake on the power of religion.

From the eighteenth century onwards, the Paris basin, having at last become ideologically active thanks to literacy (originating in Germany), defined its own values, which were liberal, egalitarian and in fact hostile to all religious ideas. In other words, it abandoned catholicism. The latter – and here is a paradox – took refuge in regions which would probably have gone over to protestantism if they had not been prevented from doing so by the weight around them of regions where the egalitarian nuclear family prevailed in the sixteenth and seventeenth centuries.

Catholicism, therefore, in France identifies itself with the stem family. The move to the Counter-reformation, therefore, seems to have been random, but irreversible. In places where protestantism had not triumphed, the catholicism of the Counter-reformation established itself.

IDEOLOGICAL AND RELIGIOUS TERRITORIES

So several stable ideological territories emerge from France's pre-industrial past, covering the whole territory (see map 21):

1   The largest territory was centred on the Paris basin, the political heart of the country. It consisted of dechristianized regions whose special character asserted itself on the occasion of the French Revolution.
2   A minority territory, but still a large one, situated in the outlying regions, consisted of areas where religious belief persisted and sometimes increased. This second territory itself embraced two subdivisions:
    a The regions which remained basically Catholic.
    b The development areas of various forms of religious dissent between the twelfth and sixteenth centuries, e.g. Catharism, the Waldensian heresy and the Protestant Reformation.

The two subdivisions which made up the 'religious' territory were not watertight. The frontiers separating them were blurred, and overlapping

Map 21
Religious areas

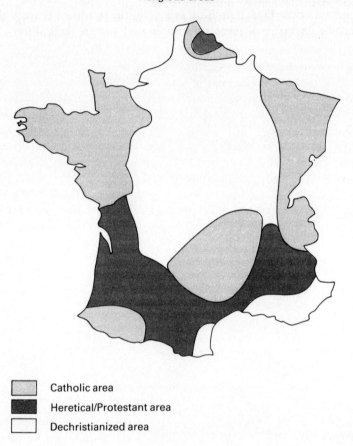

▨ Catholic area
■ Heretical/Protestant area
☐ Dechristianized area

Derived from maps 1, 15 and 16.

was frequent. On the other hand the dividing line between the dechristianized and the religious territories was quite distinct.

These broad ideological territories were a fairly good reflection of ancient anthropological areas defined in terms of family types and agricultural systems. The dechristianized territories cover the regions of the egalitarian nuclear family and of large farming estates. The religious territory consists of regions of the stem family and peasant proprietorship. The minority anthropological types in France have had to align themselves with the dominant systems. The community family, which was associated with share-cropping, has joined the dechristianized territory. The absolute nuclear family, associated with tenant farming, has merged itself with the religious territory.

Analysis of the French political system in the twentieth century shows the lasting character of these anthropological and ideological territories.

PART II

THE TRADITIONAL POLITICAL SYSTEM

So far in this book the concepts of Left and Right, which are of such importance in French political life today, have not been put to use. It has been a question of revolution and counter-revolution, of dechristianization and catholicism. But the revolutionary and counter-revolutionary forces were never explicitly equated with the parties which dominated French political life between 1945 and 1980. Neither the socialist Left, nor the communist Left, nor the classic Right, nor the Gaullist Right, has ever been put forward as the legitimate heir of the French Revolution or the counter-revolution which ensued. At first sight, all instant identification of present-day political forces with the great founding ideologies is impossible.

The French Revolution affirmed two basic values – liberty and equality. The counter-revolution opposed them with their opposites – authority and inequality. It is quite clear that neither the Parti Socialiste (PS), nor the Parti Communiste (PC), nor the Union pour la démocratie Française (UDF), nor the Rassemblement pour la République (RPR), can identify itself fully with one or other of these value systems.

The nineteenth-century republican was a liberal in the strict sense. He was not red, but blue. He rejected social authority in the shape of God, the king, the bishop and the priest. It is true that he wanted equality among men, but before the law rather than within the economy. *He disliked the State*, and in particular its most powerful element under the *ancien régime* – the Church. Moreover the sale of church property provided some expansion of the private sector during the Revolution. The man of the counter-revolution, who was a monarchist in the nineteenth century, respected authority, – the authority of God, the king and the noble. He proclaimed at the same time the notions of authority and inequality, blending them in fact in a single principle of *hierarchy*.

The Left of the second half of the twentieth century, socialist and communist, cannot logically recognize itself in the anti-State liberalism of the revolutionary vision. The Right, whether classic or Gaullist, cannot recognize itself in the Revolution's virulent egalitarianism. There is only one conclusion to be drawn. The historical link between the 1789 Revolution on the one hand and the system of present-day parties on the other, is not straightforward. There are masses of contradictions between the values of today and those of yesterday.

The most glaring contradiction concerns the communists' and socialists' identification with the 1789 Revolution, and the relationship between *Left* ideas and *authority*. If one considers the 1789 Revolution to be a left-wing phenomenon, one has to admit that liberty is a value of the Left. However, according to the Right of today, authority, which in our time has been particularly prized in the communist countries, is a value of the Left.

If you combine these two observations, you can only come to one conclusion – authority as a value belongs neither to the Left nor to the Right, and the same goes for the value of liberty. There is no clear and necessary connection between the pairs authority-liberty and Left-Right. A rigid association of the Left with liberty or authority would be an absurdity. Yet one feels that a total separation of the Left from the idea of liberty and of the Right from the idea of authority would be no less fundamentally absurd. Only a more subtle analysis of the notion of authority could enable one to escape from this conceptual labyrinth, and define accurately the respective logical positions of the concepts of Left and Right, and those of liberty and authority.

THE RIGHT–LEFT CONFLICT AND THE NOTION OF AUTHORITY

An authority relationship brings together two individuals, of whom one is considered superior to the other and empowered to act on him. It indicates clearly a ruler and a ruled. This formulation is absolutely general and does not define the degree of authority exercised, which can be strong or weak. One can imagine a ruler–ruled relationship in a system that is feebly authoritarian, and a similar relationship in a system that is strongly authoritarian.

On the anthropological level, for instance, the nuclear family, which is liberal in its fundamental values, does however at a given moment define the rulers (the parents) and the ruled (the children). The domination is of low intensity, but it does exist. At the very heart of the notion of liberalism a ruler–ruled polarity can be discovered. In the same way the stem family, one of whose fundamental values is authority, defines at a given moment rulers (the parents) and ruled (the children). The domination here is of strong intensity. At the very heart of the notion of authority a ruler–ruled polarity can be discovered. So in the liberal family type, as in the authoritarian, there exist two *positions* in the domination link.

This split perception of the authority relationship, which has just been detected at the family level, can also be seen at the ideological level. In this sphere, as in the family sphere, the authority relationship lays down in effect two poles *a priori* – that of the rulers and that of the ruled. Every individual can identify with the former or the latter. At this stage of the analysis, a hypothesis can be put forward on the origin and significance of the Left–Right conflict:

If the individual identifies with the ruled, the attitude is Left.
If the individual identifies with the ruler, the attitude is Right.

As in the case of the child-parent relationship within the family, the Left–Right relationship on the ideological plane can exist at different levels of authority intensity. One can imagine a Left–Right relationship in a liberal system, and a Left–Right relationship in an authoritarian system:

In a family and ideological system that is liberal a Left and a Right can come into being, born to fight one another, but sharing the same idea, i.e. weak, of the degree of authority required.

In a family and ideological system that is authoritarian a Left and a Right can come into being, born to fight one another, but sharing a same idea, i.e. strong, of the degree of authority required.

As the very notion of authority implies the existence of rulers and ruled, the Left–Right polarity is universal. It is the ideological expression of *a priori* mental categories. But because the various anthropological systems lay down different intensities of authority, the Left–Right relationship is very diverse. To each intensity of authority there corresponds a specific Left–Right pairing.

If one confines oneself to the two degrees of authority intensity used in this book, i.e. weak and strong, which define liberal and authoritarian ideological systems, one must postulate the existence of four possible ideologies – a liberal Left, a liberal Right, an authoritarian Left and an authoritarian Right.

SYSTEMIC VALUES AND LEFT–RIGHT POLARITY

This hypothesis on the origin of the Left–Right antithesis refines, without modifying, the exploratory model put forward in my book *The Explanation of Ideology*. The logic of the model is not altered as the ideological categories remain the reflection of family categories. The values of liberty and authority, of equality and inequality, continue to define local and regional ideological systems, that is to say mental structures, liberal or authoritarian, egalitarian or inegalitarian. From now onwards I shall call these values systemic, because they define ideological *systems*. Liberty and authority, equality and inequality are pairs of systemic values.

The notions of Left and Right are independent of these systemic values. They stem from a secondary antithesis, which is *internal* to each ideological system. Every authority mechanism, whether it be strong or weak, can give rise to two attitudes – the Left springing from identification with the ruled, the Right from identification with the rulers. This conceptualization only refines our understanding of a single pairing of systemic values, that which opposes liberty and authority. To the systemic values of liberty there corresponds one liberal Right and one liberal Left. An authoritarian Right and an authoritarian Left correspond to the contrary systemic value of authority.

The systemic values of equality and inequality do not come into play in this new conceptual set-up, which makes them absolutely independent of notions of Left and Right. I am aware of the surprising and brutal character of such an interpretation, which dissociates the notions of Left and equality. Doesn't the defence of the ruled imply in itself a claim for equality?

The experience of Soviet communism has certainly prepared people to accept the idea of an authoritarian Left. But must one by the same token accept the improbable idea of an inegalitarian Left and (why not?) an egalitarian Right? At this point one must pass from the conceptual to the real, from the model to history. The first European Left that one can situate historically was at the same time *authoritarian* and *inegalitarian*. We refer of course to protestantism.

THE FIRST LEFT: PROTESTANTISM

All the essential elements which enable us to identify protestantism as an authoritarian and inegalitarian Left have been put forward in earlier chapters. Inegalitarianism and authoritarianism as systemic values reflect the family values of inequality among brothers and paternal authority in the stem family regions, where protestantism developed. The absolute authority of God and the sense of humanity's inability to work out its salvation alone are typical of an authoritarian doctrine, and give rise to an insistence on submission. Certain people's predestination to election, and others' to damnation, is characteristic of an inegalitarian doctrine. Yet protestantism, which is authoritarian and inegalitarian, veers to the left. Why is this? It is because of its negative attitude to an authority that it can only see as strong. Historically protestantism arises out of a violent rejection of the most powerful authority of its time, that of the Church. It identifies itself with the oppressed, who are defined not so much in material as in spiritual terms. For Luther the oppressed were above all the German laymen, dominated by Romish priests. The 'left' character of the first Lutheran reforming texts – notably *The Appeal to the Christian Nobility of the German Nation*, which dates from 1520 – is undeniable. In it Luther demands the end of a domination, and he asserts the right of each individual to read the Scriptures for himself. This right to Scripture embodies an idea that is 'left' without being 'egalitarian'. Protestantism claims for everyone the right to establish direct contact with God. However, it is only interested in the direct vertical relationship of the soul with its Creator, and scoffs at the idea of equality of souls among themselves.

The subsequent history of protestantism shows that the stability of an authoritarian and inegalitarian Left is no easy matter. The 'open' authoritarianism of protestantism, which ultimately recognizes only direct submission to God as legitimate, can only end up with mongrel solutions: Protestant man must oscillate between obedience to his conscience and obedience to civil authority, whether it be prince or State, according to period.

One could at this point maintain that the violent snatching of Protestant regions from the Pope's authority represented no more than a transition between a spiritual authority and a temporal one, and that established protestantism, such as came about in the nineteenth century for instance, became 'right' because it respected civil authority. The political history of Protestant regions in the twentieth century shows that this was not the case, for they all inclined to the left when the working-class movement expanded. Protestantism is indeed structurally a doctrine of the Left, but it is authoritarian and inegalitarian.

The simultaneous use, therefore, of *systemic values* and *Left–Right dualism* provides an effective approach to the Protestant phenomenon. The latter represents the left pole of a dualism that corresponds to the systemic authoritarian and inegalitarian values of the stem family. This formal approach makes possible a rigorous analysis of the French political system in the seventies.

THE FRENCH POLITICAL SYSTEM: TWO LEFTS AND TWO RIGHTS

The French political system, as it appeared during the seventies, combined a Left–Right opposition, regarded as natural, with certain secondary cleavages whose fundamental origins were unknown. The PC–PS confrontation on the one hand, and the RPR–UDF split on the other, were the most notable of these cleavages.

A simple examination of the relations between the PC and the PS in the course of the last sixty years suggests that what separated these two forces was in fact more important than what drew them together. Since the schism at Tours in 1920, the PC and PS have spent more time fighting each other than governing together. The rapid and repeated breakdown of all attempts at governmental collaboration in 1936, 1946 and then in 1981 suggests that an alliance of the two forces of the Left is contrary to nature. It is this nature that we must define. The persistent disunity of the Right, less distinct but equally mysterious in its origins, also needs explaining.

The facts are there. France, which professes to have only one economy, one bourgeoisie, one working class, in fact has two Lefts and two Rights. An anthropological analysis of the political system will enable us to understand the origins of this superabundance of ideology.

REGIONAL RIGHTS AND LEFTS

The diversity of the anthropological fabric of France is, of course, responsible for the diversity of the various Lefts and Rights. Everywhere in France, between 1880 and 1980, dualist opposition between Right and Left was set up and maintained. But the existence of different systemic values in different provinces of France – liberal and egalitarian at the heart of the Paris basin, authoritarian and inegalitarian in the south and on the frontiers – led quite logically to the emergence of Lefts with varied systemic values and Rights no less varied in their attitudes towards liberty and equality. The universal presence of the Left–Right antithesis makes one think that the Lefts should unite, and the Rights likewise. But an alliance of Lefts deeply divided in their fundamental values is not easily achieved, and an alliance of Rights is hardly less problematical. All the complexity of the political game in France arises from the existence of two levels of conflict – between systemic values and between Right and Left.

A geographical examination of the two French Lefts and the two French Rights confirms this anthropological interpretation.

● The egalitarian nuclear family in the eighteenth and nineteenth centuries occupied a dechristianized territory. It gave rise in the twentieth century to a specific Right and Left.

● The stem family maintained a religious territory from the sixteenth to the nineteenth century. It created in the twentieth century a specific Right and Left.

The analysis set out here is empirical and based on statistics. It contradicts a large number of generally accepted notions, both current and long-standing, on the nature of Right and Left. Indeed the Right produced by the egalitarian nuclear family seems devoured by egalitarianism, while the Left that goes with the stem family seems quite indifferent to the ideal of equality.

6

The Catholic Right

Political geography, a French speciality which came into existence at the beginning of the century, has for a long time revealed the existence of a stable geography of the Right. André Siegfried had already shown in 1913 in his *Tableau politique de la France de l'Ouest*,[1] how impervious certain provinces were to the republican ideals of liberty and equality. Even before the First World War the electoral and political history of France seemed to have frozen into a mould. François Goguel, a disciple of the electoral geography invented by André Siegfried, showed in his *Géographie des élections françaises sous la Troisième et la Quatrième Republique*[2] that in France, even since direct universal suffrage was finally established, there had been a permanently fixed grouping of provinces which constantly and massively voted Right (see map 22). Between 1900 and 1987, the inland West, Brittany, Vendée, the Basque country, Alsace and Lorraine, part of Savoie and of the Jura Mountains, and the southern part of the Massif Central between Ardèche and Aveyron voted for the Right, with amazing constancy. In fact, over a long period, all these regions had no political history.

THE IMPACT OF THE CHURCH

There is an obvious resemblance between this picture of the Right and the map of catholicism. The oldest Right in the French political system is firmly situated in traditionally Catholic territory. Because of its almost religious geography, the stable Right is one of the heirs of the counter-revolution which took place at the end of the eighteenth century.

Like catholicism, this solid Right gets its support from the regional bastions which correspond to a precise anthropological category, the stem family. To this may be added, as in the case of the Church, the absolute nuclear family of the inland West. The Catholic Right, however, does not dominate in all the stem family regions. The major part of the South-west, where the stem family dominated, voted Left, exceptions

Map 22
The Right in 1936

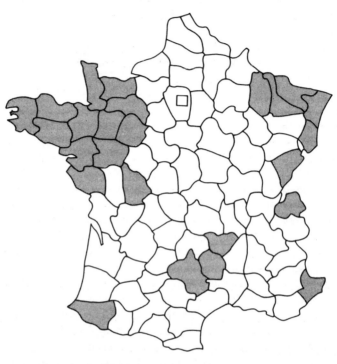

25 *départements* in which candidates hostile to
the Front Populaire obtained more than 50 per cent
of the votes cast.

Based on the map provided in Goguel, F. 1970: *Géographie des élections françaises
sous la Troisième et la Quatrième République*. Paris, 57.

being the Basque country and the southern part of the Massif Central. A
division of the stem family regions took place during the nineteenth
century, some opting for the Right and others for the Left. Their
common values of authority and inequality, as we have seen, could incline
them to the Left or the Right. Protestantism was in accord with a left
orientation, while catholicism implied a right orientation.

Unlike protestantism, catholicism shows no ambiguity in its relationship
with the principle of authority. It insists on formal submission to the
Church, the Pope, the bishops, the priests, and also to the social and civil
authorities, to the extent that the latter do not oppose the wishes of the
Church. The right-wing orientation of most of the Catholic regions of
Europe, whether Bavaria, Ireland, northern Italy, northern Spain or

Portugal was not the result of pure accident or tactical alliances. It was a visible demonstration of the very nature of catholicism, which is in essence a right-wing religion. Acceptance of this total identification of catholicism and the Right naturally presupposes acceptance of the notions of Right and Left as defined above. To be right-wing is to accept authority and identify with the dominating power: to be left-wing is to contest authority and identify with those who are dominated. If positive obedience is a prerequisite of fidelity to the Church, the terms 'catholicism' and 'Left' are contradictory. It is possible to imagine 'a Christian of the Left', but one cannot speak of a 'Catholic of the Left'.

This authoritarian and inegalitarian Catholic Right has a stable base, anthropological in origin, shown by the specific place it holds in French territory. It also has, at the national level, a history. Political, economic and social evolution as well as domestic and international conflicts have caused the growth of many parties and groups as reactions to the problems of one period or another. They all, however, have in common certain fundamental characteristics.

The royalist Right, the Right that rallied to the Third Republic, the MRP of the Fourth Republic, and the so-called 'classic' Right of the Fifth Republic must be considered as successive embodiments of the Catholic Right.

It is not possible here to study systematically all the changes and adjustments of the Catholic Right. We must, however, mention a particularly important episode which will allow one to grasp the autonomous role of catholicism and its moderating influence on the behaviour of the French Right.

RALLYING TO THE REPUBLIC

During the nineteenth century Catholic thought was simultaneously royalist and Catholic. Restoration of the monarchy and defence of the Church seemed inseparable objectives. The stabilization of the Third Republic finally raised the question of dissociating royalist ideals from those of catholicism. In 1890 Pope Leo XIII ordered French Catholics to rally to the Republic – an important turning-point. Royalism was dead. The Catholic Right survived, but became republican.

It was, of course, an ambiguous and very curious form of republicanism. The Church, attached as it was to the principle of authority, detested the liberal and egalitarian values of the French Republic. It saw, however, that the republican environment, pluralist by definition, was not a bad solution for the survival and defence of a catholicism which remained strong but enjoyed only a minority status. So Catholic support for the idea of liberty could only be a tactical posture, coming from an ideological body that exalted the virtue of obedience.

As a result, the stability of French institutions was enhanced, but became grounded in a contradiction. After the 1893 elections, which followed the rallying of the Catholics, the principle of authority, which meant so much to the Church, contributed to the strengthening of republican institutions. The Church encouraged political and electoral involvement. The various catechisms insisted that it was the duty of every Christian to vote, but of course for the candidate backed by the Church. The integration of essentially disciplined Catholic voters at once had a positive effect on republican institutions. The internal instability of the French political system, so typical of the nineteenth century, greatly decreased after the Catholic Right became integrated. Revolutions became a thing of the past.

So the Catholic Right became the classic Right. Respectful of the Church, it claimed to be liberal. Its liberalism was not, however, the result of deep convictions but of having to adapt to circumstances. It was born by accident from a wish to defend the freedom of a minority whose temperament was authoritarian. The regional societies on which the classic Right depended were characterized by the people's massive loyalty to the principle of authority. To submit to celestial and earthly powers seemed natural in Brittany, Rouergue, the Basque country and Alsace. Nor was the attachment of the Catholic Right to decentralization the expression of a truly liberal inclination, but rather the result of geographical circumstances. In France the Church controlled fragmented and peripheral strongholds. Any increase in the independence of the provinces, and any decrease in the role played by Paris and its region, increased the relative power of catholicism and its Right in the national system.

The anti-individualism of the regions from which the classic Right got its support can be clearly seen in the field of morals as well as in social and economic life.

THE MORAL ORDER

It is probably in the emotional and sexual spheres that the discipline exercised on the individual is at its strongest in regions of stem families and Catholic tradition. The eternal power of the family made it possible to put into practice the Catholic concepts of marriage and procreation. The combined authority of parents and priests encouraged the establishment and furtherance of a specific morality, clearly expressed through certain classic demographic parameters.

A few great principles summed up the attitude of the Church towards sexuality:

First principle: Sexuality is bad in itself.

Second principle (which derives logically from the first): Celibacy and chastity are the noblest state of man and woman.

Third principle: For those men and women who do not possess the necessary control of their sexual urges, marriage is an acceptable solution. As Saint Paul said, 'Better marry than burn.'

Fourth principle: Marriage must definitely not be regarded as a means to enriching sexual life. 'A wife must not be her husband's prostitute.'

Fifth principle: Marriage is indissoluble.

Sixth principle: The Christian function of marriage is the reproduction of the species. A Catholic couple must accept the children God sends it, and must in no circumstances practise contraception or resort to abortion.

All these principles had a certain moral coherence. The ethical aspect of the Catholic conception of marriage must not, however, hide the existence of a utilitarian rationality, which satisfied the stem family. The horror of marriage, and the value set on celibacy, facilitated the harmonious functioning of the principle of primogeniture. The celibacy of the children who did not inherit from their parents was legitimized by religion. The luckiest entered the Church or the Army. Many, the majority perhaps, were transformed into bachelor aunts or uncles, living in their brother's family, condemned to having no descendants. This social sterilization of younger sons was an efficient demographic brake, which to some extent compensated for the prohibition of contraception in the Catholic world. The Church was hostile to individualistic birth control by couples, but it encouraged an overall social control through the celibacy of certain categories. Here the Church fully assumed the non-egalitarian imperatives of the stem family. Inequality was not fundamentally material but sexual, for certain of the elect were entitled to a sex life, others not.

With perfect logic, the map of late marriages and celibacy in France between 1850 and 1965 coincides with that of catholicism. Moreover, the proportion of permanent bachelors was higher where the action of the Church and the stem family was combined. In stem-family regions where catholicism did not wield its maximum power, e.g. the North and the valley of the Garonne, people married young. In Catholic regions where the stem family did not exist – the inland West with its absolute nuclear family structure – the celibacy rate was distinctly lower than in other regions controlled by the Church.

The frequency of divorce was, of course, much lower in the Catholic regions than in those which had been dechristianized. Between 1850 and

1960 the peasants, workers and bourgeoisie of the Catholic regions were subjected to a remarkable sexual and emotional discipline. Certain individuals did not have the right to marry. The duty of the rest, who were married, was simply to bring up an indefinite number of children. It was a strange world where we find bachelors side by side with large families, a world fundamentally hostile to the expression of the individual will.

ECONOMIC AND SOCIAL LIFE

In the economic and social fields catholicism accepted the idea of property and defended the bourgeois order, but it was not liberal. The Church respected the land, but hated money and trading in goods. It considered that, in general, economic interests should be subordinated to moral principles. It was anti-capitalist. It could not accept the overall vision of an individualistic and commercial society free of constraint.

Respecting property but not money, the Church was in fact favourable to a moderate form of state intervention in economic life. Catholicism has always encouraged certain social and charitable attitudes, and insisted on the moral responsibility of élites. This trend persisted from the social catholicism of the nineteenth century to the MRP of the post-war years, and with the passage of time this attitude was reinforced.

The Church developed a vertical vision of society, in which the bourgeoisie exercised a paternalistic and benevolent authority over its workers. The obedience which the workers owed to their employers did not prevent the organization of a powerful Christian trade-union movement, which in most Catholic regions wielded more power than the left-wing unions. The Church did not like to leave the individual isolated and free. It surrounded him with a tight network of social relationships and specialized social organizations such as the Jeunesse Agricole Catholique and the Jeunesse Ouvrière Catholique.

Catholicism expresses in the social context the anti-individualist tendencies of the stem family, which finds it hard to imagine the existence of an individual who is independent of all authority, whether parental or social. This is a far cry from the right wing of the English-speaking world, which is truly liberal and individualistic.

THE PROBLEM OF RACISM

Of the two great ideological values adopted by the stem family, the Church really accepted only one, i.e. authority. The Church rejected republican egalitarianism, but stopped short of positive promotion of the principle of inequality. The Church – universal, Roman, Catholic – has never, because of its conservatism and no doubt because of its respect for the authority in power, brought itself to declare that men are not equal, as many racist doctrines which flourished all over Europe during the nineteenth century did not hesitate to assert. Maintaining a universal dogma was not easy. The stem family is really a carrier of inegalitarian ideals. Its obsession with lineage often degenerates into an obsession with purity of blood and race. Aristocratic primogeniture encourages the myth of blue blood.

From the time of the Dreyfus affair, the race myth began to influence French catholicism. But the anti-Semitism which spread amongst the faithful was not of the traditional type. It was no longer directed against Jewish particularism in the name of a universalism which insisted that all should be converted. The Jews were no longer reproached for their splendid isolationism, but for having finally accepted the assimilation offered by republican universalism: they should not be allowed to become ordinary French citizens. This new anti-Semitism was based on the new belief in the inequality of races. This tendency to reject the idea of universal humanity could already be seen in the works of Joseph de Maistre. It grew from 1899 onwards, with the increase in influence of Action Française.

Charles Maurras, who in effect ran the movement throughout its history from 1900 to 1940, was himself an agnostic. It was, however, the Catholic world which provided Action Française with its leaders and followers. Better than the Church, Action Française realized, in its interpretation of 'the Right', the full ideological potential of the authoritarian and inegalitarian stem family. The Maurras doctrine was monarchist, asserting the values of order and inequality. It was nationalistic and racist, anti-German and anti-Semitic. Its fate is a clear measure of the independent power of the Church.

In 1926 and 1928, Pope Pius XI condemned Action Française in the most uncompromising terms. Catholics were forbidden to read the movement's paper, on pain of exclusion from the sacraments and from the Church's blessing at marriage or burial. This was a comforting and wonderful example of authority, that of the Pope, exercised to repress an anti-liberal, anti-republican, anti-egalitarian and anti-Semitic movement. The Catholics obeyed; Action Française collapsed. France was never to develop her own Nazi-type movement.

The inegalitarian principles of the stem family were broken by the unqualified application of the principle of authority. The member of the Catholic Right is not a liberal. In a sense he is not a free man, for he is ruled by an ethic, that of Christianity.

7

Socialism

When socialism first appeared during the 1848 revolution, it showed a marked preference for the southern half of France. A social form of republicanism, entirely different from the traditional form, made its appearance during the 1849 elections (see map 23). It seemed to avoid the nuclear-family regions of the North, and instead it penetrated the provinces of the complex family of the South. The movement came from the East: this new form of socialism followed in the tracks of advancing literacy, originating in Alsace, Franche-Comté and Savoie. It was in the mid-nineteenth century that Occitania, whose cultural dynamism had been crushed during the seventeenth century, finally attained mass literacy.

This social republicanism, different from the traditional revolutionary dogma, was not fundamentally anti-religious. A well-known characteristic of the 1848 revolution, clearly distinguishing it from that of 1789, was the absence of anti-Catholic feeling. This contrast between historical periods masked a territorial difference. The 1789 revolution reflected the ideological awakening of the Paris basin, which was a dechristianized area, while the 1848 revolution showed the ideological growth of the South, which was not dechristianized except for the Mediterranean rim.

It was then that new and ambiguous doctrines, which would have been incomprehensible to Robespierre and Condorcet, made their appearance. The social catholicism of Lamennais was typical of that period of wavering, when the difference between catholicism and socialism seemed less strong than the difference between catholicism and egalitarian liberalism. Later this first image of socialism became confused. It was neither clear nor stable. The *coup d'état* of 2 December 1851 put an end to freedom of expression and consequently to the possibility of our setting up an electoral map. The subsequent history of socialism, however, shows that this first territorial localization in the southern part of the country reflected a profound logic.

Map 23
The democratic socialists in 1849

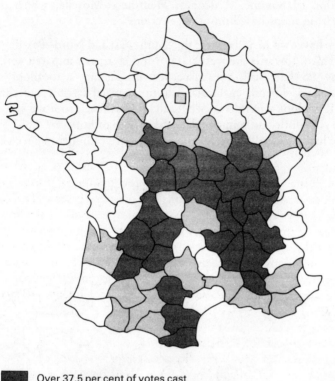

Over 37.5 per cent of votes cast

Between 22.5 and 37.5 per cent of votes cast

Based on the map given in Dupeux, G. 1959: *Le Front populaire et les Elections de 1936*. Paris, 169; taken from Bouillon, J. 1952: *Les Elections du 13 mai 1849*. Paris: Faculté des Lettres, unpublished dissertation for the Diplôme d'Etudes Supérieures.

SOCIALISM IN 1978

On the eve of the Left's return to power in 1981, the geography of the new Parti Socialiste was still very similar to that of the old SFIO (see map 24). The PS appeared to be strong in two bastions, unequal in size but equally peripheral:

● The whole of a 'greater South-west', extending towards the Alps and Jura and putting out a tentacle towards La Rochelle, and also one towards the Paris region without actually reaching it.

- A zone made up of the extreme north of the country – the *départements* of Nord and Pas-de-Calais, increased in 1978 by the addition of Somme, Ardennes, Meurthe-et-Moselle, which do not appear on maps based on other elections.

So we have two main centres: the South-west and Nord–Pas-de-Calais. A movement towards the west and north is clear, as compared with 1849. Yet the PS had still not succeeded in gaining a foothold in the revolutionary, liberal, egalitarian, dechristianized territory of the Paris basin. If we look carefully at where the PS has taken root we see, on the contrary, a subtle and refined relationship with catholicism. The PS seems to have had a special liking for the areas where catholicism survived, but

Map 24
The Socialist Party in 1978

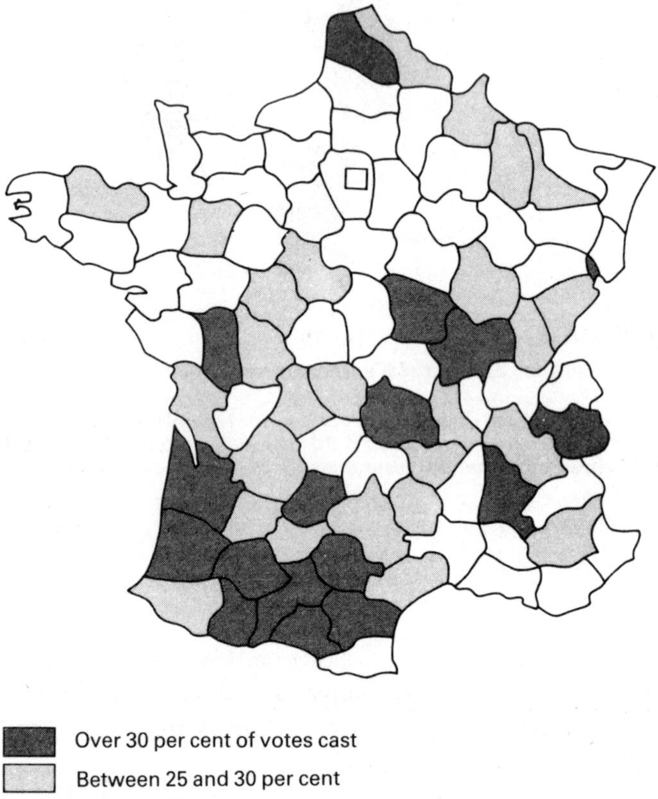

☐ Over 30 per cent of votes cast
☐ Between 25 and 30 per cent

Based on the parliamentary election results of 12 March 1978, published in *Le Monde*.

in a reduced form. This was the case in the Nord–Pas-de-Calais and in the valley of the Garonne. Consequently there is no negative correlation (indicating a repulsion relationship) between socialism in 1978 and attendance at mass around 1965. These two forces seem to be able to coexist locally, or at any rate regionally.

So French socialism, though of the Left, does not appear to be the heir of the Revolution from a geographical point of view. In fact the southern regions penetrated by socialism between 1848 and 1978 were originally royalist. This royalist orientation is stressed by Stéphane Rials in a book on legitimism: 'The common people, from Toulouse to Marseille, generally loved *lou rei goi* – the lame king.'[1] Before becoming socialist, Occitania was not republican but royalist.

SOCIALISM WITHOUT WORKERS

The passage from royalism to socialism cannot, in the case of the SFIO, be attributed to industrialization or to the development of a proletariat, conscious of its strength and of where its interests lay. The Nord–Pas-de-Calais is certainly one of the oldest and most densely populated working-class regions in the country, but the South-west, the core of the socialist system in France, is hardly a working-class region. Indeed it is, and has always been, the least industrialized part of the country. It has been a well-balanced regional society made up of executives, employees, craftsmen, tradesmen, peasant proprietors, a few farm labourers and share-croppers, who have provided the loyal troops of the Second (socialist) International. From the point of view of Marxist theory, which associates economic polarization and class war with the rise of socialism, the adherence of the South-west to the PS was an aberration. If we move from working-class mythology to anthropological analysis, we shall understand the history of the South-west and the North, and we shall be able to explain the relationship which exists between royalism and socialism. It is undeniable that, ideologically, socialism does not appear to be the heir of the Revolution, but rather of the counter-revolution.

THE AUTHORITY OF THE STATE

More distinctly even than the Catholic Right, which garnered absolute nuclear family regions, French socialism made headway in stem-family regions – the extreme North and South-west of France. This anthropological type at the same time preached authoritarian values resulting from close parent–child relations, and inegalitarian values derived from the principle of the sole heir.

What led the stem family to socialism was the principle of authority shared by the anthropological type and the ideological system. The power of the State in a modern urban setting, even if not industrial, replaced the feeling of security provided by the father. Socialism conceived and put into application the dependency of the individual on the administration. This was a depersonalized copy of the traditional dependency of the individual on the family organization in a three-generation family system. The intervention of the State in economic and social life succeeded that of the parents in professional and private life. It is this fundamental authoritarianism that establishes a parallel between socialism, royalism and catholicism, all of them grafted on to family structures of the stem type.

This authoritarian and inegalitarian family system has never shown itself capable of giving birth to a liberal conception of private and social life. It will always assume anti-individualistic and integrating forms which favour submission of the individual to a form of authority, which can be either concrete or very abstract. In the case of royalism, authority is very concretely incarnated in the image of the king, father of his subjects, or of the aristocrat, the local father of his dependents. In the case of the Church, authority is also very material and visible. The power of God is represented on earth by the Pope, and by the priests who very officially assume a father-image: 'Forgive me, Father, for I have sinned.'

Socialism makes a greater effort at transforming parental authority. The state tries to be impersonal, the abstract agent of the common good, and it conceals its paternal character. The Sécurité Sociale official does not treat those who apply for the reimbursement of their medical expenses like his own children. But subjection is no less real, for all that. It acts through financial mechanisms rather than through interpersonal relationships: the taxpayer considers a high level of fiscal pressure as normal. It is true that his peasant ancestor readily agreed to work for his father and to have no personal income at the age of thirty or thirty-five.

In stem-family regions, this dependence was accepted as a natural phenomenon. On this point, royalism, catholicism and socialism were all in opposition to the passionately individualistic ideal of the French Revolution, which originated in the liberal and egalitarian aspirations of the Paris basin.

INEQUALITY

The stem family, applying the rule of the sole heir, favours the existence of inegalitarian social values. The latter are indispensable if the socialist ideological mechanism is to function.

Of course, inequality is never an absolute value for socialism. But we have to admit that neither is equality a fundamental value for socialism. Unlike communism, socialism is not *heterophobe*, or hostile to the idea that differences exist among men. It establishes a vertical relationship with the State, but does not insist on total homogenization of the social system. It is in favour of heavy taxation, but does not reject the idea of private property. Such a rejection would make socialism unacceptable in the South-west and in all the stem-family regions. This anthropological type is in fact obsessed with the idea of the direct transmission of property. The three-generation household exists to transmit a specific inheritance – land and real estate in a peasant context, cultural and professional property in an urban context. This family patrimony separates human beings and implies the existence of differences and inequalities.

As in the case of catholicism, the relationship that socialism maintains with the concept of universal Man is ambivalent. Like catholicism it is universalist by habit, but internally tormented by the inegalitarian values of the stem family, which over and over again whisper to the subconscious that men are not equal, for some are eldest sons and some are younger.

Historically the PS is descended from the European movement and is still a member of the Second International. However, at no time has it shown any great capacity for international action. The SFIO, which in 1914 voted in favour of war credits and passively accepted the colonial wars, was never capable, as were the French Revolution and the Communist Party, of rising for better or worse above a narrowly national concept of political life.

On the doctrinal level, the SFIO of the thirties was far more affected than the Communist Party by the new inegalitarian, élitist doctrines then fashionable all over Europe.[2] At no time, however, did this lead to a serious crisis. Action Française had never succeeded in impairing the cohesion of the Catholic Right; nor did 'neo-socialism' seriously threaten the unity of the SFIO. Obviously it was not the authority of the moribund International which braked socialism in its drift towards anti-universalism. It was socialism's identification with the poor, the weak and the underdog, and its attachment to the Left, that blocked the development of the stem family's inegalitarian concepts. Here one can detect friction between systemic values (authoritarian and inegalitarian) and Right–Left dualism. Faced with an inegalitarian vision of social life, the socialist, a man of the Left, spontaneously identified with the weak, worker or Jew, whereas the man of the Right identified with the strong, the aristocrat and the 'true' Frenchman.

BELONGING TO THE LEFT

Despite their identical systemic values, authoritarian and inegalitarian, the Catholic Right and socialism nevertheless represented two opposing interpretations, right and left, of the ideological system favoured by the stem family. Belonging to the Catholic Right implied identification with the dominating power, while socialism implied identification with the underdog.

The ideal twentieth-century underdog is socio-economic – the proletarian, as defined by Marx as early as 1848 in *The Communist Manifesto*. To be a socialist in the twentieth century was thus to belong to the workers' party. Study of the Socialist Party in practice shows that this identification was largely subjective and did not imply actual membership of the working class. The Nord–Pas-de-Calais region, with its strongly industrial and proletarian population, is the only area where the impact of the Socialist Party can, at a pinch, be said to be the consequence of the normal Marxist pattern. The society of the South-west is, however, essentially *petit-bourgeois*, and yet it identifies itself no less than the Nord–Pas-de-Calais with the working class.

Moreover, the existence of a theoretical Left–Right polarity did not imply the actual division of the local societies into left and right wings, matching the interests of the exploiter and the exploited. From 1880 onwards, we can see, locally, the emergence of virtual right or left unanimity. At the time of the 1936 Front Populaire elections, in twenty-one *départements* the left-wing vote represented 70 per cent of the total, while in twenty *départements* the Right obtained 60 per cent of the votes cast.

These 'unanimist' societies whether of the Left or the Right, frequently had identical socio-economic morphologies and should have had similar class conflicts. Thus Ariège and Pyrénées-Atlantiques had comparable socio-economic structures – peasant proprietors and some workers. In 1936, however, Ariège voted 98 per cent for the Left, while Pyrénées-Atlantiques voted 61 per cent for the Right. One must draw the conclusion that all Ariégeois consider themselves to be working-class, and that a majority of Basques see themselves as rulers.[3] Objectively both are *petit bourgeois*. Socio-economic perception undoubtedly helps to structure the conflict between Left and Right, but it seems to be more an instrument than a cause.

The socialism which rules in Ariège is an *image*, which exists independently of the proletariat so dear to Marx.

The differing Left–Right political orientations which show up in *départements* with identical socio-economic structures are a classic exercise for French political scientists. They correspond to a reality, but one whose importance must not be exaggerated. The conflict between Left and Right is in fact secondary. It in no way casts doubt on the existence of systemic values which, as shown, are common to Ariège and the Basque country.[4] In both cases the stem family nourishes authoritarian and inegalitarian values. In the case of the Basque country the Church and the social authorities are respected. In Ariège the attachment to power has been massively transferred to the State – a State which is almost equally respected by the Catholic Right.

One important difference must be underlined – the socialist attitude towards authority is less consistent than the Catholic attitude. The mentality of the Right is simple – a powerful authority exists, and it must be obeyed. The left-wing mentality in an authoritarian system is less straightforward. The mechanism of the stem family fuels the need for authority, but this does not prevent questioning of the actual authority of the traditional rulers. Ideally, according to the socialist system, this authority should be handed to the people or the proletariat. As this proletariat is not a material, conscious being, transfer of power presents practical difficulties. Who are the proletariat? On a purely logical level the problem of socialism is that of protestantism. The Reformation has taken authority away from the Church to hand it to God. But how can this transfer of power be made to a being whose existence cannot be proved?

Socialism removes authority from the bourgeois to hand it over to the proletariat. But how can power be handed over to a purely theoretical being, an imaginary aggregate of very real workers, each of whom ceases to be a worker once he is given management of a factory?

In practice the Reformation and socialism find the same answer. For Protestants the State replaces God. For socialists the State replaces the proletariat in the day-to-day or long-term organization of earthly matters. This difficulty in defining authority leads us to consider the left-wing conception, whether Protestant or socialist, of a strong but impersonal authority as *non-harmonic*. The logical simplicity of the mechanism approved by the Right leads us to qualify it as *harmonic*. The relationship between protestantism and socialism is not, however, limited to a structural analogy, an identity of systemic, authoritarian and inegalitarian values and a common orientation towards the Left. There is an obvious historical link. Socialism in the twentieth century flourishes in regions which were of a Protestant temper in the sixteenth century.

IN THE FOOTSTEPS OF PROTESTANTISM

At this stage we must explain the divergence, between 1880 and 1980, of those stem family regions which tended to the Left from those which tended to the Right. The study of ideological maps, both old and new, suggests that the actual process of orientation has, on the causal level, nothing to do with class war, even if the left-wing vote implies identification with the underdog. In practice French socialism is located in the territory defined by the great religious dissents of the South, whose history extends from the twelfth century to the seventeenth. Modern socialism flourishes where the Cathars, the Waldensians and the Protestants made their appearance. There is an obvious continuity of left-wing tendencies in these regions, leading from religious dissent to socio-economic dissidence. This persistence in heresy has its correlative in the stability of Catholic orthodoxy in the other stem-family regions.

The SFIO thus reanimated the old geography of the heresies and the Reformation with its two most important bases: the South between Agen and Grenoble, between the Garonne valley and the central Alps, and the extreme North between Arras and Lille. This connection links socialism to the would-be majority creed of *sixteenth century* protestantism, and not to the residual and different twentieth-century version which persists in Alsace, Ardèche and Deux-Sèvres.

The possibility of an historical link between protestantism and the socialist vote is clearly brought out by Maurice Agulhon, the historian of nineteenth-century attitudes, in his *La République au village*. In the town of Luc, in Provence, which played an important role in the revolutionary events of 1848–51, he notes the existence of a protestant substratum.[5]

This continuity must not be exaggerated. It does not lead directly from one positive doctrine to another, but rather from one negation of authority to another. The refusal to acknowledge the power of the Roman Catholic Church became the rejection of the bourgeois. The Protestant and socialist solutions to the problem posed by this transfer of concrete authority are, as we have seen, the same. The civil and impersonal authority of the State replaces either that of God or of the proletariat.

The emergence in the nineteenth and twentieth centuries of political dissidence in the formerly Protestant regions (but where the Protestants were no more than residual minorities) suggests that the Church's resumption of control had consisted more in a crushing of the Reformation than in a real revival of catholicism. Between the revocation of the Edict of Nantes and the stabilization of socialism, there seems to have been a certain ideological void in the valley of the Garonne, with no great force imposing fully its conception of social life. Certain demographic data suggest that a specific way of life at the family and individual level persisted right through the eighteenth century. From this period onwards we note in the valley of the Garonne signs of birth control, inconceivable in entirely Catholic regions.[6] People marry young, and the latent malthusianism of the stem family is expressed by a control of fertility within marriage, an idea repugnant to the Church.

The coincidence of maps of religious dissent and of socialism is fair, but insufficient statistically. It makes the hypothesis of continuity plausible, but is not a rigorous demonstration from the point of view of probability theory. A glance at the link between protestantism and socialism throughout Europe can alone provide sufficient proof. In Europe, most of the Protestant countries and regions show a swing towards socialism. In all the Lutheran countries of the north, in Norway, in Denmark, but particularly in Sweden, socialism is the strongest ideological movement. We find the same alignment in the very authoritarian kingdom of Prussia where, prior to 1914, social democracy was the dominant electoral force.

In present-day West Germany, a region of Europe where the stem-type family structure reigns supreme, the Left–Right dualism continues to oppose socialism and Catholic Right. A correlation coefficient of +0.67 links the percentage of Protestants to the Social Democrat vote around 1970. The same phenomenon exists in Switzerland where the correlation coefficient is +0.53, and in the Netherlands where it is +0.87.

The case of France shows that the continuity of a left-wing orientation does not require an actual survival of protestantism. All that is needed is a certain identification with the underdog, the negation of an authority that can only be conceived as powerful. This is a purely mental attitude, independent of objective social and economic circumstances. The story of left-wing Occitania is not unique. In Bohemia, another stem-family region which was Hussite in the fifteenth century and Lutheran in the sixteenth, the resumption of political power by the Church during the seventeenth and eighteenth centuries did not prevent the emergence at the end of the nineteenth century of a particularly strong social-democratic movement. The Counter-reformation failed to take control of social behaviour in Bohemia, and the rejection of authority, leading from protestantism to socialism, persisted as it did in the valley of the Garonne.

8

Gaullism

Traditional French conservatism, obtaining its support from catholicism and its peripheral strongholds – Brittany, Anjou, Alsace-Lorraine, the Basque country, Rouergue and Savoie – ceased immediately after the Second World War to represent the overwhelming majority of the Right. Because of the strength of its regional positions, it continued to provide the general map of the political system with its outstanding features. Actual experience, however, shows that between 1945 and 1978, the Right, like the Left, was made up of two important tendencies. The origins and reasons for this division are not much less obscure than the opposition between socialism and communism. The call of 18 June 1940, which symbolically marked the split between the traditional Right and Gaullism, must be considered the founding myth, the right-wing equivalent of the Congress of Tours which marked the separation of the SFIO and the Communists.

Gaullism was not an accident of history, the work of a single man. It was based on deep and stable forces. It succeeded in getting the better of the Fourth Republic and, without being in an overall majority, established itself and survived in the Fifth. The clash between Giscard and Chirac in 1981, which largely contributed to the defeat of the Right, was not merely the result of a conflict of men and ambitions. Two images confronted one another, two sets of opposing values, and they were as strong and stable as those which, since 1921, have been responsible for the struggle between communism and socialism.

THE GEOGRAPHY OF GAULLISM

An empirical and cartographical approach shows that the Gaullist phenomenon, like other ideological forces in the country, is situated in a specific territory. The shape of this second Right appeared more clearly during de Gaulle's presidency, the moment of the new movement's maximum strength, rather than at the time of the Giscard–Chirac clash, which coincided with a weakening of Gaullism.

It was in November 1962, during the parliamentary elections, that Gaullism came closest to acquiring an ideal geographical shape. At that moment the UNR–UDT was opposed to all other political forces – the PS, the PC and the traditional Right. Its results – quite remarkable as it obtained 32 per cent of the votes cast – give a typical map centred on the Paris basin, the political heart of the nation (see map 25). Certain Catholic regions were affected, but not the majority of them. The most remarkable was the East, where Gaullism represented something different from its

Map 25
Gaullism in 1962

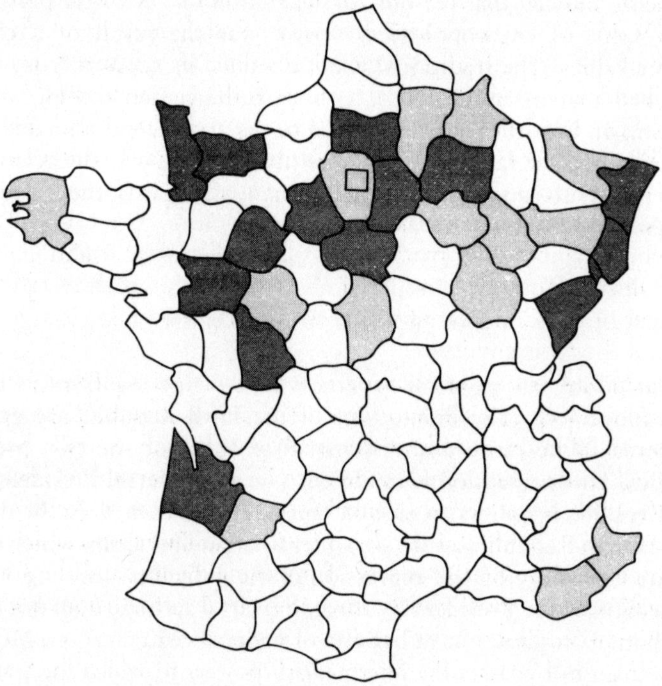

Départements in which the UNR-UDT received,
at the November 1962 elections:

Over 40 per cent of votes cast
Between 32 and 40 per cent

Based on detailed data provided in Goguel, F. et al. 1965: *Le Réferendum d'octobre et les Elections de novembre 1962*. Paris.

nature in the rest of the country – a very special brand of patriotism in a province which had been particularly shaken and ravaged by the centuries-old conflict between France and Germany. On the whole, however, it was the revolutionary and dechristianized territory (minus the Mediterranean littoral and the Limousin) which followed de Gaulle after 1958.

In time this very simple image became blurred, and the opposition between Gaullism and the traditional Right weakened. A 'neo-Gaullist' conglomerate took shape, which endeavoured to weld the two components of the Right. In 1965, de Gaulle obtained majorities in the Paris area and in the old strongholds of the Catholic Right. The blending of the two right-wing movements was not a merger. The RPR–UDF, Chirac–Giscard conflict which raged from 1980 onwards, in spite of the Union de la Gauche, showed that reasons for separation on the Right persisted.

This split, of anthropological origin, was the result of a clash of systemic values. The traditional Right obtained its support from regions which had a stem-family structure, both authoritarian and inegalitarian. Gaullism, on the other hand, appealed to the provinces dominated by the egalitarian nuclear family, which was liberal as regards the relationship between parents and children, egalitarian as regards the relationship between brothers.

THE PROBLEM OF LIBERALISM

Without doubt few political experts would define Gaullism as being a liberal movement. The institutions of the Fifth Republic are generally considered to be more authoritarian than those of the two preceding republics. This perception is muddled. The all-powerful President of the Fifth Republic is no less an elected representative than were the deputies of the Fourth Republic, a sure sign of egalitarian liberalism, which confers absolute legitimacy on the expression of the individual and popular will. The election of the President by direct universal suffrage does not express an authoritarian ideal, but rather one of national centralization. Moreover, this mechanism bypasses the intermediary powers to which the traditional Right is so attached. In a sense it represents the final victory of Jacobin and revolutionary hostility to local power. The election of the President by direct universal suffrage does not increase the authority of the State. It concentrates in the hands of a single man the authority which was previously fragmented and decentralized.

De Gaulle, the first incarnation of this new form of authority, was, through certain aspects of his personality and career, the living negation of the principle of authority. To understand the real connection of

Gaullism with authority, we must go back to the basic myth, the call of 18 June 1940. At that moment de Gaulle, a regular army officer, belonging to a corps founded on the ideal of discipline, refused the armistice order given by Pétain, his superior officer. He was a rebel and an anarchist. Although not a man of the Left, de Gaulle rejected the principle of authority in the name of higher personal ideals.

For decades de Gaulle was incomprehensible to the traditional Right. His opposition to Nazi Germany and the armistice were acceptable to the Catholic Right, which fifteen years earlier had refused to follow the inegalitarian, anti-Semitic doctrines of Action Française. What was inconceivable was de Gaulle's scorn for the hierarchy and for the principles of authority. He did something which the officers of the Third Republic had never dared to do at the time of the Dreyfus affair, namely flout legal authority. One of the miracles of the Third Republic was the absolute obedience of a largely royalist and Catholic officer corps. In reality this miracle was simply one of the stabilizing effects of the Catholic principle of authority, within a liberal and republican framework. As for de Gaulle, he did not submit. His choice was a personal one, but to identify with the man and the Gaullist legend implied a certain indifference to the principle of authority, which the General had flouted. So it was natural that the Paris basin, with its liberal temperament, should consider the basic myth of Gaullism as perfectly acceptable.

The Gaullist conception of power must thus be considered as centralizing and personal rather than authoritarian. The Gaullist voter finds it more natural to give his loyalty to a man, a transient and mortal being, than to a fixed doctrine with unchanging principles. This choice of a person rather than a dogma seems characteristic of an individualistic mentality. De Gaulle was not the first to benefit from this attitude, which is both personal and volatile, and which is characteristic of voters in egalitarian nuclear family regions. Bonapartism[1] seems to have appealed to the same areas and the same temperaments.

Here anthropological analysis confirms an important aspect of René Rémond's description of the various right-wing parties in his book *Les Droites en France*. A link between Bonapartism and Gaullism is clearly established.[2]

POPULIST EGALITARIANISM

The existence of an egalitarian mentality in the Gaullist electorate, reflecting the family egalitarianism of the Paris basin, is even easier to prove. It cannot be dissociated from the liberal conception of social life which is typical of popular Gaullism. The association of the ideas of liberty and equality produces a special mentality, which is dominant in the north of France and is characteristic of the Revolution. This combination and this mental structure can also be found in a barely modified form in the Gaullism of the years 1960–80.

The average Gaullist, like the traditional *sans-culotte*, likes neither authority nor social inequality. He is against the traditional principle of the Catholic Right, which is the ideal of hierarchy. The Catholic voter respects the social authorities, and is both deferential and 'correct'. The Gaullist voter is not deferential: he is independent and loud-mouthed. He does not accept the principle of submission to the aristocrat or the bourgeois, and even less to the priest. The Gaullist regions are dechristianized, and it was there that contraception developed early, in fact as early as the eighteenth century. The divorce rate is high, and individualist behaviour the rule. On all these points Gaullism did no more than reproduce or continue the revolutionary tradition. This was the origin of the movement's populist image, which opposed the bourgeois image of the classic Right. The General's jeering tone was the opposite of Giscard's correctness.

Examination of opinion polls show that around 1978, for example, the 'Gaullist' RPR electorate was really no more 'popular' than that of the 'classic' UDF – 38 per cent employees and workers as against 35 per cent.[3] The populist image of the RPR comes from the fact that it attracted people and regions whose typical social behaviour fitted, in certain respects, the idea that the more traditional Left had of the people. The 'true man of the people', not that of the Catholic provinces of the periphery, never submits to social and religious authority. But we are talking about the 'people' of 1789 to whom, in certain fringe provinces, is now opposed another 'people', Catholic this time, which upholds the principles of authority and inequality.

A LIBERAL AND EGALITARIAN RIGHT

Gaullism, whose systemic values are close to the Revolution, differs from it by its right-wing orientation, i.e. by a subjective identification with the rulers. This orientation made possible a belated alliance with the classic Right. This was an historic moment, which fulfilled the Napoleonic dream of a reconciliation between Church and Revolution. The Paris basin's swing to the Right and its liberal and egalitarian values did, however, raise theoretical and practical problems.

Whatever its degree of conceptual precision, the distinction between systemic values and Right–Left dualism should not mask the existence of frictions and contradictions. Empirical study conclusively proves the necessity of the distinction – in the Paris basin a Right of liberal and egalitarian temperament *does* exist. But we must also admit that this orientation towards the Right is in conflict with the egalitarian tendency of the value-system, and this creates structural instability. Egalitarianism and identification with the rulers are not easy ideals to reconcile. In practice, Gaullism presupposes a certain cooling-off of the principle of equality.

As we have seen, it was in 1962 that the liberal and egalitarian Right of the Paris region best asserted its power and its independence. But Gaullism is only one of its possible means of expression. Born in a specific anthropological territory, that of the egalitarian nuclear family, this Right appeared well before the establishment of the Fifth Republic, and it survived General de Gaulle's death. It is a constant force, of which Gaullism is but one historical phase. In its most general form it is a type of conservative republicanism. It is as if the French Revolution of 1789 had been achieved and then halted. One of the branches of the Radical Party had a fairly strong hold on the Paris basin.[4]

Study of the electoral history of post-war France shows the relative stability of this force. In 1946, at the time of the first constitutional referendum after the war, the Catholic Right was no longer alone, as it had been as in 1936, to confront the socialist and communist Left. The latter had briefly joined forces to ensure that the constitution, which they alone had drafted, would be adopted. Loiret, Seine-et-Marne, Eure-et-Loir, Seine-et-Oise and Eure went over to the Right as early as this. The authoritarianism of the Marxist Left aroused the liberal principles of the Paris basin, which rebelled. After the departure of de Gaulle the liberal, egalitarian, non-Catholic Right continued to exist. To distinguish this second, non-Catholic Right from its Gaullist incarnation, I shall from now onwards call it the 'non-religious Right'.

THE NON-RELIGIOUS RIGHT IN 1978

The relative unity of action of the right-wing parties between 1965 and 1978 makes it difficult for us to attempt a direct analysis of the respective Catholic and non-religious components for that period. Also, the existence of numerous single candidates at parliamentary elections makes it difficult to identify these ideological forces, which were less solidly structured than those of the Socialist and Communist parties. A map showing the votes obtained by the RPR or the UDF in 1978 does not give a precise idea of the territories actually occupied by the two tendencies.

This is all the more so because neither the UDF nor the RPR can be considered as the clear-cut representative of one tendency or the other.

The UDF, because of certain historical accidents which must be looked upon as theoretical imperfections, garnered the remnants of a type of radicalism which had very little connection with catholicism, and even less with the Church. As for the RPR it subverted the loyalty of certain Catholic voters in the East and the West.

An indirect technique of evaluation makes it possible to define with greater precision the strength and territory of the non-religious Right around 1978. A fairly simple calculation enables us to estimate the relative weight of this second Right at that date. We shall take it that the vote for the non-religious Right was equivalent in each *département* to the difference between the percentage of right-wing voters in 1978 and the percentage of people who attended mass in the middle of the 1960s. This is obviously an approximation which rests on a triple simplification:

1   The figure for the percentage of people attending mass is rather out of date.
2   We are assuming that only people who attended mass were Catholics.
3   We are assuming that all who attended mass belonged to the Right.

The first and third simplifications tend to an overestimation of the weight of the Catholic Right. The second simplification leads to an underestimation of the weight of the Catholic Right. The approximations being in opposite directions, we can hope that they partly compensate each other, and in consequence do not excessively distort our estimate of the non-religious Right's strength.

The map of the *départements* where the non-religious Right obtained more than 25 per cent of the votes (map 26) is simpler and more regular than that of the UNR–UDT in 1962. Drawn with the help of certain conventions, it has the territorial regularity of the map of catholicism (map 16) and of the overall map of the Right (map 22). It eliminates short-term political vicissitudes. Somewhat detached from the realities of politics, it illuminates a fundamental structure. The whole Paris basin is clearly visible, with the usual downward movement of the dechristianization maps towards Bordeaux. The most notable difference concerns Provence and central Limousin, where the non-religious Right appears relatively more powerful than Gaullism in 1962. These are areas which are like the Paris basin, but where family structures are not egalitarian nuclear but community, so that the local systemic values are egalitarian and authoritarian. To be absolutely precise, an anthropological analysis must postulate the existence of two distinct non-religious Rights, corresponding to two types of family structure favourable to dechristianization. The community type should in theory define a specific Right – an authoritarian ideological force more like Italian Fascism than Gaullism. One senses in the case of Gaullism, with egalitarian nuclear territory being more

Map 26
The non-religious Right

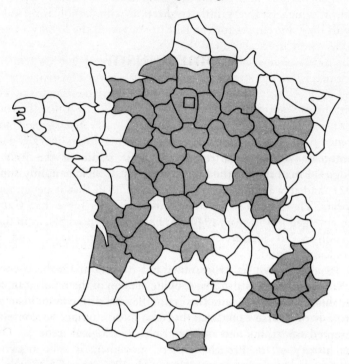

Départements in which the non-religious Right takes over 25 per cent of votes cast

Derived from maps 16 and 24.

favourable to it than community territory, a subtle difference of outlook. In the case of communism, the left antithesis of the non-religious Right, the community territory appears on the contrary to be more favourable to it than egalitarian nuclear territory.

9

Communism

Communism is the most recent and least stable of the four great ideological forces sharing the French territory. Officially it only appeared in 1921, and it was only between 1936 and 1946 that it penetrated the electorate. These dates make communism an older force than Gaullism, which emerged in the years 1940–65; but it is not possible, as in the case of Gaullism, to identify communism with an ancient and stable ideological tradition.

By its aspirations, its programme and its action, Gaullism connects with Bonapartism. It is also a right-wing version of the republican, liberal and egalitarian temperament. This is not the case with communism whose doctrine is of course egalitarian, but also authoritarian. So communism represented something new on the French ideological scene.

The history of the French workers' movement is split in two by a fundamental ideological break. Around 1900 the CGT, the most important trade union, was a stronghold of 'anarcho-syndicalism'. It expressed egalitarian and libertarian aspirations. Its militants were individualistic, undisciplined, in fact not unlike the stereotype of the typical Frenchman. The anarchism of the beginning of the century seemed a natural variant of the republican temperament, a left-wing version meeting the needs of the working class.

Immediately after the Second World War and the split which separated Force Ouvrière (socialist) from the CGT, the latter seems to have changed its nature. It became no more than the trade-union arm of disciplined and organized communism. An ideological and mental inversion seems to have taken place in a section of the French Left between 1921 and 1945. The anthropological analysis of stabilized communism in the 1970s makes it possible to describe, and moreover to explain, this disconcerting evolution.

THE MAP OF COMMUNISM

The map of communist votes in 1978 (map 27) reveals two distinct levels of maximum strength for the Parti Communiste Français:

Level 1: Communism obtained 20 per cent of the vote in a vast zone spreading tentacles towards the south-east and south-west, the centre obviously being Paris.

Level 2: The PC polled more than 24 per cent of the votes cast in three peripheral strongholds – the Mediterranean littoral, central Limousin, Nord–Pas-de-Calais, Somme, Seine-Maritime, Aisne and Ardennes.

The existence of these two levels suggests that two distinct factors were at work, even if the strongholds of level 2 are included in the level 1 zone.

Map 27
Communism in 1978

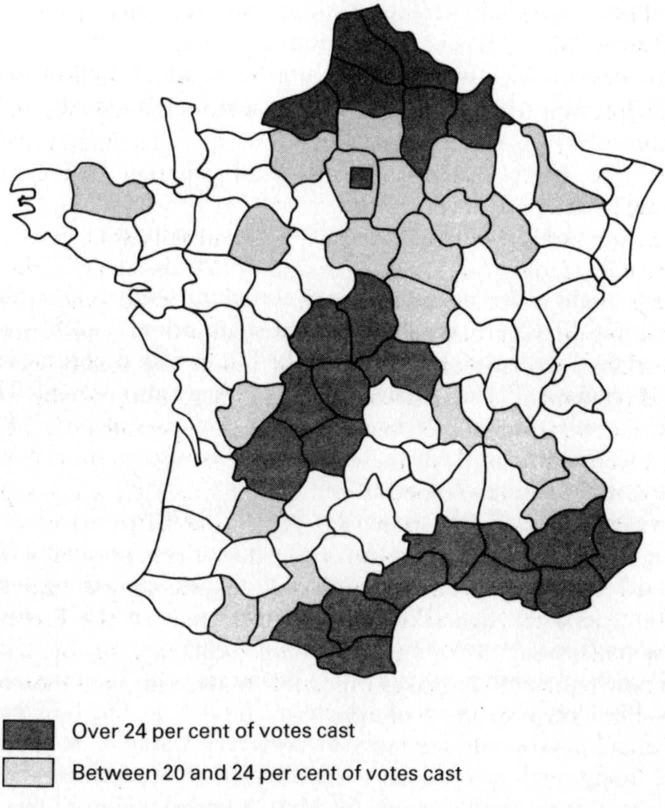

Over 24 per cent of votes cast

Between 20 and 24 per cent of votes cast

Based on the parliamentary election results of 12 March 1978, published in *Le Monde*.

Cartographic analysis does not reveal any impact by economic factors on the political pattern.

The industrial regions of the East are on the whole impervious to the communist phenomenon. The red bastion of central Limousin is fairly rural, if we exclude the *départements* of Haute-Vienne and Allier.

As for the Mediterranean littoral, it is neither industrial nor rural, belonging more to the service sector. An urban, commercial and crafts tradition has long dominated the socio-economic structure. The existence of this Mediterranean and Roman heritage did not prevent the flourishing development of communism between 1921 and 1978. Only the Nord stronghold suggests a link between the growth of industry and the regional penetration of communism.

If we move from the maximum strength level (above 24 per cent) to level 1 (more than 20 per cent), again we note that an economic interpretation cannot explain the territorial distribution of communism. The Paris basin, which was not the centre from which French industry took off, was nevertheless the centre from which communism spread.

FROM DECHRISTIANIZATION TO COMMUNISM

With a few slight differences, the map of communist influence reproduces the territorial structure typical of dechristianization, which was also centred on the Paris basin. In the case of the PC, as with dechristianization, the Mediterranean, Provençal and Audois poles are also present. The PC is strong in only one non-dechristianized region, that of Nord–Pas-de-Calais, the only region where communism is strong in a massively industrialized working-class area.

Generally, however, the regions where in 1978, shortly before its collapse, the PC obtained more than a 20 per cent vote produce a familiar shape: the reverse of the map of catholicism. A strong negative correlation (−0.56) linked the communist vote in 1978 with the proportion of people attending mass around 1965.

So French communism did not penetrate the majority of the industrialized regions, most of which are located in the East between Lorraine and Savoie, and are fairly or even very Catholic. It established itself in traditional revolutionary territory, that of dechristianization. Maps do not show the PC as one of Marx's offspring, but as *one* of the legitimate heirs of the French Revolution, alongside Gaullism.

EQUALITY WITHOUT FREEDOM

The general strength zone of the PC (level 1, more than 20 per cent of votes) coincides, as did the Revolution, with the egalitarian nuclear family region of the Paris basin. Relations between brothers were egalitarian, Relations between parents and children liberal. Between these systemic values and communism, there existed only a partial affinity, resting on a single ideological and anthropological trait – equality, a value which is present in the family structures of the dechristianized zones and in communist doctrine. On the other hand, the authoritarian characteristics of Marxism-Leninism do not have their counterpart in the family structures of the Paris basin. This absence explains the incomplete and very minority attachment of this region to the communist ideology. In a general minority in France, the PC is equally so at the centre of the national system, which is merely a zone of relative strength. More than 70 per cent of the electorate voted for other parties.

In the old dechristianized regions, communism appears merely a belated manifestation of the French revolutionary tradition, vitiated by its abandonment of the liberal principle and by its reduced size. In fact communism is accepted in this region because it is the tenuous heir to a brief paroxysm of the Revolution – the dictatorship of the Committee of Public Safety. From a Marxist-Leninist point of view, the French Revolution was fully acceptable only during the few aberrant months of the Terror. Communism would like to view this accident of history as a fixed and stable structure. However, in the great liberal tradition, the Terror was ended by the Assembly movement of Thermidor.

Because it corresponded with egalitarian but liberal regions, the anthropological implantation of French communism in the heart of the Paris basin was rather unnatural and consequently fragile. In these areas, joining the Communist Party meant a reversal by the individual of certain family values, as well as an internal repression of the desire for freedom. This abnormality undoubtedly explains a certain neurotic quality of communist support in France. It also makes it possible to understand certain characteristics of the PC within the Communist International, i.e. exceptional dogmatism and relative instability.

The strength of the French Communist Party organization, established and maintained by a system of filtering and close supervision known as 'democratic centralism', should not lead us to overestimate the PC's authority over its outer areas, and over its voters and the working class of those regions where the party dominates the Left.

Communist trade-unionism, very different from the social democratic or Christian democratic trade-unionism of the northern European countries, is weak at the organizational level. It has difficulty in controlling its rank and file and is not completely free of the anarcho-syndicalist tradition, which prefers spontaneous mass action to bureaucratic centralism. It is quite remarkable how incapable the French PC has always been of starting up or guiding strike movements. The incapacity of Stalinism to master the fundamental anarchism of the workers was particularly notable in May 1968. As a result the action of the masses has never been guided by the party organization. It has obeyed the unconscious anthropological determinants, egalitarian and liberal, which are found in the heart of France.

THE COMMUNITY STRONGHOLDS

In two of the three peripheral strongholds where the Communist Party controls 24 per cent of the electorate, it finds its exact anthropological counterpart in an egalitarian and authoritarian 'community' family structure. This family model, always significant but not necessarily dominant, exists along the north-west edge of the Massif central, between the *départements* of Saône-et-Loire and Dordogne. It is equally characteristic of part of the Mediterranean littoral, particularly in Provence. On the agricultural level the community family is associated with share-cropping. These two regions are zones of maximum strength for the PC. The 'party of the working class' has penetrated the peasant world, particularly west and north of the Massif Central.

In the Limousin, communist influence does not preclude a very large socialist influence. This ideological overlap coincides with an anthropological superimposition. Family structures of both the stem and community type exist in Limousin where, at the agricultural level, they are reflected in a juxtaposition of peasant proprietorship and share-cropping. Although less noticeable, this type of coincidence is also characteristic of Provence, in the *départements* of Bouches-du-Rhône and Var.

This peripheral communism, well anchored like catholicism in its strongholds, does not quantitatively dominate the movement at national level. It is to the north, in the Paris region, that we find the true centre of gravity of the PC, in egalitarian and liberal areas that do not subscribe whole-heartedly to Marxist-Leninist ideas. The peripheral strongholds, a minority in the movement but perfectly adapted to communism because of their authoritarian and egalitarian structures, nevertheless make a considerable contribution to the stability of the party.

THE DISUNITY OF THE LEFT

We are now in a position to explain the separation of communism from socialism, made official by the Congress of Tours in 1920 and confirmed by incessant political and electoral competition. Here is no difference of degree, but of nature. The separation does not oppose a revolutionary trend to a reformist trend, a hard-line party to a 'wet' party. Each of the two ideological forces of the Left has its own logic and values, and there are distinct ideological expressions of differing anthropological systems.

Communism is grafted on to egalitarian family structures, socialism on to inegalitarian ones. Linked by a shared identification with the underdog, which marks them both as left-wing, the PS and PC are divided by differing systemic values.

The ideological autonomy of the Socialist Party, thought to be constantly threatened by communist outbidding, was in fact invulnerable between 1936 and 1981. It was not the expression of a weaker determination, but rather of a special quality. The anti-communism of the socialists of the South-west was not the result of a lukewarm reformism, but of the ideological power of the stem family, which has a certain affection for the State, but respects private property and rejects dogmatic egalitarianism.

. Supported by these specific values, a weakened SFIO was reduced between 1946 and 1958 to its strongholds of the North and South-west, but nevertheless resisted the ideological pressure of the PC. Allied with the classic Right, the SFIO defended the institutions of the Fourth Republic against both communism and Gaullism. It was able to resist the PC, which was in a majority on the Left, because it was 'different' at the anthropological level. It could not be made more radical by communism, because it was the ideological expression of an autonomous anthropological system, the stem family.

Immediately after the Second World War, the PC appeared more powerful because it gathered its support from regions – dominant and central – of egalitarian nuclear family structure. This power was fragile, for the anthropological implantation of communism was imperfect, as we have seen. The liberalism of the family structure of the Paris basin in fact rejected the communist concept of authority.

EXCEPTIONS: NORD–PAS-DE-CALAIS AND GARD

In densely populated working-class areas, communism seems to have been capable of developing on the back of the socialist movement, by attracting part of the SFIO electorate. This is what happened in Nord–Pas-de-Calais, where one of the three communist strongholds was situated. It was also the only one which was really working-class. This local Marxism did not derive its support from favourable family structures, for the stem family dominated the local scene anthropologically. In this particular case, the ideology developed independently of the family substratum. We must, however, be precise about the limits of this autonomy.

The partial drift towards communism in socialist regions must not be regarded as the direct effect of a working-class presence. The numerical strength of the proletariat is not the only explanation of communism's ability to encroach locally on socialism and develop independently of family structures. In most of the industrial regions of the East, the proletariat, orientated towards the Right by catholicism, remained largely impervious to communist influence. Two conditions must be satisfied for the communist ideology to develop outside the anthropological moulds that are favourable to it: a large working class and a left-wing tendency already in existence. In this case communism did not penetrate the working class, but the workers' socialism of Nord–Pas-de-Calais.

Another case of the spread of communism outside its ideal anthropological territory, in Gard, enables us to describe even more precisely the mechanism of the ideology's autonomous development. Gard, a stem-family region, does not on the anthropological level belong to the Mediterranean world. The communist electorate, however, accounted for 24 per cent of the votes cast. Here it was protestantism, another left-wing doctrine, which had become radicalized without either passage through a socialist phase or the presence of a mass working class. It is true that it was a particularly hard form of protestantism, shaped by the struggle of the Camisards against Louis XIV's absolute Catholic monarchy. In this case we are not dealing with a socialist working class drifting towards communism, but with a specific Protestant world, both persecuted and aggressive because of memories of the past.

In Nord–Pas-de-Calais, as in Gard, communism did not radicalize the working class. It grew parasitically on a different form of the Left, not very egalitarian, whose opposition to the Right had been intensified by special historical conditions – the toughness of industrialization in Nord–Pas-de-Calais and the brutality of repression in Gard. The communism resulting from these secondary developments is of a rather special kind. In Gard, for example, the PC in 1978 had a large number of voters, but few militants. It was a superficial phenomenon, superimposed on a fundamental loyalty to protestantism. Once more, however, protestantism showed that it belonged essentially to the Left. On the other hand, where catholicism dominated, the working class, whatever its size, resisted communist influence.

Generally speaking, electoral communism, when it escapes anthropological determinants, does not radicalize a specifically working-class outlook, but rather a left-wing outlook. What communism, socialism and protestantism have in common, and which distinguishes them from catholicism, is certainly not an implantation in a working-class setting, but a general, abstract identification with the underdog. Catholicism, on the other hand, identifies with the ruling class. These parallel identifications can lead to a certain electoral confusion; but they never open up the possibility of sharing government. The clash of systemic values is paramount, and the identification with the Left of secondary importance. Between 1921 and 1981, communism and socialism spent more time fighting each other than governing together. Their most recent alliance in government entirely confirmed the fact that an invisible wall separates the two great French left-wing tendencies.

10

The Traditional French Political System

The complexity and apparent disorder of the French political system, which consists of two right wings and two left wings, is simply due to the existence of two distinct anthropological systems within the national territory, each producing its own Left and Right.

The unification of the Lefts and the alliance of the Rights are perpetually threatened by the opposition of the systemic values inherent in the two anthropological systems. The authoritarian and inegalitarian Catholic Right finds it difficult to get on with the liberal, egalitarian, non-religious Right. Authoritarian and non-egalitarian socialism has difficulty in co-ordinating its efforts with those of the Communist Party, which is egalitarian, and whose authoritarianism reflects the necrosis of a liberal temperament – a neurotic inversion, rather than a natural aspiration resulting from direct anthropological determinants. Consequently both the Left and the Right pursue their chaotic existences, with agreements and splits following each other at a rhythm which varies according to the period.

The union of the Left is made particularly difficult because of its desire for social change. Power-sharing between socialism and communism presupposes agreement on positive objectives and plans for reform. Agreement on the right is easier because conservatism, i.e. absence of change, defines everyone's programme *a priori*.

The difficulties of the Left in uniting are made worse by the communist anomaly. Anthropological theory would expect an egalitarian and liberal tendency, of the *radical* type, to predominate in the Paris basin. The communist domination of this region, albeit temporary, upsets the dynamic of the system. The alliance of a 'socialist' Left, authoritarian and non-egalitarian, with a 'radical' Left, liberal and egalitarian – in other words of two moderate forces – would hardly raise more problems than that of the Catholic and the non-religious Rights.[1]

THE ALLIANCE OF LEFT AND RIGHT

What divides the Left and separates the Right brings certain right-wing and left-wing parties closer to their opposites. Indeed, the Right and the Left that are produced by the same anthropological systems accept identical systemic values. The four great forces which make up the French ideological scene can thus be regrouped two by two, no longer according to a Right–Left criterion, but according to their anthropological origin:

- The Catholic Right and socialism are both products of the stem family.
- Gaullism and communism emerge from the same background of the egalitarian nuclear family.

In practice an alliance between communism and Gaullism is impossible. Each of them stands for an accentuation of one of the egalitarian nuclear family's systemic values: the non-religious Right lays claim to the liberal principle, the PC to the egalitarian principle. Here the clash between the Right and the Left also reflects, for special historical reasons, a clash of systemic values which are separate rather than contrasted. The liberalism of the Right is not the opposite of the egalitarianism of the Left.

Despite this heightened antagonism, it is well known that there are certain affinities between the Gaullist and communist electorates. Gaullism has been structurally infected by an egalitarian dynamic, communism by a liberal instability. In 1958 Gaullism encroached widely on the traditional communist electorate, a sure sign of an ideological relationship between the two electorates. However, at the level of programmes and leaders, all political alliance was out of the question.

Alliance between the Catholic Right and socialism is, on the other hand, not an impossibility. The Right–Left dualism cannot hide the fact that the systemic values of both forces are, identical, i.e. authoritarian and non-egalitarian. In practice, the classic Right and socialism have, in spite of noble efforts to keep up appearances of separateness, often governed together and for a considerable time. The temporary stability of the Fourth Republic, which stood for opposition to both Gaullism and communism, rested on their underlying accord. There was agreement on a moderate programme of social and economic intervention, respectful of private ownership and of the Church and its schools. In France this socialist and Catholic majority represented a belated triumph of the stem-family fringe regions over the central zone of the Paris basin, which was egalitarian, liberal and in favour of centralization.

LOCAL SYSTEMS

The complexity of national political life contrasts with the relative simplicity of local political life, founded on Right–Left dualisms which are regionally uniform. Locally there is *one* anthropological system, *one* Right and *one* Left. The national political game makes it possible for the four great ideological forces to survive in all regions. But in each *département* there is a dominant left-wing and a dominant right-wing faction. In the West, the Basque country, Alsace and Rouergue, the Catholic Right controls the Right. In the Paris basin, Gaullism dominates the Right. In the South-west, socialism controls the Left, while in the Paris basin the communists hold a privileged position. This preponderance of one of the two left-wing parties over the whole of the Left can also be observed where the Left is in a minority: thus in the right-wing West, socialism controls the Left. In the same way, one of the two right-wing forces can dominate the whole Right when the Left is in the majority: in the South-west, a Catholic Right controls the whole Right.

A general model can be set up. In each *département* we identify a dominant Right, which can be either Catholic or non-religious, and a dominant Left, either socialist or communist. The local confrontations between the dominant Right and dominant Left bring out the underlying tendencies of the local political system. Four combinations are possible a priori:

Table 10.1

	Dominant Right		*Dominant Left*
1	Catholic Right	against	socialist Left
2	Catholic Right	against	communist Left
3	Non-religious Right	against	socialist Left
4	Non-religious Right	against	communist Left

An examination of existing local systems shows that all types are not equally possible or frequent. This is perfectly natural: the non-religious Right and communism stem from the same anthropological territory and fight each other locally, and the same goes for the Catholic Right and socialism.

In practice (see map 28), around 1978

- In 48 *départements*, a Catholic-dominated Right faced a socialist-dominated Left.

- In 21 *départements*, a majority non-religious Right faced a communist-dominated Left.
- In 18 *départements* a majority non-religious Right faced a socialist-dominated Left.
- In 2 *départements* a Catholic-dominated Right faced a majority communist Left.

Two types of local confrontation thus seem to be most typical – the Catholic Right – socialist Left and the non-religious Right – communist.

Map 28
Local political systems *c.*1978

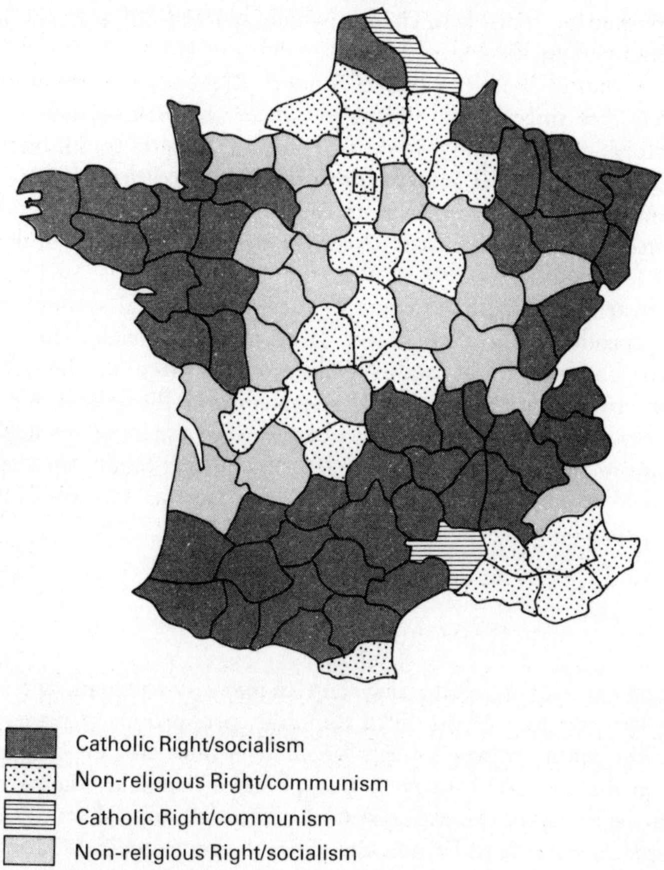

Catholic Right/socialism
Non-religious Right/communism
Catholic Right/communism
Non-religious Right/socialism

Derived from maps 16 and 24.

CENTRE AND PERIPHERY

The conflict between the Catholic Right and socialism occupies a vast fringe area; and this is logical because, according to the statistics, we are concerned here with non-dechristianized France.

The opposition between the non-religious Right and communism dominates the central area stretching from Somme to Haute-Vienne, following of course the principle axis of dechristianization. The non-religious Right–socialism duet was quantitatively far from negligible in 1978, and was represented in eighteen *départements*. However it occupied too visibly an intermediate area between the two major zones for it to be considered an ideal type. It corresponds to a recent phenomenon – the penetration of dechristianized territory by the socialists at the expense of the communists. This is a change which sparked off a break in the traditional system.

An encounter between the Catholic Right and communism is extremely rare since it only occurs in two *départements* which we have met before – Nord and Gard, two regions where communism has succeeded in developing in stem anthropological territory as a parasite of socialism or protestantism. In both cases it confronts a Catholic Right, which itself corresponds closely to the theoretical possibilities of the stem family.

The distribution within France of the local political systems on the whole reproduces the map of the large family systems. The conflict between Catholic Right and socialism takes place in the territory occupied by the stem family and its satellite of the inland West, the absolute nuclear family. The conflict between the non-religious Right and communism finds its way to the egalitarian nuclear family (in a slightly diminished form because of recent changes), and its Centre–Limousin satellite, the community family.

THE EFFECTS OF VOTING SYSTEMS

The importance of the electoral system – a majority vote with two rounds during the first part of the Fifth Republic, proportional representation during the whole of the Fourth Republic – must not be exaggerated. Never in the electoral history of Europe has a change in the method of election really upset the expression of profound political attitudes. The geographical stability of French ideological forces between 1880 and 1980 proves this. It resisted two changes in the constitution and an even larger number of changes in electoral systems.

The change from a majority to a proportional system does, however, have certain effects, which, without altering the basic nature of the conflicts, modify the way they are perceived. The majority vote with two rounds makes arrangements to withdraw in the second round inevitable. The proportional system, on the other hand, ensures complete independence for each of the ideological forces in face of all the others. The majority vote maximizes the importance of Left–Right dualism, whose mythology provides the easiest way to legitimize withdrawals. Proportional representation, on the contrary, abolishes the necessity of an alliance of the Left and an equivalent right-wing agreement. In fact it gives rein to the divisive power of systemic values – liberty or authority, equality or inequality.

In the French context the conflict between Right and Left appears as a unifying myth. It creates a fictitious relationship between distinct regional left wings. It pointlessly dramatizes class and religious conflicts, but it partially absorbs regional differences.

The majority vote, which maximizes the importance of the conflict between Right and Left, thus acts as an economic and religious divider, but a territorial uniter. Proportional representation, which reduces the conflict between Left and Right, is a better economic and religious integrator, but a territorial separator.

RIGIDITY OF THE STEM FAMILY, FLEXIBILITY OF THE EGALITARIAN NUCLEAR FAMILY

Universal although diverse, the Left–Right division can be stable or unstable according to the region and the anthropological types. There are *départements* where the balance of power between Right and Left did not fundamentally change between 1880 and 1980. Ariège, Creuse and Tarn-et-Garonne have always voted Left. Pyrénées-Atlantiques, Lozère, Alsace and Morbihan have remained eternally faithful to the Right. On the other hand, in certain *départements* changes in the majority can be observed. Loiret, Aube, Côte-d'Or and many others have changed their allegiances several times during the twentieth century. A fatal line is then crossed, that of 50 per cent of the votes cast, which sometimes go to the Right and sometimes to the Left. These identifications with the oppressor and the oppressed are consequently variable. This variable stability can be measured and mapped if we compare three series of electoral results – the three great contests during which Right and Left achieved their respective unities, in 1936, 1965 and 1974. The Popular Front, the de Gaulle–Mitterrand duel and the first Mitterrand–Giscard clash were for both Right and Left an occasion to measure their respective strengths.

The map of the *départements* whose majority did not change either between 1936 and 1965, or between 1965 and 1974 (map 29), is absolutely characteristic. A well-known fringe situation is shown up. The stem-family regions appear as the key points of political stability, independently of their 'Right' or 'Left' orientation. The South of France, the East and the West reveal the same tendency towards electoral inertia. The Paris basin, on the contrary, represents the centre of a mobile system, in which changes of majority are possible.

The correspondence between stability and the stem family, between instability and the nuclear family, is not perfect. In the Nord–Pas-de-Calais and the Rhône–Alpes region the proximity to the Paris basin produces some instability in the systems based on the stem family.

Map 29
Zones of political stability

Départements in which political orientation, left or right, was the same in 1936, 1965 and 1974

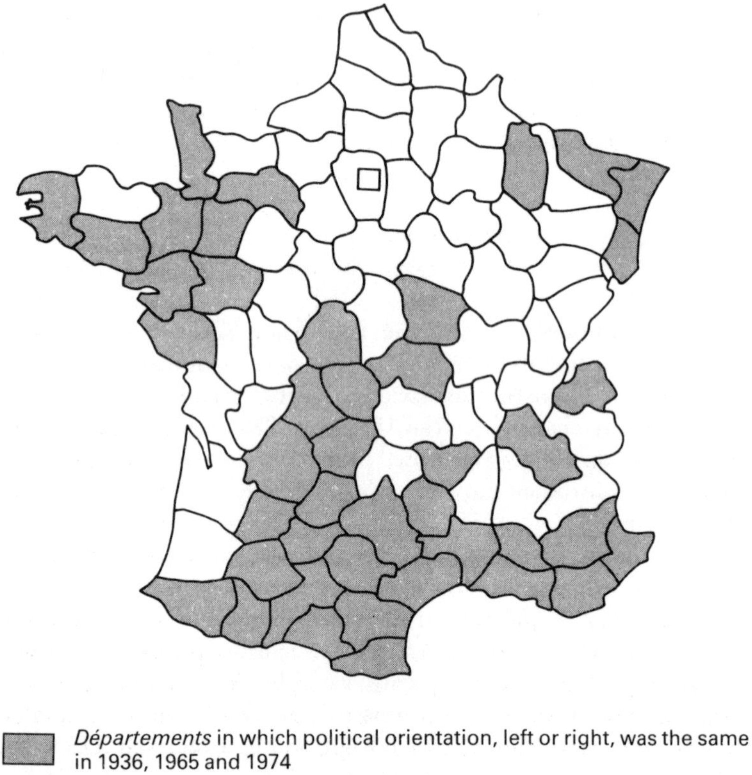

For 1936, see map 22; for 1965, results of presidential elections of 19 December; for 1974, results of presidential elections of 19 May – both published by *Le Monde*.

Generally speaking, at the European level, great stability of electoral behaviour is characteristic of anthropological systems in which there exists an authoritarian component in the relationship between parents and children, be it either in the stem family or the community family. In France, the regions with the community family structure of the Centre–Limousin and Provence resemble those of the stem family in their stability.

Different left- and right-wing orientations can reflect political authoritarianism, but they have their rigidity in common. This ideological stability of authoritarian family systems can be found in Sweden, where people perpetually vote for the Social Democrats; likewise in Bavaria, where in 1980 as in 1900 people continued to vote for the Catholic Right.

In France, the electoral stability of the inland West, with its absolute nuclear family, is not explained by this model. It is an anomaly, the consequence of the special influence of catholicism on the local population through the educational system. One of the characteristic features of the nuclear family system is in fact a certain fluidity of political behaviour. In the centre of the Paris basin, as in England and the United States, one notes majority swings from Left to Right and vice versa. The instability of the 'Left' or 'Right' label at the political level reflects the fluidity of the attitude towards authority in the family sphere.

The peripheral regions of France have in a way no political history between 1880 and 1980. They express loyalty rather than an aspiration towards change. The Paris basin, on the contrary, has a history, which in practice corresponds with that of the country as a whole. When it turned left in 1936, so did France. When, with de Gaulle, it swung right, so did France. Although it lacks stability in its attitudes, the geographical and political centre of the country plays its role well as ideological director of the nation – even because of its fragility. But it plays the role on a mythical plane, that of the Right–Left conflict, which is not fundamental.

ECONOMIC POLARIZATION, RELIGIOUS POLARIZATION

The polarization of local societies into a right and a left wing is not always effected in the same way. Although it is an a priori mental structure, Right–Left dualism must find, in the objective social universe, concrete instances of opposition in order for it to organize itself. Several systems of antagonism exist, of which the most important are economic and religious.

One of the two important polarities which can be used dates from the nineteenth century. It was then that the Industrial Revolution gave birth to a working class, distinctly separated by its way of life from the middle or bourgeois classes. In *The Communist Manifesto*, Marx suggested that the clash between the bourgeois and the proletariat should become the modern form of the eternal duel between the oppressor and the oppressed. He had a fairly wide audience. From 1880 onwards the European left-wing parties saw themselves and defined themselves as workers' movements.

But another, older polarity, less self-conscious but more stable, grounded in geography rather than in economics, also made an effective platform for the conflict between Left and Right. It opposed catholicism to the various forms of religious dissent which have left their mark on French territory. In practice, two forms of structure combine to organize the Left–Right dualism. But each dominates one of the two major anthropological systems. The economy structures the Right–Left encounter in the egalitarian nuclear family regions, religion in the stem-family regions.

IN THE CENTRE – AN ECONOMIC FRAMEWORK FOR RIGHT–LEFT CONFLICT

In the heart of the Paris basin, the clash between the non-religious Right and the PC took on the aspect of a class war. In that area the alignment of each individual on the right or left depended closely on the various socio-professional categories. A detailed electoral geography, either at the district or municipal level, shows that the working-class suburbs voted for the Left. This was a spectacularly clear phenomenon in the Red Belt of Paris between 1880 and 1980.

The appropriation by the Right of the systemic value of freedom and by the Left of the systemic value of equality in egalitarian nuclear family regions has, in this context, a certain logic. The confrontation between a liberal bourgeoisie and an egalitarian proletariat is not a theoretical absurdity. Seen from the inside, the Paris basin of the years between 1945 and 1978 seems to respect the simplest Marxist pattern. We can estimate that the absolute majority of workers there always voted for the Left, in spite of a Gaullist thrust in 1958, and even if this proletarian bias was not sufficient to drag the whole of the non-religious and republican region to the left. The working class in the Paris basin is not a sufficiently large proportion of the whole working population, and its vote is not slanted enough to the left, to be a decisive factor in a global alignment of the region. But the proletariat of the central part of France has at all times belonged to the Left, with communism dominating between 1921 and 1980.

This leftward orientation of the working class seems to Parisian intellectuals to be logical and necessary. They live in a village, which is itself located at the heart of a homogeneous anthropological region. When Jean-Paul Sartre climbed on to a barrel in order to harangue the Boulogne-Billancourt proletariat, he was not being absurd. But he was being neither an historian nor a philosopher. He was an intellectual plunged into a particular anthropological system, and he did not understand that the 'Parisian worker' was not a 'worker in general', but a particular type of worker, with specific family values and political ideals corresponding to these values. Elsewhere, on the edges of the country, the workers are sometimes neither left-wing nor communist. Elsewhere it is not economic conflicts that lead to a Left–Right dualism, and yet one does exist.

AT THE PERIPHERY: A RELIGIOUS FRAMEWORK FOR LEFT–RIGHT CONFLICT

The Catholic Right–socialist duet, which makes up the political system of the periphery, is not created basically by an economic polarity – even if in all the regions concerned the workers vote slightly more left than the executive class; even though the socialist Left claims to represent the spirit of Marxist theory. It is not difficult to trace a different, older and legitimate line of descent for the conflict between Right and Left. It descends directly from the religious clashes of past centuries, which set heretics and Protestants against orthodox catholicism.

In this peripheral world the conflict betwen ruler and underdog does not project itself on class antagonisms. In most of the Catholic regions the working class probably up to 1967 voted in its majority for the Right. This was the case in the West, in the south-east of the Massif Central, in Haute-Savoie, and in part of Lorraine and Alsace. The right-wing orientation of the working class in the East of the country has for a long time been particularly spectacular. For this has long been one of the most heavily industrialized regions in the country. In this industrial and reactionary world Marxist theory flounders. In a highly Catholic world the working class is generally impervious to class war. On the other hand, the middle classes of the stem-family regions, orientated leftwards, more particularly in the South-west, vote massively for the Left – against catholicism rather than against capitalism. This does not mean that they vote against Christianity or religion in general.

This religious structuring of the Right–Left conflict encourages, as the economic structure does not, the appearance of local consensus in left- or right-wing societies, integrated vertically in a stable membership with either a socialist or a right-wing majority. The conflict between Right and

Left in stem-family regions represents a clash of theoretical principles rather than the antagonism of two genuine human groups.

At the heart of the nuclear-family regions, the Right–Left dualism is embodied in the composition of two genuine human groups – the working class and the middle class.

TOWARDS A CRISIS

So, in certain aspects, ideological life in France resembles some facts of psychic life, as described in psychoanalysis. The most important determinants are those that are most hidden. Visible conflicts are the least profound.

The link between family structures and ideological systems is the most powerful, but also the most hidden. It is never mentioned by either politicians or voters, but silently determines the segmentation of the French ideological scene, through the values of liberty, authority, equality and inequality. It defines the oppositions – of socialism to communism, of the Catholic Right to the non-religious Right. It is one of the unmentioned factors of French political life.

The conflict between Left and Right is a conscious and even a noisy phenomenon. It organizes official political life, the clash between majority and opposition – a simplified game, the very simplicity of which has a unifying effect on the French political system. To organize itself it makes use of the different polarities in stem-family and nuclear-family regions. The rivalry between the Catholic Right and socialism extends an old religious antagonism into the twentieth century. The opposition between the non-religious Right and communism rests on economic antagonism. This is a conscious and important element in French ideological life.

The system which has just been described was active during the hundred years between 1880 and 1980. But between 1965 and 1980 exceptionally rapid and violent transformations almost all at once destroyed the religious and economic structures and the working class, giving rise to a total disorganization of Right–Left dualism in the country.

PART III

THE SOCIAL TRANSFORMATION

At the very moment when western societies thought they had reached the end of history – a final state of peace and plenty – they suddenly rediscovered what it was to be frightened. The classic trio – economic crisis, unemployment, racism – struck France harder between 1974 and 1985 than it had done during the thirties, after the 1929 crash. At that time France remained sufficiently underdeveloped in the industrial field to be fairly protected from international economic movements.

The crisis of the thirties and that of today are not, however, of the same nature. The 1929 collapse was economic in the narrowest sense of the term. It was due to the inability of economic circuits to match demand and investment to the productive potential of the period. The present crisis is a much deeper one. Above all, it is a complex one – technological, cultural, economic and sexual. It is a revolution of attitudes of mind rather than simply of economics.

It is, in fact, much easier to compare the 'crisis' of today with the Industrial Revolution, which tore the traditional peasant world away from its habits, than with the 1929 crisis which merely jammed for a time the already existing industrial world. Like the present economic crisis, the Industrial Revolution was but one aspect of a general transformation of society.

Europe's take-off between 1850 and 1914, a true crisis of modernity, was made up of three essential elements, the Industrial Revolution being only one of them.

The first element was a cultural revolution, the mass elimination of illiteracy. The process of teaching the entire European population to read and write, which started in the sixteenth century, but which grew in momentum and was completed at the end of the nineteenth century, activated and disturbed all cultural and ideological life. In France the literacy rate rose from 50 per cent in 1866 to 86 per cent in 1906.

The second element was a sexual revolution, indeed a demographic transformation. The decrease in the death-rate, brought about by the improvement of sanitary conditions, was accompanied (with some time-lag) by a decrease in fertility. The spread of contraceptive techniques implied a questioning of religious dogmas and in particular of Catholic ideas. In France, the first massively dechristianized country, the decrease in the birth-rate came early in the central regions. It began during the second half of the eighteenth century, but it was in the course of the nineteenth century that the major part of the transformation took place.

The third element was the Industrial Revolution. The perfecting of standardized methods of manufacturing, using coal and iron, made mass production possible. It meant that peasants were uprooted from their villages and transformed into a proletariat, docile servants of the new machines.

The three revolutions which took place between 1850 and 1914 – cultural, sexual and economic – together made up the process of entrance into the modern world. They took place during the same historic period, but they showed a certain autonomy in relation to one another, even if literacy (a cultural revolution), sparked off during the sixteenth century, must in the long term be regarded as the driving force.

France, advanced with regard to the drop in her birth-rate, was far less so when it came to literacy. England shone for her industrialization, but did not occupy first place either for literacy or for the drop in fertility. Germany, very advanced with regard to her rate of literacy, was behind England for industrialization and behind France for birth control. With various discrepancies, both national and local, the three revolutions nevertheless took hold of all western Europe gradually between the sixteenth and the eighteenth centuries, with a dramatic acceleration during the second half of the nineteenth century.

The three components of this general transformation in European societies – cultural, sexual and economic – also explain the present crisis of the western world, which may simply be a passage to a superior form of modernity. The present crisis is merely phase II of a permanent and many-sided revolution, in which mass literacy, demographic changes and the Industrial Revolution constitute the whole of Phase I.

PHASE II

The development of primary education, characteristic of Phase I, was succeeded in Phase II by a spectacular advance in secondary education. According to the French 1982 census, the percentage of people with a diploma equal or above that of the *baccalauréat* rose from 6.6 per cent in the 65–74 age-group to 25.4 per cent in the 25–34 age-group. The percentage of men and women with no diploma fell from 66.4 per cent in the 65–74 age-group to 24 per cent in the 25–34 age-group.

The demographic change characteristic of phase I is succeeded in phase II by a second decrease in the birth-rate, which puts the fertility index below the theoretical threshold, allowing a net reproduction of the population. The fertility index oscillated between 1.75 and 1.90 per woman in France during the years 1976–86.

To the Industrial Revolution of phase I there succeeds in phase II a tertiary post-industrial revolution, whose driving force is automation. The industrial proletariat has become tragically superfluous. The development of secondary education and the collapse of fertility seem to be the logical continuation of mass literacy and the first demographic change. On the other hand, the tertiary revolution reverses the trends of the

Industrial Revolution. It implies a very real destruction of the working class formed in France between 1850 and 1975.

The development of secondary education and the collapse of fertility, two transformations shown by cartographic analysis to be closely linked, also have their destructive aspects (cf. chapter 1, p. 14 and 18, maps 2 and 4). These changes, which are mental rather than technological, do not directly affect the economic organization of the country. They attack its religious structure head on. Catholicism, which in certain areas survived the Protestant crisis and the French Revolution, seems today to be succumbing to the invisible blows of a cultural and sexual revolution. This revolution is all the more irresistible in that it does without an ideological framework or an appearance of doctrine.

As a result, the transformation of French society between 1965 and 1980 cannot be summarized, as has been suggested by most current political thinkers, by an analysis of the unemployment rate. The increase in the unemployment rate is only an *incidental* measure of current changes, the passing effect of new and massive adjustments in the socio-professional structure. Fundamental and irreversible movements are at work in French society – the decline of the working class, the rise and diversification of the middle classes, the terminal crisis of catholicism.

The problem of immigration, a fundamental one, is at the same time both new and old. The importing of foreign labour is more typical of an advanced phase of the Industrial Revolution, which required unskilled workers for its factories. But the destruction of the unskilled working class, which brutally affects immigrants, is typical of the post-industrial age.

The sum of all these transformations, at times painful, sometimes beneficial, makes up the very march of progress. It was these upheavals, rather than withdrawal agreements between the Socialist and Communist Parties at elections, which led from the start to the advance of the Socialist Party, the collapse of the communists and François Mitterrand's election in 1981. It was these upheavals which, continuing and spreading in a second phase, led to the rise of the Right and its subsequent split due to the emergence of the Front National, a xenophobic movement of a new type for France. French political life is now more than ever dependent on unconscious political forces.

11

The End of the Manual Workers

In France, the Industrial Revolution took the form of a slow but continuous transformation. Around 1946 it was not yet over. In that year the manual workers represented only 30 per cent of the working population. During the years 1946–75, which spanned the period between post-war reconstruction and the crisis, the end of the Industrial Revolution in France coincided with the emergence of a society of plenty. In the 1975 census the manual workers represented 38 per cent of the active population, a peak figure that was never to be exceeded. The working class was far from being in the majority in the country, as 62 per cent of the French were not manual workers. It was, however, by far the largest socio-professional class. In 1975, the peasants amounted to 9.3 per cent of the working population, white-collar workers 17.6 per cent and middle management 12.7 per cent. The French working class never dominated the national system numerically, as did the English working class until fairly recently. In 1961, the English and Welsh proletariat represented 54 per cent of the working population of their countries.[1]

The French working class looks weak by comparison. Yet around 1975 it was the largest socio-economic group. In electoral terms it represented a relative, but not an absolute majority. This marked the end of the French Industrial Revolution. Then began an incredibly sudden process of deindustrialization, when one thinks of the slow development of the secondary sector between 1850 and 1975.

The change in the socio-professional nomenclature effected by the INSEE between the censuses of 1975 and 1982 – a particularly badly chosen moment – makes a precise comparison of the workers' numbers at these two dates impossible. However, an examination of the number of people employed in industry, in fact a similar concept, gives a striking idea of the evolution which has taken place. In seven years, the number of people employed in industry fell from 38.6 per cent to 34.2 per cent of the working population.

A detailed examination of the sectors affected by this vast decrease in workers shows that the present transformation is indeed an *industrial*

Table 11.1

	The three sectors in 1975 and 1982		
	Numbers in 1975	*Numbers in 1982*	*Change 1975–82*
Agriculture	2,108,680	1,759,220	−16.6%
Industry	8,074,040	7,344,680	− 9.0%
Services	10,761,180	12,362,060	+14.9%

	Relative share of the three sectors in the working population in 1975 and 1982		
	1975	*1982*	*Change 1975–82*
Agriculture	10.1%	8.2%	−1.9%
Industry	38.6%	34.2%	−4.4%
Services	51.4%	57.6%	+6.2%

counter-revolution. It was the main sectors of the nineteenth-century Industrial Revolution which collapsed, i.e. the coal mines, iron-ore extraction, metal industries, textiles, leather. But the crash of the basic chemical industry, mainly devoted to the manufacture of textile synthetic fibres, shows that it was also the belated industrial revolution of the fifties which was partially overwhelmed, rendered obsolescent by worldwide technological and economic developments. Very few industrial sectors managed to avoid this reduction in the numbers of workers employed. The entire secondary sector shrank in numbers of workers between 1975 and 1982. In the old sectors – coal, textiles, ferrous metals, leather – more than a quarter of the workers disappeared in seven years. In France the industrial counter-revolution was astonishingly rapid and bloody.

The collapse of specific sectors went hand in hand, on the regional plane, with a devastation of the old industrial areas. All the coal, iron and steel and textile regions were affected (see table 11.3). Doubs, Meurthe-et-Moselle, Ardennes, Loire and Nord recorded a decrease of more than 7 per cent of their population employed in industry in seven years. But it was the entire industrial society of the North and East of the country which fell apart in terms of working population in employment.

Running between 1975 and 1982, this evolution more or less coincided with Giscard d'Estaing's seven-year term of office (1974–81). However,

Table 11.2

Decline of the various industrial branches
Changes in the numbers of personnel employed (1975–82)
as a percentage of initial numbers

Solid fuels	−32	Building	−8
Minerals and ferrous metals	−29	Oil and Gas	−7
Leather and shoes	−27	Cars	−6
Textiles and clothing	−26	Naval construction and	
Basic chemicals	−23	armament	−5
Paper and board	−22	Electrical and electronic	−4
Construction materials	−18	Rubber	−2
Foundries and metal working	−15	Wood and furniture	0
Mechanical construction	−14	Printing, publishing, press	+3
Glass	−13	Agricultural and food	
		industries	+4
		Light chemical	+11

it was caused by fundamental trends that no government could in practice control. After a three-year resistance between 1981 and 1984, of interventionist inspiration, the socialist government finally accepted the inevitability of the industrial sector's decrease. The next census will probably register an acceleration of the decline in more recent industrial sectors, which during the fifties and sixties were symbols of economic dynamism. The motor-car sector, in particular, is heading for a crisis, a bare ten years after the engineering sector.

Table 11.3

Proportion of the working population
employed in the secondary sector (%)

	1975	1982	Change 1975–82
Doubs	54.3	45.0	−9.3
Meurthe-et-Moselle	44.4	35.8	−8.6
Ardennes	47.2	40.0	−7.2
Loire	52.0	44.7	−7.3
Nord	48.9	41.3	−7.6

FROM RURAL EXODUS TO INDUSTRIAL EXODUS

One of the main elements of the Industrial Revolution had been the rural exodus, i.e. a movement of the population from the countryside to the towns and developing areas of the secondary sector. The regions dominated by the primary sector, the rural world located in the West of France, then showed a negative balance of migration. The industrial world, an immigration region, was characterized by a positive balance of migration.

The industrial counter-revolution reversed these trends. Between 1975 and 1982 it was the industrial part of France which could no longer maintain its population, and which slowly emptied it out towards other regions (see map 30). In a vast area situated in the North and East of the

Map 30
The industrial exodus

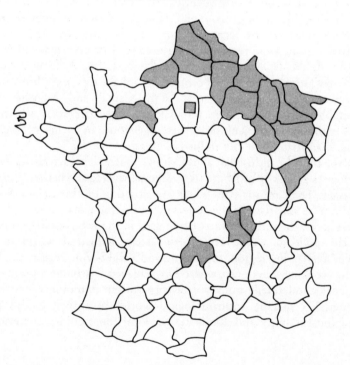

The 18 *départements* with the severest loss through migration between 1975 and 1982

Based on data from the 1975 and 1982 censuses.

country, the balance of migration was negative between 1975 and 1982; so much so that one can speak of an industrial exodus, just as one once did of a rural exodus.

The industrial worker of the nineteenth century was for Catholic moralists as well as for revolutionary socialists an uprooted individual, the son of a peasant removed from the stable world of the countryside and projected into a shifting urban universe of great uncertainty. The manual worker of the late twentieth century, if he makes his living like his nineteenth-century ancestor working in a coal mine, a textile factory or iron works, in no way fits this description. At the end of more than a century of industrialism, he is no longer uprooted. On the contrary, he is too deeply rooted. The industrial exodus, which is slowly emptying out the traditional North and East of the country, should not hide the real effects of emigration on local communities. In these areas from which people flee, quite naturally very few people come to settle. If we exclude a few foreign workers, immigration from within metropolitan France is very low, close to nil. Consequently, the North and the East at present have a remarkably homogeneous and stable population, autochthonous in the Greek sense of the term, i.e. born on the spot. In 1982, the old industrial regions were remarkable for the very low percentage of people born outside the *département*. In Nord–Pas-de-Calais, Ardennes, Moselle and Vosges, more than 90 per cent of the inhabitants were born in the *département*. Among rural areas, only Cantal and Manche reach comparable percentages. The population of *départements* which are mainly rural is at present more heterogeneous, in terms of regional origins, than that of the old industrial areas.

Today, the old industrial world shows certain characteristics which ethnologists generally attribute to traditional societies, whether primitive or peasant. They are societies which are closed in on themselves. So one should not be surprised at the appearance of a true working-class culture in these areas, the term 'culture' being used in the anthropological rather than the political sense. The north-eastern industrial world in fact includes a left-wing region, the North, and a right-wing region, the East. But the working class everywhere has achieved – around its mines, its steel works and textile mills – a density and an immobility which has engendered a specific anthropological world, because it enjoys great geographical stability and dominates the local communities numerically.

INDUSTRIALIZATION AND CULTURAL BLOCK

Here we find ourselves at the heart of the problem of decline. This tendency to close in on oneself can be interpreted in terms of fossilization. There exists a direct and close relationship between the shutting-in of the most traditional working class and the collapse, without hope of recovery, of the areas concerned.

The French example is perfectly clear, but admittedly this is a phenomenon of the whole western world. Everywhere the oldest working class faces problems of reconversion. The most dramatic case is obviously that of Britain, where the traditional proletariat, between 1900 and 1950, represented more than half the working population. Its economic fossilization has been that of Britain as a whole. In Belgium, the United States and Germany, the miners, steel-workers and those employed in the textile industry have raised or continue to raise problems of reconversion.

The blockage phenomenon, in fact, only seems mysterious to economists whose eyes are glued to national accountancy charts, financial circuits and capital investment and who tend to forget that, above all, economic health is a question of *men*, with their capacities, both intellectual and manual, their habits and their tastes.

Over a long period industrialization of the old type (along the lines of the English Industrial Revolution) has inevitable and often destructive effects on behaviour. The first industrial revolution required brawn rather than brains, manual workers and labourers rather than skilled workers. One cannot reject Engels' horrifying picture of the brutalization induced by factory life in the Britain of the mid-nineteenth century – women and children at work, the destruction of the family and of child-rearing systems. All these elements are part of classic Marxist dogma and must be accepted. What this side of Marxism lacks is a vision of the future consequences of this devastation, which were not only political, but above all anthropological. The brutality of nineteenth-century industrial life gave rise to a double reaction. Mutual aid among workers was made humanly necessary by the harsh conditions of production. But a cultural decline emerged almost automatically from this dense industrial world, where scholastic and intellectual achievement served no purpose. Traditional industry above all produced economically passive human beings.

Here a certain caution is necessary. It is out of the question to assert that the old industry on its own destroyed cultural effort. Its action was only effective where it crushed the social landscape by its mass. This occurred where the majority of the population lived off a single industrial activity, where the factory or mine with their working-class housing became villages as culturally homogeneous as the Breton or Provençal parishes of the eighteenth century.

The cultural collapse of dense working-class societies shows up in the educational statistics of the 1982 census. Certain factors can retard the collapse, others make it irresistible. Different types of industrialization imply varying degrees of gravity for the syndrome.

The mining sector is the most destructive. It creates a world of its own, partly underground, particularly dangerous and not highly qualified. It produces warm-hearted, inert, closed communities. No positive factor seems able to counteract the culturally regressive consequences of coal-mining when there is a dense implantation. No anthropological structure can resist it, not even the stem family, which, wherever it can, encourages the transmission of culture and success at school. Its lineage ideal is unable to resist the habits of a closed, unskilled working class. Neither in Pas-de-Calais, Belgium, the German Ruhr nor in Scotland has the dynamic of the stem family really stood up to coal-mining.

In all the regions concerned, this family type favours, on the political level, social democracy or social catholicism, both authoritarian but non-egalitarian political ideologies. It has not, however, retained much of its educational potential. The Nord–Pas-de-Calais, which in France is the most characteristic example of this combination, is a zone of cultural weakness, which produces very few graduates and very few teachers.

The general engineering sector, which requires a certain level of qualification in at least part of its work-force, is less destructive, even if it is based locally on heavy metal-working, which demands little intellectual competence. In this intermediate context, the family differential can play a part. A family system such as the stem family, with its strong attachment to cultural transmission, is in a better position than the nuclear family to resist the passivity induced by industrial mechanization. It makes a point of handing on the competence of skilled workers, an industrial echo of the craft skills of former times. This mechanical sector–stem family combination is typical of the extreme East, between Alsace and Savoie, and throughout the whole Rhône–Alpes sector. In these regions the cultural drive is generally positive and even strong. The growth of school attendance is comparable to what is found in the stem-family regions of Occitania.

However, when the general engineering industry develops in nuclear family areas, as it does in the north-eastern part of the Paris basin, it shows a low cultural activity, fairly typical of all nuclear-family regions, whether or not there is industrial development. In these regions the cultural passivity of the industrial proletariat simply follows on from the torpor of the agricultural proletariat.

A map simultaneously representing industrial decline and cultural

Map 31
Industrial decline and cultural advance

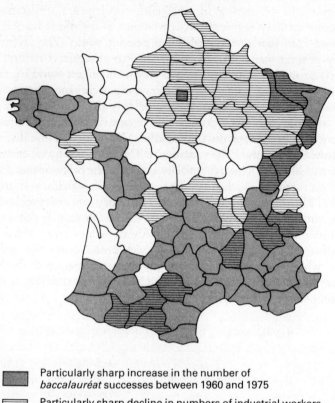

▓ Particularly sharp increase in the number of
baccalauréat successes between 1960 and 1975

▤ Particularly sharp decline in numbers of industrial workers
between 1975 and 1982

Based on data from the 1975 and 1982 censuses.

growth in the France of 1982 (map 31) shows that the two phenomena are independent of one another, one having its centre of gravity in the North and the other in the South. However, coincidence is possible. It is visible at the eastern edge of the country. Simultaneously in Alsace and in Savoie there appears a decline in industrial manpower and an increase in the percentage of individuals with the *baccalauréat*. There is a secondary pole which consists of Haute-Garonne, Tarn and Hautes-Pyrénées, where the same two phenomena can be observed. In these regions the decline of an industry which does not lean too heavily on the mining sector has neither destroyed nor even hampered the cultural drive that is typical of the local anthropological system.

The disintegration of the economic and anthropological fabric created by nineteenth-century industry has been a drama comparable in its intensity to the destruction of nineteenth-century rural civilization. But one cannot entirely regret the disappearance of the old industrial world any more than that of the traditional peasant world. The seventeenth-century peasant was the slave of a frequently destructive nature, which regularly produced famine as often as crops, and infant mortality as much as folklore. Mining and heavy engineering were and remain deadly sectors. Coal and iron did not merely destroy the natural landscape and create a world that was gloomy and weird, consisting of tips, blast furnaces, mining villages, dust and smoke. This world was not just ugly, it was medically harmful. The statistics of INSERM (National Institute of Health and Medical Research) cruelly highlight the carcinogenic action of the old industrial fabric through the very air itself, which was thoroughly polluted. The map of the incidence of respiratory cancer coincides almost exactly with that of the old industry of the North-east. It skirts the old but cleaner industry of the Jura and Rhône–Alpes area, which is not dependent on mines and iron and steel production. The industrial exodus, which has emptied the humanly shattered regions of the North-east, can be regarded to a certain extent as a rational reaction. It was the abandonment of an artificial but hostile environment.

The percentage working in each field/sector* (1982)			
	Technical and managerial staff	Skilled workers, foremen and supervisory staff	Unskilled workers
Textile and clothing	4.2	23.3	55.8
Mining	6.1	43.4	41
Household goods and furniture	11.9	25.6	49
Motorcar industry	12.1	41	35.7
Engineering	15.3	42.8	20.9
Light chemicals	17.9	24.8	24
Electrical and electronic industries	29.6	29.3	22.7
Aeronautical industry and naval construction	26.1	45.9	10.6

* Since employees in the commercial, administrative and social sector have not been included, the totals in each column do not add up to 100 per cent.

A NEW INDUSTRY WITHOUT A NEW WORKING CLASS

This repellent effect of the environment, working through human factors, aesthetic, medical and cultural, rather than economic ones, enables one to understand the move of the working population and of industry towards the West and South. The revival of industrial activity, as we have seen in chapter 2, has taken the form of a geographical move towards those areas. Industry is the contrary of a phoenix rising from its own ashes. Modernity does not reappear on the same soil; or, if it does, it does so badly. The latest industrial sectors – automobiles, household appliances, the light chemical and electronic industries – are developing along the Seine–Rhône axis flanking the old industrial regions on the west. In the centre and to the west of the Paris basin this growth of new sectors is to a great extent taking place on virgin soil. A new industry finds the fresh blood necessary for its expansion in a clean, neat world with no set ways. It is, of course, an industry which is much less harsh, less destructive and, in particular, less thickly concentrated than that of the nineteenth century. But make no mistake, it often demands no more of the workers' intelligence than did its predecessor. In the automobile and household-appliance industries the skills required are minimal, and the number of specialists and technicians is limited. On the assembly lines it is easy to use illiterate immigrant workers and, in the West, the under-educated children of Norman, Breton or Anjou peasants. This redevelopment of the economically tranquil societies of the centre and west of the Paris basin has not, however, been really destructive. It has in fact been a minority movement. Automation and increases in productivity make a massive uprooting of the population unnecessary. The semi-skilled workers in these newly revived regions will remain a social minority from the industrial point of view. The new industry is developing in regions which will never be classed as 'industrial'. The automobile, light chemical and household-appliance industries have started up in areas where the main development is not that of industry but of the services. A tertiary rather than a secondary revolution characterizes the centre and west of the Paris basin.

12

The Two Middle Classes and the State

Between 1975 and 1982 the 55 per cent threshold of the working population employed in the service sector was crossed. In 1982, 57.6 per cent of the French were working in the service sector, i.e. trade, transport, telecommunications, insurance, banking, medical and social services, teaching and public administration. What all these branches have in common is that they produce intangible services, rather than manufactured or consumer goods.

Around 1982, in fifty-five out of ninety *départements*, the service sector engaged more than half the working population (see map 32). The thirty-five *départements* where services were not in an absolute majority belonged to two different worlds. Twenty of them were in the partly rural West of the country, while the other fifteen were located in the East and, on the contrary, represented the former industrial world. Services have indeed progressed very quickly everywhere, but have not reached their maximum growth speed in the most industrialized regions. The culturally devastated regions of the North-east show a lower rate of growth than the national average. These regions are handicapped in their race towards the service sector by the weakness of their educational drive. If we leave to one side the less sophisticated trade branches, the service sector, both in public and private organizations, is a world of executives and office workers who unceasingly shuffle figures and paperwork. These professions generally require knowledge above the level of elementary primary education. The service sector is peopled with graduates holding certificates ranging from the BEPC to the *agrégation*. The interaction between education and the service sector is naturally closer than between education and industry.

Taken by itself, the map of cultural advance shows the emergence of the South and of the border regions in general, but does not explain the development of the service sector. The areas where the 'service population' has grown fastest, with a few exceptions, correspond to the regions of the most recent industrial development. Between 1975 and

Map 32
The service sector in 1982

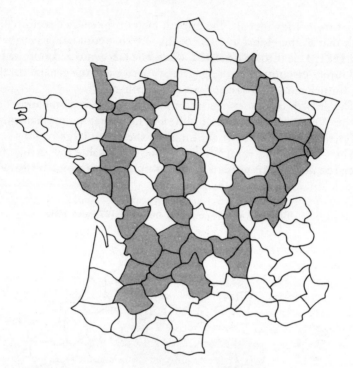

Départements in which the service sector engaged:

☐ Over 50 per cent of the working population

■ Under 50 per cent of the working population

Based on data from the 1982 census.

1982 the increase of labour employed in the service sector is over 20 per cent in two large but clearly delimited areas (see map 33).

The first describes a semi-circle starting from a broadly based Paris area (Beauvais–Orléans–Rouen) towards the inland West (Rennes–Nantes–Vendée) crossing the Loire region.

The second area where there has been an acceleration of services is a south-eastern triangle extending from the Rhône–Alpes region to the whole of the Mediterranean littoral.

The geographical movement of the service sector delineates two very dynamic zones – one in the West, the other in the South-east. In both these geographical areas the movement is both economic and cultural, bringing with it particularly clear political changes.

DEMOGRAPHIC GROWTH AND MIGRATION

Apart from a few details, the growth map of the service sector coincides with that of the global increase of the working population between 1975 and 1982. This is to be expected, when one takes into account the present and future insignificance of the primary sector and the general paralysis in the former industrial societies of the North-east.

The growth of the service sector and the working population depends in the West and the South on different demographic mechanisms. Two different types of take-off are found in these two large regions.

The Catholic and rural West was long remarkable for its high fertility rate. The decrease of peasant labour in an area with a high birth-rate frees

Map 33
Rise of the service sector between 1975 and 1982

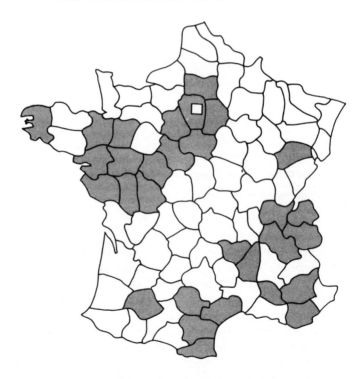

Increase of over 20 per cent in numbers of
the working population engaged in the service sector

Based on data from the 1975 and 1982 censuses.

a great deal of manpower for the development of new economic activities. This demographic potential of the West was recognized by planners and industrialists after the Second World War. It was consciously exploited when Renault installed a factory in Le Mans and Citroën in Rennes. But, contrary to the expectations of those in favour of decentralization, the economic activation of the West has led more to a growth of the service sector than to industrialization.

The South-east, on the contrary, did not produce large demographic surpluses between 1945 and 1982, except perhaps in the Rhône–Alpes region, which is mostly but not exclusively Catholic. In the Languedoc–Roussillon–Provence–Côte d'Azur region the increase in the service sector and the working population resulted from immigration rather than from fertility. Where the service sector was concerned, this immigration came from the North, the principal motivation often being a search for the sun and the Mediterranean climate.

These migratory movements have made the south coast culturally one of the most heterogeneous regions of France. It is, quite as much as the Paris region, an area remarkable for cultural change and the merging of traditional provincial anthropological systems. In the narrower Paris region – the inner and outer circles plus Seine-et-Marne – the proportion of inhabitants born outside the *département* reached 25 per cent in 1982. In Var, Alpes-Maritimes, Alpes-de-Haute-Provence, Vaucluse and Hautes-Alpes, the proportion was not much lower, being around 20 per cent.

In the Paris region, the Mediterranean rim and the Rhône valley, immigration has thus not only been foreign. It has also – in fact mostly – been French. This is an important factor to consider when one analyses the cultural and political evolution of these regions.

THE LIMITS OF ECONOMIC RATIONALITY

The expansion of the western and south-eastern areas can only partially be interpreted in terms of economic logic. The concentration of manpower and activity along the natural means of communication is clearly visible. It runs along the Seine, the Loire and the Rhône. The establishment of new activities in these areas, however, has involved a movement away from the European centre of economic gravity. To explain fully this slide of the French economy towards the South, one must take into account irrational factors, which are to some extent aesthetic. The populations are escaping towards the Mediterranean sun.

What the Paris region, the West and the South-east have in common is that they were not devastated between 1850 and 1960 by the industrial revolution. The present economic dynamism of these regions is explained by their former lack of dynamism. Here we are very far from the logical and continuous pattern leading from an agricultural economy to industry, and from industry to the service sector. Industry seems rather to be a historical dead-end, a stage both necessary and destructive. Indispensable as it has been for the European take-off, traditional industry blocks the future where it is too powerful. In order to progress, the second economic revolution, dominated by the service sector but also including the development of new industrial activities, requires virgin soil, untouched by industry.

ECONOMIC SECTORS AND SOCIAL CLASSES

Any structural evolution of branches of the economy changes the relative weight of the various socio-professional categories. Industry generally lives off the effort of workmen, i.e. manual workers, be they skilled or not. The service sector mainly needs office workers and executives. This contrast should not be exaggerated, for in all industrial branches there are designers, managers, administrators and salesmen, who in practice represent the service sector within industry. The people who work in this incorporated service sector are executives and employees whose activities do not greatly differ from those of their opposite numbers in the service sector. Conversely, the service sector includes some manual work dependent ultimately on the industrial sector. Transport and shopkeeping in particular give manual work to a great many people.

Consequently the description of economic sectors provides a simplified and imperfect idea of the country's socio-professional morphology, especially when technology is on the move. At present, merely to measure the overall drop in 'industrial' manpower, dramatic though it is, leads to an underestimation of the transformation which is taking place.

The new industries, whose expansion or tenacity reduces the overall drop in industrial manpower, employ fewer and fewer production workers and more and more white-collar workers and executives. They are being eaten up from within by the service element. Even when in the production of goods, the weight of the designing, administrative and marketing personnel continues to increase in relation to that engaged in the manufacturing process.

In the old industries – mining, iron and steel, leather, paper and cardboard, the engineering and building industries – the percentage of manual workers is still between 55 per cent and 80 per cent; in mining it is 76 per cent, in textiles 75 per cent, and only 58 per cent in engineering (see table 12.1). The sectors which sprang up during the expansion period of

Table 12.1

Proportion of manual workers in industry
The number of manual workers as a percentage of all
employees in each branch in 1982

Leather and shoes	79	Agriculture and food	
Solid fuels	76	industry	59
Textiles and clothing	75	General engineering	58
Glass	73	Heavy chemicals	53
Paper and board	72	Aeronautical and naval	
Motor cars	71	armament	52
Household equipment	71		
Rubber and plastics	70	Newspaper and book	
Foundry and metalwork	69	printing	49
Building materials	69	Electrical and electronic	
Iron conversion	67	material	47
Wood and furniture	67	Light chemical and	
Building	64	pharmaceutical industries	44
Non-ferrous		Electricity	35
ore and metals	61	Petroleum	29

the fifties and sixties have not yet contradicted this traditional tendency (which was natural only in appearance) of industry to use mainly manual labour. In 1982 the motor-car, household-appliance and plastic industries still had a perfectly traditional employment structure – 71 per cent manual workers in motor cars, 71 per cent in household appliances and 70 per cent in plastics. But certain small, old-established industries and a few rapidly expanding ones already show a reversed employment structure, a working class in a minority within a specific industry – 47 per cent in the light chemical and pharmaceutical industries, 35 per cent in the production of electricity, 29 per cent in the oil and gas industries.

The geographical parallelism of new industry and the service sector is consequently not surprising. The most progressive enterprises consist mostly of people with service-sector functions. The world of executives and office-workers is invading industry. These proliferating middle classes are now to be found everywhere. But are they homogeneous?

BUSINESS MIDDLE-CLASS AND SOCIALIZED MIDDLE-CLASS

The spectacular entry of the service sector into the economy has been a massive and many-sided phenomenon. The increase in manpower

Table 12.2

	Growth of service branches (1975–82)		
	Numbers in 1975	Numbers in 1982	% Growth
Commerce	2,353,740	2,542,660	8.0
Transport & telecommunications	1,271,845	1,358,160	6.8
Retail services	3,159,030	4,032,100	27.6
Real estate and mortgages	56,260	68,800	22.2
Insurance	127,535	147,920	16.0
Financial services	378,300	429,540	13.5
Non-trade services	3,414,470	3,782,880	10.8

between 1975 and 1982 was strong in all branches, but varied from 8 per cent in shopkeeping to 27 per cent in commercial services. The increase in non-commercial services, i.e. those provided by the State and its directly dependent bodies, was not spectacular, contrary to what recent ideological debates have suggested. It reached 10.8 per cent. Just before the Left came to power, the development of the service sector in France assumed a traditional American form. It is in no way a bureaucratic cancer. It is doubtful whether the brief experience of real socialism between 1981 and 1983, which was halted by the government of Laurent Fabius, had much effect on the long-term development of these parameters.

The interpretation of these figures cannot, however, be pushed too far. Certain of the most remarkable growth sectors of the economy, such as health, simply cannot be included in the categories defined by the INSEE or by economists in general. Medicine in France is neither public nor private, neither commercial nor non-commercial. Financed by the social security system, it is practised mainly by private doctors. It is a mixed organization, difficult to define. There are few economic sectors where the French genius for rationalized simplification plays such a small part. Is that why it works so well? French performance in medicine, as indicated by the very low rate of infant mortality for example, is amongst the most impressive in the world, and puts France up with the leaders amongst developed countries.

Our inability to make a perfect classification of complex social and economic activities that become more and more varied cannot, however, mask the existence of two distinct service sectors. Two middle classes, with very similar qualifications, have made their appearance, but their economic functions and ways of life are different. One deals with the State and social services, the other with business and commercial activities. Their supremacy has succeeded that of the peasants which was absolute, and that of the industrial workers, which was relative. However, the relationship with the State – close or distant – splits this social order in two at the very moment of its appearance. The economic crisis, which emphasizes the security of the State sector and the uncertainties of the business sector, has dramatically heightened awareness of the existence of two middle classes, one of which lives off the redistribution of taxation and the other off the income of free enterprise.

The fundamental distinction is less the public or private characteristics of employment, than the true origin of the salaried worker's income. Renault, the EDF, the SNCF and the firms nationalized by the Left in 1981 belong to the public sector; but even when they are state monopolies, they produce goods which must be bought by consumers. The civil service, education and the hospitals operate outside the market because their services are free. The salaries paid to the operatives of this truly 'socialized' sector of the economy come entirely from the redistribution of taxes.

Neo-liberalism attacks the State business sector and the State social sector indiscriminately, without really distinguishing between them. In practice one has to admit that a fundamental difference separates the public *business corporations* which can be denationalized because they draw their income from the market, and the public *social services* which cannot be denationalized because they draw their revenue from taxation.

This hard core of the State, enormous, but not as all-encroaching as people like to say, nevertheless creates a new middle class, whose life is socialist of its own accord. The executives and employees living off the revenues of business represent another middle class, whose life implies the achievement of a liberal ideal.

Discussions about the future role of the State must take into account the objective existence of two groups within these middle classes which are becoming the social centre of gravity of the country – two poles, one social and the other business.

Contrary to some commonly accepted ideas, the growth of the *business middle class* tends to be much more rapid than that of the *socialized middle class*. There do exist, however, two massive blocks, unequal but on the same scale, whose relative weight is not the same in all the regions of France. The socio-professional classifications of the INSEE, here logical and effective, make it possible to study the territorial distribution of these two large socio-professional blocs and to calculate, for each French *département*, a *rate of dependence on the state*, or rather *on taxation*, of the new middle classes.

The business middle class/socialized middle class dichotomy is far from being perfect. It does, however, show up certain fundamental contradictions in the French economic and ideological situation.

The social sector, as we have said, is not the public sector; the business sector is not the private sector.

The large public corporations, the SNCF, EDF–GDF, RATP and Renault, which in the public mind are associated with the Left, belong to the business world.

The members of the clergy and of the armed forces, which the public associates with the conservative Right, are now part of the social sector.

The staff of the SNCF, RATP and EDF thus find themselves hand in hand with the employees and executives of the private sector, motivated in principle by the search for profit.

Priests and officers join non-religious teachers because they too fulfil social, non-commercial functions financed by fiscal-type mechanisms.

The socialized middle classes, although numerous in the Paris area which contains the core of the French State mechanism, occupy a generally peripheral position in the national territory (see map 34). They represent more than 12 per cent of the working population in a large part of Brittany, and particularly along the southern Bayonne–Nice axis. Most of the eastern border is also fairly well provided with executives and employees of the social and teaching services.

The middle classes of the business sector, a little more numerous overall, are on the contrary concentrated in a central region, grouped around two poles (see map 35): first the greater Paris region between Beauvais, Rouen and Orléans, and second the entire Rhône–Alpes region. The Rhône, Loire and Rhine valleys appear as secondary but still important expansion zones of the business middle classes. There is nothing mysterious about this distribution. It repeats the general map of the growth of services and the new industries, both young sectors whose executives, technicians and employees make up the human content.

Very logically, the socialized activities seem to have been pushed out of the main zone of economic activity. The independent action of the State makes up for natural or acquired disadvantages. The contrast between the two maps shows on the whole the result of a conscious policy. Parliament and the government have always tried to direct State social investment towards the underprivileged areas, showing a legitimate concern for equalization.

Only the weight of the socialized middle classes on the Mediterranean littoral may seem to be an anomaly. There is no question here of an underprivileged area, peripheral in the widest sense; the sunward rush of immigrants from the North and tourists has placed the Mediterranean at the centre of the French economic system. So we must look for a special

Map 34
The socialized middle classes

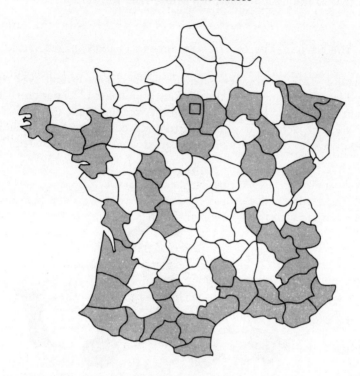

Départements in which the socialized middle classes accounted for
more than 10 per cent of the working population in 1982

Based on data from the 1982 census.

explanation for the great number of civil servants, the category
responsible for the size of the social sector in the South of France.

One cannot help supposing that there exists in this region a particular
style of municipal organization which produces local government officers
in large quantities. The very ancient urban tradition of the Roman South
has perhaps been revived by the revenues from tourism. One can imagine
a model (which would have to be checked by detailed local studies) in
which the money collected from tourists by local taxes is generously
redistributed to the population in the form of municipal sinecures. The
verification of this hypothesis might reveal the existence of a most
impressive historical continuity from Roman Provincia to French
Provence and Languedoc: the survival from Roman times to the age of
the French Republic of small-scale socialism at the municipal level,

grafted on to the tradition of the ancient city-state, large or small, rather than that of the nation-state born of the 1789 Revolution.

THE DEPENDENCE OF THE NEW MIDDLE CLASSES ON TAXATION

Generally speaking, the new salaried middle classes around 1982 represented less than a quarter of the working population (22.5 per cent). They remain numerically less weighty than the working class, mainly because they are here defined in a very narrow sense. The professions and the tradesmen who do not depend on salaried work are not included. These

Map 35
The business middle classes

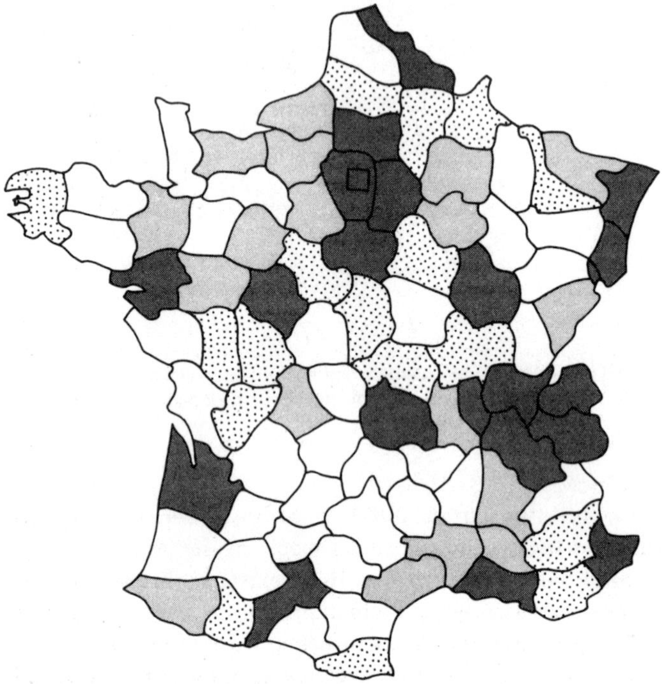

Proportion of the working population in 1982:

■ Over 14 per cent

▢ Between 12 and 14 per cent

▨ Between 10 and 12 per cent

Based on data from the 1982 census.

Table 12.3

<table>
<tr><td colspan="2" align="center">The two salaried middle classes as laid
down in the socio-professional categories
of the INSEE</td></tr>
<tr><td align="center">Middle classes in private
enterprise</td><td align="center">Middle classes in state
enterprise</td></tr>
<tr><td>Administrative and commercial
  executives (37)</td><td>Executives in the government
  sector (33)</td></tr>
<tr><td>Engineers and technical
  executives (38)</td><td>University and secondary school
  teachers; scientific professions (34)</td></tr>
<tr><td>Intermediary administrative
  and commercial professions (46)</td><td>Primary school teachers and
  equivalent (42)</td></tr>
<tr><td>Technicians (47)</td><td>Intermediary professions in
  health and social work (43)</td></tr>
<tr><td>Administrative staff (54)</td><td>Clergy, monks and nuns (44)</td></tr>
<tr><td>12% of the population over
  15 years old</td><td>Intermediary administrative
  professions in the public service (45)</td></tr>
<tr><td></td><td>Subordinate staff in the public
  service (52)</td></tr>
<tr><td></td><td>Police and military (53)</td></tr>
<tr><td></td><td>10.5% of the population over
  15 years old</td></tr>
</table>

The individuals are graded according to the socio-professional category of the head of the household. The figures between brackets refer to the INSEE nomenclature.

new, rapidly expanding salaried middle classes, however, already represent the centre of gravity of French society. An increase in their relative mass in the national system is likely to take place in the next decade.

It is possible by experiment to evaluate the respective strength of the socialized middle classes and the business middle classes in a society exclusively consisting of salaried middle classes. The two groups more or less balance each other out – 10.5 per cent for the socialized middle classes, 12 per cent for the business middle classes in the whole of the population. A homogeneous salaried middle-class society would thus consist of 47 per cent socialized middle class and 53 per cent business middle class. A simple reading of these figures shows that the present debate on the part played by the state would not enable any conclusions to be drawn on a clear majority in this imaginary middle-class society, even if the ideological behaviour of the individual were dictated by short-term economic advantages, which is not the case. One would merely obtain two blocks of more or less equal size, i.e.

- 47 per cent of the salaried middle class living off the redistribution of taxes
- 53 per cent of the same middle class living off business activities.

The numerical collapse of the working class, therefore, does not really threaten the ideal of a redistributive socialism, for the simple reason that socialism also concerns the middle classes, or at any rate a part of them.

The variations in French territory of the balance of power of the socialized and business middle classes are evident:

Map 36
Dependence of the salaried middle classes on the State

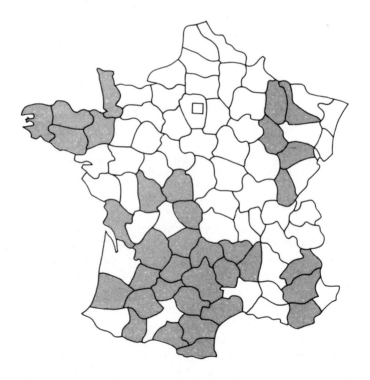

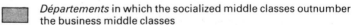 *Départements* in which the socialized middle classes outnumber the business middle classes

Based on data from the 1982 census.

- In 36 out of 90 *départements* the socialized middle class makes up the local majority within the salaried middle classes.
- In 54 out of 90 *départements* it is the business middle class which dominates.

Such a calculation shows up the difference in France between the centre and the periphery (see map 36). The Paris basin as a whole, the valleys of the Loire, the Rhône and the Rhine make up a large region in which the business middle class predominates. Brittany, the South-west taken in its widest context, the Southern Alps and a part of the East between the Meuse and the Jura are, on the contrary, strongholds where the socialized middle classes make up a majority in the salaried middle classes. The relative strength of the socialized middle classes in the South-west is particularly remarkable. In this region the stem family seems to have fully achieved its ideal of dependence on the state.

A promotion of the neo-liberal theme by the Right can only provoke different reactions in the various French regions – positive in the centre of the country, negative on the periphery where the redistribution of taxes ensures the very life of the middle classes. This contradiction is all the more interesting in that nearly half of the 36 peripheral *départements* dominated by the socialized middle classes are traditionally orientated towards the Right. Politics depend as much on myths as on economic advantages. One must, however, underline the probable ineffectiveness of Reagan-type neo-liberalism in most of France, and the potential dangers it harbours for the peripheral (i.e. Catholic) regions of the Right.

13

The Strangers in the City

The immigration phenomenon in France has been a logical development in two ways – one traditional and on a national scale, the other recent and on a world scale.

First of all, the traditional form. The birth-rate in France went down a century before that of the other European nations, and it very soon had need of help from outside to ensure growth, or even, after the First World War, simply to maintain the population level of the country. From the twenties onwards, one wave of migration followed another, and the largest ones were Italian, Spanish, Portuguese and finally North African. This last Portuguese and North African stage cannot, however, be regarded as specifically French. In the course of the sixties the immigration phenomenon became general in Europe, even before the fall in fertility, which dates from the years 1965–75. Great Britain took in Pakistanis and West Indians, Germany Turks and Switzerland Italians. Later on, in the course of the seventies, the United States, who had started in the twenties a policy of restricting immigration from Europe, saw their defences circumvented. A large-scale clandestine migration started up, coming from South America and Mexico, and it was still far from being controlled in 1988.

In Western Europe, the general migration phenomenon of the sixties was the response to a certain logic, both cultural and economic. Far more than their pre-war predecessors, recent immigrants took up a special position in the social hierarchy of Europe. The past should not be idealized. The integration of immigrants in France has generally occurred via the bottom rung of French society, i.e. by the factory. But there were exceptions before the war. The Jews of Central Europe were assimilated at the middle levels of the country's economic and social structure. Manual workers coming from Italy, often Tuscans, joined the ranks of qualified artisans as much as of factory workers. In practice, the level of integration of a group coming from another country is not mainly the result of the receiving community's degree of resistance. It depends above all on the cultural and professional level of the incoming families. A family from Central Europe, in which there has been a tradition of secondary or higher education, will in no circumstances provide unskilled workers for French society. A Tuscan family, in which members know how to read and write, and where there is a solid tradition of manual skill, will not contribute to the creation of an unskilled proletariat.

The cultural level of immigrants settling in France is not constant, but a slight tendency towards a lower level can be observed. It is difficult to obtain the exact literacy level of immigrant populations, but one can, as a first approximation, quote the literacy rate of the countries of origin at the departure time, in order to grasp this evolution.

Table 13.1

Rate of literacy in the countries of origin of the main categories of immigrants			
Portugal (1970)	71%	Portugal (1930)	30%
Italy (1930)	77%	Algeria (1970)	26%
Spain (1920)	58%	Morocco (1970)	21%

This drop in the cultural level, which we are measuring here from the French point of view, should not make us forget that in Algeria and Morocco, as in the rest of the Third World, the literacy rate is rising rapidly.

It is a fact that the cultural difference between the immigrant population and the host country has never been as great as it is now. When the first Italian workers arrived in southern France in the middle of the nineteenth century, large tracts of the country still contained very many illiterates. Nowadays, the arrival of North African workers, mostly illiterate and possessors of a purely oral culture, is happening in a country which has reached Phase II in its cultural revolution, in which the most typical phenomenon is a rising number of people with a secondary education. One has simply to look at the education statistics to see that a new rift is coming into existence, and there is a serious possibility of North African workers becoming marginalized.

A SUB-PROLETARIAT

The entry of foreign workers into the French socio-professional hierarchies reveals no surprises. In the 1982 census foreigners make up 6.6 per cent of the working population, 13.3 per cent of workers, 17.7 per cent of unskilled workers, and 18.3 per cent of agricultural workers.

An internal hierarchy is also visible from immigrant statistics. The more the country of origin is literate, the greater is the proportion of skilled workers – 57.2 per cent skilled workers among the French, 55.3 per cent among the Italians, 51.1 per cent among the Spanish, 40 per cent among the Portuguese, 36.1 among the Algerians, 31.5 among the Moroccans. These figures reveal that the cultural variable explains a great deal.

THE GEOGRAPHY OF IMMIGRATION

The distribution of immigrant workers in French territory at the time of the 1982 census, however, gives very little support to the idea that the import of labour has followed a purely economic logic (see map 37). Even if they are mostly manual workers, the foreigners have not settled where the oldest and least qualified form of industry was to be found. The correlation coefficient between the proportion of foreigners in the working population and the percentage of individuals working in industry is only 0.27, i.e. it is of very little significance.

The map of the proportions of foreigners in France does not therefore coincide with that of industry. It does, however, have an absolutely familiar look. It follows the main lines of communication (Rhône, Rhine, Seine) and the first network of autoroutes. In 1982, as at the time of the Roman conquest, the western half of the country was hardly affected by immigration. The permanence of spatial constraints, after 2000 years of technological progress, is very striking. The present distribution of immigrants over French territory is astonishingly like that of the Roman settlement during the centuries which followed the conquest of Gaul. The Rhône-Rhine-Seine system, then as now, was absolutely fundamental.

It is, however, difficult to assert that we have here a number of causes that are purely and simply spatial. This is not the first appearance in this book of the Rhône-Rhine-Seine socio-geographical system. If you widen it towards the lower valley of the Loire, you can see that it has also been drawn on the map which shows the business middle classes. There is here more than a simple coincidence. In these same regions the simultaneous expansion of the number of employees and executives of French nationality and of the number of manual workers of foreign origin is complementary in the highest degree. Statistical data confirms the visual reading. The correlation coefficient linking the relative strength of the business middle classes in the working population to the percentage of immigrant workers is high, amounting to +0.65. The new business classes and the immigrants together amount to a new type of society, and it foreshadows problems.

Map 37
Immigration

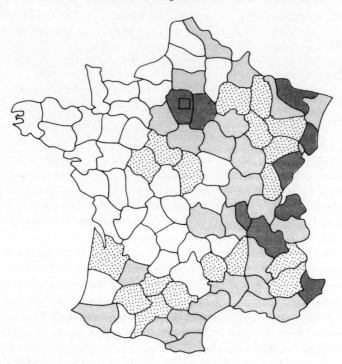

Proportion of foreigners in the population in 1982:

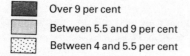

Over 9 per cent
Between 5.5 and 9 per cent
Between 4 and 5.5 per cent

Based on data from the 1982 census.

A NEW CASTE SYSTEM?

The new, economically dynamic society, which came into existence between 1960 and 1980 along the axes of the rivers and autoroutes, is turning France into a tough world because there is polarization. On the one hand there is a new middle class, French in origin and rising rapidly in the social scale, which occupies the clean world of offices, ball-point pens and computer terminals. On the other hand there is a crowd of manual workers, who are illiterate and specialized in the dirtiest and most repetitive tasks of manufacture and maintenance. A whole host of differences and inequalities follow. Here is a table that highlights this new polarity:

Table 13.2

Immigrant workers	Middle classes
Poor knowledge of French	Mother language French
Illiteracy	BEPC standard qualification or better
Non-qualified manual labour	Office work
Moslem religion	Catholics or lay tradition

This simplified table only applies in its entirety to North African workers. Portuguese immigrants occupy a middle position because they are more literate and are Catholic in religion.

Never has French society, which in 1789 gave birth to the idea of universal man, been so near to erecting a caste system of the Indian type, allotting certain economic tasks considered impure to a category of men considered to be outside society itself. This point has not yet been reached, but it was in sight when the economic crisis of 1974 started. The rise of the National Front must not make us forget the main fact that an unacceptable society was coming into being amid general indifference on the eve of the crisis, and this was particularly evident around the Rhône–Rhine–Seine zone.

PROLETARIAN SCHIZOPHRENIA

The polarization of French society along the Rhône–Rhine–Seine system has created two categories – the new middle classes and the immigrants – and their roles, whether satisfying or not, are equally clear. The real distress is born of ambivalence and uncertainty. The 'French' manual workers in the regions most affected by the ethnological polarization of the economic system are subjected to a socio-cultural stress that is hard to bear. They are Frenchmen, and they have been left behind by the cultural expansion and social improvements of the preceding twenty years. Their present situation resembles that of the immigrant workers, whereas they might have profited from this arrival of foreign labour. They do not benefit from the work of the new slaves of French society. On the contrary, they feel themselves threatened by a relative diminution of their status, even when their standard of living rises.

Immigration, therefore, contributes in its own way considerably to the decay of the working class. To the general reduction of their numbers is added the menace of internal division. This works along ethnological, religious and cultural divisions that are particularly marked and clear. The arrival in large numbers of immigrant labour devalues the fundamental ideas of socialism and Marxism. The proletariat is no longer a mystic being brutally exploited and ripe, in its distress, for regeneration. It becomes purely negative, an object of decay rather than of moral rehabilitation. It is something which a man wants to leave.

IN THE WEST: THE IMMIGRANTS OF THE INTERIOR

The only region in which the business middle classes and the immigrant workers are out of step concerns the West of France. Within the Caen-Rennes-Nantes-Tours quadrilateral the business middle classes are increasing rapidly, but the foreign workers are very few in number. This exception confirms a rule, i.e. that new industry is fed by labour that is without work habits. The West in France is the last region with a rural exodus. This has transferred its surplus population from the country to the town between 1960 and 1975. The new industries in the West, therefore, use workers of local origin who are children of peasants, but they are the equivalent of the immigrant workers in the eastern half of France.

Economically, the development of the East and of the West has been very similar. The lower valley of the Loire has taken on secondary and tertiary industries following a geographical and mercantile logic, which is no different from that which has transformed the Rhône–Rhine–Seine system. The anthropological mechanisms, however, are quite different. In the West, a classic process, more typical of the nineteenth century than the year 2000, has transformed country people into townsmen, and native peasants into native workers and executives. In the East, the specialization inherent in industrial work depends on an ethnological split. Employees and executives are native born, while workers are more and more immigrant foreigners. This difference between economic changes in the West and in the East will be of great importance when we come to explain the recent development of the Right-Left cleavage, the relative veering of the West to the left, and the relative veering of the East to the right.

NEW ECONOMIC TERRITORY, OLD IDEOLOGICAL TERRITORY

The strongly polarized society, which is coming into existence around the Rhône–Rheine–Seine system as a result of the growth of service industries and of immigration, pays no attention to anthropological differences and ancient ideologies. It brings together in the same group one region of the egalitarian nuclear family, the core of the Paris basin, two zones of the stem family, the Rhône–Alpes and Alsace region, and a region that is partly community family, Provence. On the ideological level, the Paris basin and Provence belong to the dechristianized sector, Rhône–Alpes and Alsace to the Catholic world.

One cannot assert a priori that old anthropological and ideological forces still play a role in these local societies, which have been shaken by violent migratory movements, French as much as foreign. An analysis of the crisis in the regional political systems will, however, reveal special provincial reactions, partly influenced by the most traditional ideological considerations.

REDEVELOPMENT AND ASSIMILATION – TEMPORARY PHENOMENA

The innovations of the sixties and seventies were not 100 per cent. The expansion of the automobile and household equipment industries, which used a fair amount of non-qualified workers, was probably the last appearance of old-style industrialization. Automation, depending from now onwards on the growth of electronics, made a new leap forward, whose extent foreshadowed the final disappearance of non-qualified labour. It is the factory hand of the sixties who is now threatened by automation. And in fact it was the branches of industry which employed a large amount of foreign labour, e.g. automobiles, which went into crisis during the course of the eighties. This painful transformation had one favourable effect. It put an end to the establishment of a caste society. The economic changes of the years to follow did not involve the spread of a low caste of exploited immigrants, but they did lead to an increase in the amount of robots. Therefore the question of immigration came to be posed at the very moment that it ceased to be dramatic, at the very moment when a reversal of economic tendencies guaranteed a medium-term solution and avoided a disaster for French society.

The absorption of a foreign population, amounting to 6.6 per cent of the active population at the time of the 1982 census, is not an impossible objective for French society. An anthropological analysis will enable us to evaluate the extent and limits of the problem more precisely. This analysis will preclude an abstract and optimistic approach to the subject, denying the depth of the differences between populations. It will also prevent us from considering these differences as permanent and irremediable. It will suggest that the problem of immigration will not be settled in five or ten years, but in twenty-five years, the minimum time necessary for the accomplishment of the assimilation process.

AN ANTHROPOLOGY OF IMMIGRATION

1 Italians, Spaniards, Portuguese

It is a cliché to underline the similar character of Latin immigrants of the years 1920–80. Italians, Spaniards and Portuguese speak languages related to French and practise – or do not practise – the same Catholic religion. In their case the problem of assimilation seems to reduce itself to learning a different variant of the Latin tongue. This is a correct view up to a point, but it underestimates a little the extent of cultural differences that one can measure in terms of literacy. However, we have already seen that these differences are far less extensive than those separating Frenchmen of today from North African workers. The description in terms of 'Latin-ness' does, however, oversimplify the situation and masks important differences between Italians, Spaniards and Portuguese. These differences have been significant in the ideological development of France's working class.

A description in terms of family systems gives one a much more diverse picture. The world of Latin immigrants then appears to be generally as complex from the anthropological point of view as the world of the French provinces. Three well-known family types are represented. Each of the immigrant groups – Italians, Spaniards, Portuguese – can be regarded as the main vehicle of one of these systems. The family types are not those of Italy, Spain or Portugal, but of the Italian, Spanish or Portuguese *provinces* from which the immigrants arrived in France between 1920 and 1980. In fact in these three Latin countries there does exist a families geography which, without being as varied as that of France, is nevertheless just as clear-cut.

The most usual family type amongst Italian immigrants is certainly that of the central part of the 'Boot'. It is the *community* type, authoritarian and egalitarian, founded on close interaction between parents and children and on great solidarity between brothers.

The family system of the Spanish immigrants is that of the southern half of the Iberian peninsula. It is *egalitarian nuclear*, liberal in its relations between parents and children, egalitarian in its relations between brothers.

The family system of Portuguese immigrants is that of the north of the Iberian peninsula. It is the *stem* type, authoritarian in its relations between generations and non-egalitarian in its relations between brothers.

This diversity echoes that of the French provinces. It never exceeds the number of possible variations available in France itself:

- The family system of Central Italy is close to that of Centre-Limousin.
- The family system of southern Spain is equivalent to that of the Paris basin.
- The family system of northern Portugal is identical to that of Rouergue Alsace and Pays Basque.

In each of these three cases the correspondence established between family type and agrarian system in chapter 4 is again verified:

- Central Italy, *community type*, is a region of share-cropping, as is Centre-Limousin.
- Southern Spain, *egalitarian nuclear*, is a region of *large estates*, whose population originally consisted mostly of farm workers, like the Paris basin.
- Northern Portugal, where the *stem* family is predominant, is an area of peasant property, like Rouergue, Pays Basque or Alsace.

To this variety of family and agrarian systems there is, of course, an equivalent variety of ideological systems. And, as the relationship between family structures and ideological systems is essentially universal, the correspondences in the Italian, Spanish or Portuguese provinces are the same as in the French provinces. Central Italy, with its community family type, is dominated by a Left of the communist type. Southern Spain, with its egalitarian nuclear family type, is traditionally controlled by a Left of the anarcho-socialist type. Northern Portugal with its stem family type, is one of the European bastions of the Catholic Right.

Each of these three Latin waves was, therefore, the carrier of a specific family and ideological culture, which was not immediately absorbed by the receiving community. The ideological element, in particular, was not at once cancelled by integration into the French working class, for the latter was itself fragmented by different regional ideological attitudes. A scientific study of the political integration of the different Latin working communities has never been made, but it is clear that there were definite reactions:

- The Italian immigrants in Provence swelled the ranks of the local communist party, in accordance with their traditions of origin.
- The Spanish immigrants also, but rather less definitely, lined up with the various left-wing tendencies of the French political scene.
- The Portuguese immigrants, however, Catholic and right-wing, mostly continued to resist communist influence.

These different political reactions were not studied by the Marxist sociologists, who were the only ones to have access to the facts through the medium of the Communist Party. They were, however, well known to the militants of the sixties and seventies. The reactionary passivity of the Portuguese immigrants, coming after the revolutionary enthusiasm of their Italian predecessors, was a painful surprise for the communists. One can suppose that, by pure ethnological chance, immigration strengthened the Communist Party in the years 1930–50 and weakened it in the sixties and seventies.

The picture of a peaceful Latin immigration without problems is, therefore, pure myth. None of the groups – Italian, Spanish, Portuguese – suddenly overnight ceased to be themselves or were suddenly deprived of their ethnological character by a simple train journey. On the other hand, all these groups had an immediate influence on the general ideological development of the French working class. No immigration can be regarded as purely passive.

2 North Africa

In spite of their differences, the family system of central Italy, southern Spain and northern Portugal have two things in common. Without being feminist, European systems never give women a very low status, and they never encourage cousin-marriage. The typical family system of the Arab world, on the other hand, has two characteristics. It is vigorously anti-feminist, an aspect that is perfectly well known to most Frenchmen; and it often goes with a system of endogamous marriage, in which marriage between the children of two brothers is considered ideal. In most of the Moslem world, the relative frequency of marriage between first cousins varies between 10 per cent and 30 per cent of the total.

In conventional ethnological terms, European family systems would be described as *bilateral*, because they give equal value to the paternal and maternal lines, and *exogamous*, because they require marriage outside the original family group. The Arab family system should be described as *patrilineal*, because it declares the precedence of the paternal line, and *endogamous*, because it favours marriage within the original family group.

So the main difference, unfortunately, between Europe and North Africa concerns *marriage*, a central element in the mechanism of assimilation. Two exogamous communities with similar ideas on the ideal relationship between men and women will have no difficulty in fusing, by the marriage of their children. But the existence of opposite conceptions of the ideal nature of the marriage bond, on the contrary, makes the fusion of communities by intermarriage a major problem. It is, in fact, the classic Moslem idea of woman's status which slows down the integration of the North African community in France. There is here a cultural conflict, which in itself has nothing to do with classic racism. The revolutionary traditions of France and Islam are two of the most universalist and anti-racist ideologies in the world. Confrontation does not come from a sense of superiority of one or other community, but from the existence of two anthropological structures that are different and incompatible.

The integration of the North African community involves destruction of the Arab anthropological tradition by French culture which is dominant. The Code Civil, which defends monogamy, is stricter than the Koran, which allows a married man four wives. An exaggerated respect for cultural differences, which is a fashionable attitude (though one does not know very well whether it belongs to the Left or the Right) can only have one result – the establishment of North African ghettos.

A survey of North African youth in the suburbs of Paris, Lyon or Marseille clearly shows that the process of destruction of the old family model is well under way. The survival of an anthropological system that is numerically and culturally dominated seems an impossibility. The family structure is simply not strong enough. It can resist and slow down the process, but it will end by breaking.

The second-generation immigrants, born in France and speaking French better than Arabic, are already cut off from their world of origin. They are actors and victims of the particularly violent destruction of a culture and the birth of a new one. It is even tougher for the men of Algerian or Moroccan origin that it is for the women. However attached the daughters of immigrants are to their traditional milieu, they can find emancipation and liberation by integrating themselves into French society. The young men of North African origin, on the other hand, suffer a double deterioration of status in France. They are already at the bottom of the social ladder, and in addition they have to endure the denial of their traditional status as dominant males.

THE THIRD GENERATION

The existence of important differences between European and North African family systems in no way means that a process of assimilation is impossible. It merely indicates that integration will occur in two stages, in the course of two generations rather than one, as happened with the Italian, Spanish and Portuguese immigrants. The child of an Italian, Spanish or Portuguese worker, born or brought up in France, is impossible to distinguish culturally from his French counterpart. Second-generation immigrants of Algerian or Moroccan origin on the other hand keep some specific traits, which can lead to a certain marginalization, especially for men. Their children, on the other hand, will be typical Frenchmen, 'descendants of the Gauls' just like the others.

14

The Third Crisis of Catholicism

Between the twelfth and twentieth centuries, the history of the Church seems to be a succession of regional battles and geographical withdrawals. First of all, medieval heresies and protestantism weakened Catholic orthodoxies in the non-Mediterranean South and the extreme North. During a second period the French Revolution expelled the authority of the Roman Catholic church from the Paris basin and Provence. However, up to the beginning of the sixties of this century, an austere and effective form of catholicism, which had accepted the infallibility of the Pope since 1870, remained powerful and apparently invulnerable within a constellation of peripheral strongholds in the Basque country, Rouergue, Savoy, Anjou, Brittany, Alsace and Franche-Comté. Between 1965 and 1982, even these strongholds were shaken by a mental revolution as hostile to catholicism as had been the Cathar heresy, the Waldensian revolt, the protestant Reformation or the French Revolution. The destruction of the authority of the Church in these peripheral strongholds was the crisis of French catholicism which we may regard as final, for the regions concerned were the last to remain faithful to the Church. Between 1945 and 1965, a slight decrease in religious practice was evident. But after 1965 all the figures dropped in all regions, whether as regards attendance at Mass, communion at Easter or confession.

Even more alarming was the weakening of the Church's organization, which seemed incapable of renewing its supply of priests. The Catholic strongholds ceased providing priests for the parishes or convents. The 1982 census gives a striking picture of the decline in religious personnel at the national level. We can extract the number of active members of the clergy in five-year age brackets (see table 14.1). It shows a massive and continuous decline – thirty-eight active priests per 10,000 people in the 60–40 age group, and only four per 10,000 people in the 25–29 age group.

Between 1975 and 1982 the human breakdown is particularly clear in the religious communities. They are emptying out. In seven years the number of monks dropped from 17,820 to 11,520, that of nuns from 76,500 to 35,000. This desertion of the convents irresistibly reminds one

Table 14.1

Clergy: active members in 1982					
per 10,000 persons in each age-group					
20–24 years	2.6	35–39 years	7.5	50–54 years	21.4
25–29 years	3.7	40–44 years	13.0	55–59 years	29.1
30–34 years	5.0	45–49 years	15.7	60–64 years	38.1

of the protestant Reformation, one of whose main claims and achievements was the suppression of the regular clergy. The difference is that the present crisis is a silent one. It is a spontaneous disappearance, rather than the consequence of an aggression. The absence of an ideological enemy does not, however, imply an absence of reasons. This final crisis is well explained by the changes in culture and morals.

THE SECOND CULTURAL REVOLUTION

The protestant crisis was the ideological expression, in southern France as in the Germanic world, of a rise in the cultural level. The spread of written culture outside the religious world led to questioning the authority of the priests. Luther claimed that everyone was entitled to the word of God, 'we are all of us priests'. Counter-Reformation catholicism then defined itself negatively by its desire for authority, but equally by its refusal of cultural progress. It did not wish everyone to have access to the sacred texts. It did not wish the faithful to understand or to argue about the statements of priests. Catholicism saw culture as a threat. First of all it set up schools to counter the competition of the Protestants, and later that of the Revolution, but it was fundamentally hostile to progress and to freedom of the mind in the most general sense of the word. The relative cultural decline of the Catholic regions of Europe, obvious as early as the 17th century, as compared to Protestant dynamism, shows that this basic attitude of the Church effectively blocked the development of the stem family regions, which could have begun as early as the sixteenth century.

Here we must mention Max Weber's thesis on the economically progressive character of protestantism, to underline its incompleteness. Weber exaggerates the importance of economic values, particularly the attitude towards profit. Above all he reverses the fundamental causes. In trying to explain the progress of Protestant regions and the backwardness of Catholic regions, he suggests that protestantism accelerated the change. In fact it was above all true that catholicism *slowed down* the spontaneous development of regions where it was dominant. As for protestantism, it was the natural expression of a movement of the mind. Catholicism put its authority at the service of the control of minds. Culturally it sterilized vast stem family regions, where parental authority could have been used for a good accumulation and transmission of culture.

Thus catholicism slowed down the elimination of illiteracy between the seventeenth and nineteenth centuries, without actually preventing it. In the second half of the twentieth century the increase in means of communication – radio and television – exploded the control system. In France all the stem family regions, whether Catholic or not, were in the vanguard of the cultural movement which led to a second revolution, that of secondary education and the *baccalauréat*.

Where it had survived, the authority of the priests was swept away by this over-rapid movement, as it had been by the development of primary education in the sixteenth century. Too many men and women achieved a cultural level equal to, or higher than, that of the servants of the Church for the mechanism controlling the masses to be able to survive. Confession, the central element in the Catholic system of control of the mind, in order to function properly, demands that there should be a cultural gap between the person confessing and the confessor, the authority of the latter resting on his acknowledged superiority. Fundamentally it was this second cultural revolution which destroyed the authority of catholicism in its strongholds. It was a long-term process, which explains the slow decline of catholicism in the post-war years. But the sexual revolution, which started up towards the end of the sixties, accelerated and dramatized the crisis.

THE SECOND SEXUAL REVOLUTION

The putting into practice of Catholic morality by the populations of the peripheral strongholds was not simply caused by moral preoccupations. The control of sexuality is a problem for every society. The sexual act leads to procreation, and chaotic reproduction is a threat for the reproduction of values and the transmission of wealth, a particularly sensitive problem in all anthropological systems dominated by the stem family.

The Catholic horror of sexuality and the value set on chastity both within and outside marriage are good regulators in a society which does not have at its disposal safe methods of contraception. Religious morality has been a useful aid in the age-old struggle of families against disorganization arising from sexuality and feeling. Catholicism is useful but not indispensable. In a number of French regions, between 1780 and 1900, the disappearance of the Church did not prevent the achievement of a different form of control, founded on the use of imperfect but generally efficient contraceptive techniques. The perfecting of absolutely sure methods of birth control – the pill and the coil – modified the very nature of man. From the beginning of time up to the sixties the human couple in its natural state was fertile. The spread in the mid-seventies of reliable contraceptive methods has made the human couple non-fertile in its 'natural' state, the word 'natural' not being read here in its strict meaning. It implies that human beings of the developed western world are not normally in a procreating state. A decision to stop taking the pill or eliminating the coil must take place for procreation to be possible.

In this context the Catholic contribution to the sexual security of women becomes superfluous. Parents no longer fear their daughters becoming accidentally pregnant. The control of sexuality has ceased to be a family or social problem. Chastity is no longer the safest birth control method, bachelorhood no longer useful for the population. The recruitment of priests is drying up.

More than any other religion, catholicism defines itself by a strictly negative and repressive attitude towards sexual relations. Inevitably the sexual revolution of the seventies was a particularly hard blow. It does not totally explain the third crisis of catholicism, but it makes one understand the speeding-up process which took place in the mid-seventies.[1]

THE STEM FAMILY REUNIFIED

The fade-out of catholicism has tended to abolish the division into two of the space occupied by the stem family. The valley of the Garonne on the one hand, the western Pyrenees and the Massif Central on the other cease to differ in one important characteristic, the strength of religious orthodoxy. From now onwards catholicism is weak everywhere. The reunification of the stem types simplifies the maps. It re-establishes the homogeneity of southern France, which now differentiates itself more generally and more distinctly from the North than in the past. That is why the recent fertility maps and *baccalauréat* maps (see chapter 1) show up now big North-South differences, with the nuclear system on the one side and the stem system on the other.

At the same time the collapse of the Catholic apparatus of control has liberated the inland West, where the absolute nuclear family now predominates absolutely. Anthropologically distinct from the stem type regions, it is better able to express its potential and its specific ideals. It is nuclear and in certain aspects joins up with the egalitarian nuclear system of the Paris basin. Paradoxically the latest crisis of catholicism, the result of modernity, leads to the reappearance of the simplest and most general national cleavage of all – the opposition between North and South.

PART IV

THE POLITICAL IMPLOSION

The disintegration of the traditional French political system took place in two stages. It began with an evolution which appeared to be slow to the actors on the political stage, but which on the scale of French history was fast, and it brought the Socialist party to power at the end of a political climb spread over 14 years, from 1967 to 1981. When François Mitterrand was elected President, the reorganization of the left was clear to see as the Communist party was declining fast. The disorganization of the right-wing parties, however, was not yet perceptible. Their failure was seen as a withdrawal phenomenon, a statistical complement to the socialist thrust. But as early as 1984, the appearance of the Front National showed that a process of decomposition had already started on the Right. The 'return to power' of the Right in March 1986 was the result of a narrow victory. It was the consequence of a weakening of the Socialist party, rather than a resurgence of the UDF and the RPR. In 1986, however, the Front National confirmed the disintegration of the right-wing half of the national political system. It still obtained 9.8 per cent of the votes, thus showing both its endurance and its decline, for in 1984 it had obtained nearly 11 per cent of the votes – in a context of particularly high abstention, it is true. The co-habitation episode between 1986 and 1988 showed that in France relations between Left and Right had changed.

15

Victory and Disintegration of the Left-wing Parties

The idea of a victory of the Left in 1981 was in itself a strange one. It was a tribute to the power of myth. In fact, François Mitterrand's accession to power proved in a striking manner that the French Left as an ideological unit simply did not exist. In 1981 it was the Socialist Party that triumphed, not the Left. The condition of its victory was the collapse of the Communist Party. L'Union de la Gauche was necessary because of the electoral system, i.e. a majority vote with two rounds (at that period), which made mutual withdrawal agreements necessary. But these agreements did not create a common cause for the Left. Between 1967 and 1981, the Socialists and the Communists, entrenched in their different regions and depending on contradictory systemic values, pursued separate careers. Between 1967 and 1981, the percentage of votes obtained in the first round by the Socialists rose from 18.8 per cent to 25.8 per cent. The Communist vote dropped from 22.5 per cent to 15.3 per cent. An invisible hand, that of the electorate, seemed to pay little attention to party headquarters or myths. Having gained victory, the Socialist Party immediately became all-powerful. It held the presidency and it held the absolute majority of seats in the parliament. The Communist Party's capacity to control matters was close to nil.

The 'victory of the Left' in 1981 was, moreover, the result of lack of unity at that period, as the Programme Commun no longer existed. In the summer of 1974, the 'defeat of the Left' had been the logical conclusion of a union which was superficially too coherent. If he had been the only candidate in the first round in 1981, François Mitterrand would have frightened people off. As George Marchais's opponent he was reassuring. Before swinging to the left, the electorate seem to have wanted to make sure that the Socialist Party had the capacity and will-power to curb the Communist Party. The quarrel between the PC and the PS, which broke out shortly after the Socialists' arrival in power and after a few essentially cosmetic communist ministers had been appointed to the government, was logical and necessary. The separation was achieved in 1984. The adoption of a proportional electoral system re-established the reciprocal, tactical independence of the two left-wing parties and liberated the free play of anthropological forces.

The rise to power of the Socialist Party must therefore be considered as a specific phenomenon and not linked to the Union de la Gauche. The collapse of communism had its own logic. The combination of the two movements made it possible for the socialists effectively to seize power. But the result was largely accidental. The 1981 victory of the Left was a masterpiece of false historical awareness. There was indeed hardly any relationship between the electoral themes of the forces of the Left and the real electoral evolution which brought the Socialist Party to power.

FROM CATHOLICISM TO SOCIALISM

The growth of the PS was carried out in two stages and according to two successive logical processes, which are well shown up by the changes in the electoral geography of the party between 1967 and 1981.

Between 1967 and 1981 the map of the movement of votes cast follows without any ambiguity a known shape, that of catholicism (see map 38). All the *départements* where the Socialist Party increased its score by more than 12 per cent between those two dates were, with only one exception, part of the traditional Catholic sphere. In the West we find Finistère, Vendée, Maine-et-Loire, Mayenne and Orne. In the East we find Meuse, Moselle, Bas-Rhin, Jura and Savoie. In the South we find Lozère. Between 1967 and 1978, socialism invaded the Catholic sphere.

The link between catholicism and socialism shown up during our study of local political systems is here fully confirmed. But competition was replaced by substitution. Socialism and the Catholic Right, the result of the same systemic values of authority and inequality, are ideologically related systems, although opposed on the Right–Left scale. The third crisis of catholicism destroyed the traditional authoritarian system. The populations went over to the Socialist Party, but transferred the respect and love they used to have for the Church to the state. An authoritarian Left succeeded an authoritarian Right. This left, however, was not attached to the principle of equality, and it did not preach hostility to social differentiation like the Communist Party.

The Catholic regions' swing to the left was not completely achieved at that time. Only two *départements*, Côtes-du-Nord and Meurthe-et-Moselle, changed allegiance and voted in majority for the Left in 1978. In the other Catholic regions the socialist thrust did not prevent the continuation of a right-wing majority – a smaller and smaller one, it is true.

The hypothesis of a final and definite swing of the former Catholic

Map 38
The socialist advance between 1967 and 1978

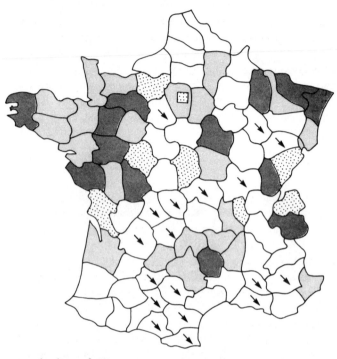

Increase in share of vote:

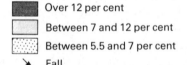

Over 12 per cent

Between 7 and 12 per cent

Between 5.5 and 7 per cent

↘ Fall

Based on parliamentary election results of 5 March 1967 and 12 March 1978, published in *Le Monde*.

regions towards the Socialist Party cannot be proved. In fact, between 1978 and 1981, the movement stopped. A slight regression of the PS can even be detected in several Catholic *départements* (see map 39). The Socialist Party, however, pursued its general progression, but less fast; and it achieved this by changing its field of expansion.

FROM COMMUNISM TO SOCIALISM

As early as the years 1967 to 1978 a second zone of development for the Socialist Party was visible. In the Paris region, Aisne, Eure, Yonne, Cher and Indre-et-Loire the PS increased its score by more than 5 per cent in 11 years. This second pole of development was situated in the centre. One can already distinguish the general outlines of the Paris basin. But between 1978 and 1981 this service growth zone became of vital

Map 39
The socialist advance between 1978 and 1981

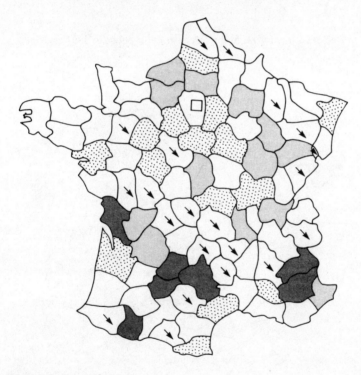

Increase in share of vote:

■ Over 10 per cent

▨ Between 5 and 10 per cent

▦ Between 3 and 5 per cent

↘ Fall

Based on the parliamentary election results of 12 March 1978 and 14 June 1981, published in *Le Monde*.

importance. The Socialist Party won votes in a few of the southern *départements* between Charente–Maritime and Aveyron, in the Alps and Pyrenees. But the large Paris basin was the real growth sector, particularly the quadrilateral of the Somme, Indre-et-Loire, Ain and Haute-Marne. Here we have one of the traditional zones of influence of the Communist Party, which the Socialist Party penetrated from the outside. The anthropological space invaded was no longer the stem family or the absolute nuclear family, but the egalitarian nuclear family.

At the time of the March 1986 elections, which for the Socialist Party amounted to a withdrawal phase, it was in these central regions of the country that socialism resisted best against the thrust of the Right (see map 40). In general it lost less than 4 per cent of the vote. From 1981 to

Map 40
Decline and survival of the Socialist Party between 1981 and 1986

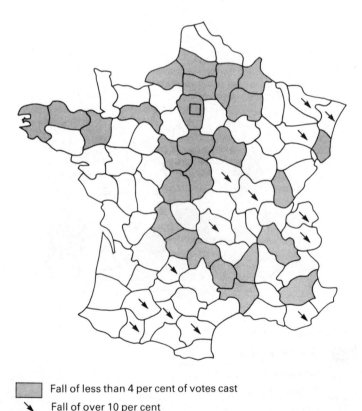

Fall of less than 4 per cent of votes cast
Fall of over 10 per cent

Based on the parliamentary election results of 14 June 1981 and 16 March 1986, published in *Le Monde*.

1986 the PS lost its electoral dynamism, but the absorption of a part of the communist electorate, which was entering into a final phase of disintegration, slowed down the fall. The PS even asserted its position in the heart of the Paris basin, and this was an absolutely new phenomenon.

THE COLLAPSE OF THE COMMUNIST PARTY

Between 1978 and 1981, the PC suddenly lost a quarter of its voters. It retreated in all the *départements* except Lozère and Corsica. This general movement did not prevent the existence of different rates of drop in the various French regions (see map 41). It was particularly swift in the Paris

Map 41
The collapse of communism

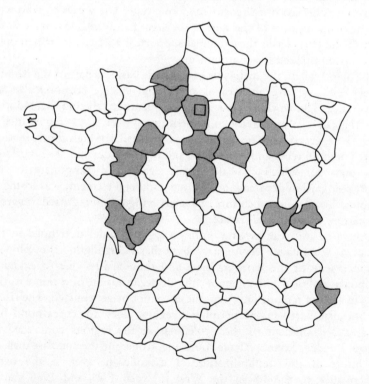

Départements in which the PC lost more than 30 per cent of its electorate between 1978 and 1981

Based on the parliamentary election results of 12 March 1978 and 14 June 1981, published in *Le Monde*.

basin, an egalitarian nuclear family region, where the losses frequently exceeded the national average. In the peripheral strongholds, from central Limousin to the Mediterranean rim and the North, the decline was large in absolute terms, but less emphatic in relative terms. So it was in the Paris basin that the proportion of the communist electorate, which did not vote for Georges Marchais in the first round of the presidential election, was the highest.

Here we find an a posteriori confirmation of the abnormal and fragile character of the communist hold on the Paris basin. The fixing of an egalitarian and authoritarian ideology on an anthropological zone that was egalitarian and liberal was an anomaly, largely eliminated by the elections of 1981. But it is equally impossible not to establish a relationship between the communist collapse of 1981 and the disintegration of the working class, which showed up between the 1975 and 1982 censuses. In egalitarian nuclear family regions the structure of the Left–Right dualism was indeed of the socio-economic type. The workers, who were not the main support of the Left in the stem family regions, were in the heart of the Paris basin the principal support of a left wing, which up to 1978 was dominated by communism.

The Seine valley, the main axis of the Paris basin, is part of the Rhône–Rhine–Seine system, an area of very rapid change economically and industrially. The working class retreated quantitatively and divided itself ethnologically, its immigrant component, moreover, not being entitled to vote. The average standard of living was particularly high there. It was a society of employees and executives, and they proliferated. The working-class message, which radicalized the egalitarian component of the anthropological system and annihilated its liberal element, was losing its meaning. Local political culture, in its left-wing version, drifted towards a rediscovery of its liberal nature.

Integrated into the general anthropological model developed in this book, a secondary 'economist' hypothesis highlights the physical disappearance of the working class and thus enables one to explain a secondary political phenomenon, the disorganization of a minority left wing in a given region. This hypothesis cannot be generalized. The rise of the Socialist Party in the peripheral regions does not correspond to a massive development of the proletariat in the regions concerned. In Anjou, Vendée, Savoie, Alsace, Lorraine, Rouergue the socialist thrust is the effect of the destabilization of catholicism, even if the better performance of the PS in the West between 1981 and 1986 can be attributed to the development of a local working class.

The decline of communism was determined by an economic crisis, whereas the socialist thrust was caused by a religious one. In origin the religious and economic crises are obviously linked. They are two phenomena of modernity, the results of technological and cultural evolution. But this link is so nebulously based that in practice it is of no great use in interpreting the movements in opinion of the French electorate. The variety of causes does not preculde a parallellism in consequences. The two crises, economic and religious, led to a parallel disorganization of the two Left–Right dualisms corresponding to the two anthropological systems of the central part of the country and the periphery – nuclear egalitarian and stem.

FROM THE RIGHT TO THE LEFT

So in 1981 France veered, a change that seemed dramatic at the time, but will not remain in history as a major mutation. To the overall national change of the Left-Right stance were added local shifts, which were not uniform. Twenty-one *départements* went over from Right to Left. One *département*, Var, went from Left to Right – an isolated case, but indicative of future events.

Here we also note a swing between the second rounds of the 1974 and 1981 presidential elections. Two types of regions changed sides. Nine traditionally Catholic *départements* situated in the extensive Rhône–Alpes region made up the first group, i.e. Puy-de-Dôme, Doubs and Haute-Savoie. A second group was made up of the *départements* with a non-religious tradition located, in particular, south of the Seine valley – Eure, Seine-et-Marne, Loir-et-Cher, Indre-et-Loire, Vienne, Charente-Maritime, Yonne, Aube, Haute-Marne and Côte-d'Or. Sarthe and Calvados with their half Catholic and half non-religious political traditions also altered their orientation, but must be considered as intermediary between the two previous types.

Thus the victory of the Socialist Party produced a majority swing in the two great anthropological and religious zones which make up the territory of France. This movement reveals the double ideological and anthropological nature of the new Socialist Party.

THE DUAL ANTHROPOLOGICAL NATURE OF THE NEW SOCIALIST PARTY

Between 1967 and 1981 the electoral progress of the Socialist Party took place in two distinct anthropological and ideological areas. The PS penetrated the entire traditional Catholic territory of the stem family, but there was included in it an absolute nuclear bastion in the West. Simultaneously, however, the party invaded the traditional non-religious, egalitarian nuclear family territory. Between 1967 and 1978 it was the peripheral Catholic territory which was attacked. Between 1978 and 1981 progress is mainly visible at the centre of the Paris basin with its non-religious tradition. The map of the local systems in the year 1978 shown in Chapter 10, however, shows that at that date the most far-flung territories of the non-religious country were eaten up from outside by the new Socialist Party. It had already taken there the place of the Communist Party as the dominant force of the Left. After the first round of the 1981 presidential elections, the PS beat the PC in nearly all the French *départements*. At that date the Communist Party stopped being the dominant force of the Left in the heart of the national system, the liberal and egalitarian regions of the Paris basin.

The development of the PS in the Catholic regions is the least interesting of the two movements. It did not imply a change in the nature of socialism. The newly conquered stem family regions differed in fact very little, where their fundamental values were concerned, from the old PS strongholds in the South-West or the North. Traces of catholicism were a little more discernible, but constantly decreasing. Dominated by authoritarian and non-egalitarian systems, these regions could only reproduce a fairly ordinary bureaucratic socialism of the SFIO type.

The crushing of the PC by the PS in the heart of the Paris basin was a much more interesting phenomenon. It announced the appearance or rather the reappearance of a liberal, egalitarian Left, much better adapted to the regional anthropological system than egalitarian, but authoritarian, communism. This change was to be the contrary of a novelty. It would be the rediscovery of the oldest historical tradition of the French Left, that of 1789, which was both liberal and egalitarian.

The totally erratic policy followed by the Socialist Party between 1981 and 1986 showed up perfectly the clash within the party and the socialist electorate, one tendency being liberal and the other authoritarian.

The first policy of the PS was authoritarian. This was normal as the party machinery was controlled by the old federations, champions of the old bureaucratic traditions. During the first phase the interventionism of the PS was multi-dimensional. A general aspiration towards control was evident. The Socialist Party simply wanted to 'change life'. Interventionism expressed itself in the economic sector with large-scale nationalizations. But the new PS then added to Marxist authoritarianism, which at least had the merit of limiting itself to the economic side of life, a degenerate form of Catholic authoritarianism, which wanted to control private and family life. The PS intervened, as had the Church, in the sexual sector. It indeed reversed the objectives of catholicism, but, just like the Church, it refused freedom to the individual. The Church forbade abortion, while the PS insisted that Social Security pay for an act which should be considered a free and private one. The Church militated against contraception, the PS in favour.

The first socialist policy on education was also part of the interventionist logic, but the wish to reinforce the control of the state in the organization of education was not a simple reappearance of former anticlericalism. It was also the consequence of the transfer of Catholic authoritarianism to the Left. The socialist teachers, who demanded that the Éducation Nationale be a large public service, were not the heirs of the radical primary school teachers of the Third Republic. They were the offspring of catholicism, renegades threatening the Church but copying its methods. The educational conflict marked the political turning-point for the socialists, but it showed profound confusion of thought. For the first time in history the secular masses came to the rescue of the private Catholic schools. The government had to withdraw, but the first, interventionist phase of socialist action was over.

Immediately after May 10th, certain liberal aspects of the Paris basin's 'socialist' aspirations became noticeable. The multiplication of free radio stations, which the government ended by accepting, was a particularly striking example. But from 1984–5 onwards, it was the whole of socialist ideology which took a turn towards aggressive liberalism, surprising the Right at the very moment when the latter thought it had a good theme. Private television channels were authorized. Industrial policy itself took a 180° turn towards liberalism. The ideological inconsistency of the Socialist Party, capable of successively pursuing two absolutely contrary policies, was not the personal inconsistency of men. It showed up the weight and contradictions of anthropological and ideological determinants. In power the PS expressed its dual anthropological and ideological nature, i.e. a mixture within itself of authoritarian and liberal aspirations, corresponding to the local values of the various French regions. The new PS inherited from the Church and from the Revolution, from the Catholic Right and from communism, a body of electors and militants whose aspirations were remarkably incompatible.

16

The Revenge and Disintegration of the Right-wing Parties

The rise to power of the Socialist Party should be seen as the result of two parallel, but distinct, movements – the dissolution of catholicism and that of the working class. The first of these movements weakened the traditional Right, while the second destroyed the Communist Party. Both these movements were negative and overthrew existing structures. The Socialist Party filled an empty space, or more precisely two spaces, which differed widely in form. The regions where catholicism collapsed were mainly of an authoritarian but non-egalitarian character, but those where the Communist Party collapsed had a liberal and egalitarian character. Obviously the policy followed by the PS immediately after it came into power satisfied no one. The Right climbed suddenly in the polls at the time of the municipal, cantonal and European elections, and the fall of the Communist Party was confirmed. The Socialist Party score dropped, and in 1986 it lost the elections. The 'socialist' reorganization of the French Left appeared as a definitive structural change, but the Right also reshaped itself at the same time.

The socialist thrust in the peripheral Catholic strongholds did not liquidate the Right in these regions, but weakened it sufficiently to destroy its traditional domination of the whole French Right. Even under de Gaulle, and in spite of the apparent strength of the UNR-UDT, the Catholic Right, invulnerable in its provincial strongholds, largely kept the upper hand. This made it possible in 1974 for Valéry Giscard d'Estaing to crush Jacques Chaban-Delmas in the first round. This period is now over. What remains of the Catholic Right is as fragile and unstable as the non-religious Right which occupies the centre of the country. At the June 1981 parliamentary elections which gave the Socialist Party an absolute majority, nearly half of the Catholic strongholds fell. The entire East (except Alsace) and the Brittany coastal area chose socialist deputies.

After the 1986 elections, the only element of the Right which covered the same area as traditional catholicism was, ironically enough, the Centre des Démocrates Sociaux (see map 42). However, the CDS represented only one of the components of the UDF, the weakest, with about 40

Map 42
CDS *députés* in 1986

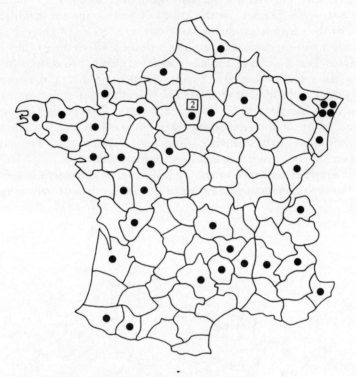

● One circle = one *député*

Based on the parliamentary election results of 16 March 1986, published in *Le Monde*.

deputies as against nearly 60 of the Parti Républicain (PR) (see map 43). The Radicaux of the UDF with 8 returned were a remnant rather than a movement. The geographical distribution of the PR deputies like that of the RPR deputies, no longer corresponded to that of catholicism (see map 44). In 1986 catholicism no longer controlled the Right.

For the first time, the Catholic and the non-religious Right showed comparable degrees of stability. Because the dechristianized territory in France was larger than the former Catholic territory, the non-religious Right for the first time absolutely dominated the entire Right. The reorganization process of the Left and Right is not yet over, and it is difficult to foresee what the final shape will be. Contrary to what appears on the media, the fundamental problem of present-day France is no longer the bitter clash between Right and Left. On the contrary, the dissolution of the two great dualisms running the conflict between Right and Left, one religious and the other economic, has created a void rather than a struggle. The love or the hatred of catholicism, the identification with, or the negation of, the working class are no longer comprehensible and important themes today, making it possible to organize or discipline passions. The division of France in two, or rather 'two times two', had given rise to two organized and stable conflicts, producing an impression of disorder at the level of the National Assembly, but providing a feeling of security for the citizen, because they were integrating factors. The disintegration of the relationship between the Left and the Right, the destabilization of the mental polarities providing structure and security, produce, in conventional sociological terms, anomy.

The Durkheimian type of anomy is defined as an absence of the rules and values that orientate the existence of an individual. It leads to mental

Map 43
Parti Républicain *députés* in 1986

●   One circle = one *député*

As for map 42.

Map 44
RPR *députés* in 1986

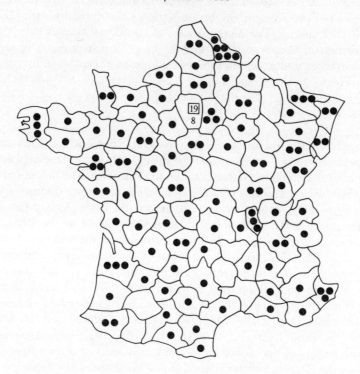

● One circle = one *député*

As for map 42.

vacillation. In France the years 1981–8 saw a brutal disorganization of the
economy, beliefs and political system, and gave rise to more ideological
anomy than the years 1945–80. The country was no longer threatened by
a violent antagonism between Left and Right, but on the contrary by their
incapacity to define a clear and acceptable political dialogue. A middle-
class society deprived of strong positive or negative religious beliefs,
France is today seeking conflictual themes, so that she may organize her
ideological life. The rise of the Front National is a transition type of
anomy, the temporary result of a disintegration of traditional themes
which marked the conflict between Left and Right. This xenophobic
thrust is not the only manifestation of such a transitory anomy. The rise
of electoral abstentionism also reveals the disarray of a large fraction of
the electorate. Ideological hesitations simultaneously affect both the

electorate of the Right and of the Left. Curiously, the rise of abstentionism seemed around 1984 the normal form of 'left' ideological anomy, and the vote for the Front National the normal form of 'right' ideological anomy. The disappearance of conflictual themes has, in fact, not completely suppressed the Left-Right clash, which seems in certain circumstances, and in certain sub-populations, to be capable of functioning in a void.

THE FRONT NATIONAL

France has never had an electorally powerful extreme Right. Even during the period between the two wars, the struggle of the Left against Fascism appeared to be largely mythical. In the 1936 elections, the united Left did not clash with a Fascist or Nazi party, but with a more traditional than ever right wing, rooted in its catholicism and having about ten years earlier rejected the Action Française at the request of the Pope. The sensational appearance of the Front National at the time of the 1984 European elections, with 11 per cent of the votes cast, was thus an undoubted historical novelty, although the rate of abstention was astonishingly high, amounting to 43 per cent of the registered voters.

It is not, however, possible to establish a true ideological link between the former extreme Right of 1900–40 – royalist, Catholic and anti-semitic – and the Front National of 1984–88, even if the personal careers of certain leaders of the movement reveal a continuity or a transition. What defines the FN much better is not the individual history of its leaders, nor the complex and hidden part of its doctrine, but the nature of its electorate. An analysis of the socio-cultural composition and aspirations of the FN electorate allows one to reach remarkably clear conclusions.

Electoral sociology and geography, in fact, rarely provide a chance of observing the instantaneous emergence of distinct and clear shapes. The stabilization of the Socialist and Communist Party maps, their insertion on deep anthropological parameters, was a gradual and lengthy process, including a great many unknown factors. On the other hand the coincidence of the FN with certain new aspects of French society's disintegration was immediate. As early as 1984, the vote for the FN lists showed a correlation coefficient of +0.89 between the proportion of votes cast and the presence of immigrant workers. This statistic defines the principal message of the FN, which is of a xenophobic type, but does not entirely describe it. In fact, the extreme right lists never obtained less than 5 per cent of the votes, even where the number of immigrants was insignificant. The extreme Right was also a vote against the Left given by voters who could no longer identify with the traditional Catholic or non-religious Right.

THE DISINTEGRATION OF THE WORKING CLASS

Few political maps are as clear as that of the Front National (see map 45). In 1984 the party obtained more than 8 per cent of the votes in a third of the country and in the whole of the Paris basin. One can recognize the immigration map and the trace of the Rhône–Rhine–Seine system, which we identified in our analysis of the socio-economic changes. The xenophobic phenomenon must be placed into the general socio-economic context, as it is not simply a racist mechanism. It is a racist mechanism in a local French society in the throes of disintegration. As we have seen, the

Map 45
The Front National in 1984

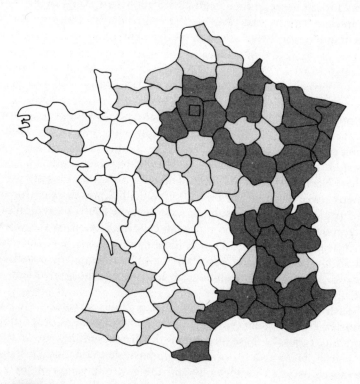

▮ Over 11 per cent of votes cast
▯ Between 8 and 11 per cent of votes cast

Based on the European parliamentary election results of 17 June 1984, published in *Le Monde*.

presence of immigrants is strongly correlated with that of executives and employees. Together, immigrant workers and the new middle classes effect a socio-cultural distancing of the workers of French origin, who were pushed to one side during the take-off years 1950–80. French workers who had not reached the level of secondary education made up a receptive, intermediate, destabilized layer – a potential area of anomy, to use Durkheim's expression.

All the public opinion polls show that these characteristics are in fact those of the FN electorate. It is more working-class, less educated than the average right-wing electorate, both RPR and UDF. It is certainly the most proletarian Right ever seen in France.

Curiously enough, the socio-economic disintegration of the working class disorganized the Right just as much as it destabilized the Left. The numerical weakening of the proletariat has been one of the immediate causes of the collapse of the Communist Party, particularly in the regions with nuclear family structures in the centre of the country. But this weakening has also led to division on the right.

THE DISINTEGRATION OF THE RIGHT

The opinion polls show conclusively that around 1984 the Front National electorate came from two different right-wing blocks. A minority fraction came from the Socialist Party. The communist electorate, in spite of its split, has remained resistant until 1986, but then produced electors for the FN in working-class areas. The polls also show that the RPR is distinctly more receptive than the UDF to the FN line. A careful analysis of the map confirms this result. At first sight the FN vote, typical of the immigration regions and the quickening disintegration of the working class, transcends the large French ideological regions, e.g. the eastern third of the country and the Paris basin in themselves constitute a summary of all the anthropological and ideological components that make up the country.

The Paris basin has an egalitarian, nuclear family structure; the East is dominated by the stem type; Provence includes a large proportion of community types. In these three zones the Front National vote is strong, but far from being in a majority. It is impossible to establish any sort of coincidence between its ideology and the systemic values of the zones concerned, which are variously egalitarian, non-egalitarian, authoritarian or liberal. The Front National is a transition phenomenon, a manifestation of anomy, hence it must be considered *void* at the systemic value level. It has no theory of man. The xenophobia of those who vote for it is empirical and concrete, the result of difficulties and clashes in daily life.

The Front National does not have Nazi anti-semitism or the aristocratic racism of the *ancien régime*, i.e. a complex and stable ideology with its literature and its dogmas.

The Front National can certainly be placed on the Left-Right scale. It belongs to the Right, but an empty, transitory, vague, perishable Right, because it is linked to an historical moment of disarray. Geographically, the Front National cuts into the non-religious and the Catholic Right at the same time. A thorough examination, however, shows that the dechristianized regions are more vulnerable than the former Catholic ones.

In certain *départements* the FN vote is distinctly higher than the proportion of immigrants would lead one to expect. In other cases it is the opposite. The *départements* where the vote for the FN is 'too high' in relation to the number of immigrants workers produce a very precise map of dechristianized France, spreading slightly east to the Meuse, the Vosges and the Haute-Saône. The whole of the Paris basin and Provence appear clearly. Reciprocally, the Catholic world, or what was up to very recently Catholic, enlarged by the addition of central Limousin, Socialist and Communist by tradition, seems more opposed to the FN message. This varied reaction of the Catholic and non-religious right-wing parties to the appeal of the Front National confirms fairly well the usual interpretation, which insists on the confused, culturally disordered character of the FN electorate.

Catholicism, as long as it exists, is indeed a powerful integrator, insisting on the submission of the individual to authority. This authority is at the service of moral values which are incompatible with xenophobic themes. The ideology of the non-Catholic Right is more vulnerable to this disintegration because of its liberalism and its tolerance of some moral indiscipline. It does not demand that the individual should submit.

In a different context and with less force, catholicism today opposes the Front National, just as it fought the Action Française, although the xenophobia of the FN cannot be compared to the anti-semitism of the Action Française; and of course catholicism is much weaker in 1984 than in 1926.

PARIS, LYON, MARSEILLE

The three largest French cities are, with their regions, the three great Front National strongholds. This topography in itself defines the movement as an urban phenomenon, often in fact associated with the human disintegration of certain suburbs, especially the large housing estates. The power of the FN in these three cities is not simply related to the number of immigrants. In Marseille, as along the entire Mediterranean coast, the number of immigrants is high, and the FN is exceptionally strong. In Lyon, the number of immigrants is distinctly higher than in Marseille, but the vote for the FN, although considerable, does not reach figures comparable to those of Provence. In Paris the situation is more complex. The FN vote is lower than the number of immigrants in the town and immediate suburbs would lead one to expect. It is, however, higher in the outer zone taken as a whole.

These differences of behaviour can be related to the sociological model which interprets the FN as a typical anomy phenomenon.

Lyon is at the heart of a traditionally Catholic region where the Church exercises a regional control. Marseille is at the heart of an absolutely dechristianized zone. The entire coast of Provence is indeed a very destabilized zone on the human level. It is a massive immigration area for people from within France, with a particularly fast disintegration of morals and values. Consequently, it is not surprising to see the Front National obtaining a score of 20 per cent of the votes cast along the whole coast, as against only 16 per cent in the Rhône region and a little less than 15 per cent round Paris.

In Paris, which belongs to the dechristianized part of the country, the vote for the FN is lower in the centre, because it is where the very concentrated elites control public opinion most closely and efficiently. On the contrary it is reinforced in the outskirts where the cultural autonomy of the working classes is higher. Here again the absence of moral authority acts in favour of the FN.

Opinion polls confirm that the FN electorate includes an even more strongly dechristianized component than that of the RPR. A study published in 1984 shows that at that date 34 per cent of the UDF electorate, 40 per cent of that of the RPR, but 53 per cent of that of the FN considered abortion to be a form of progress. The same source indicated that 47 per cent of those who backed the UDF or RPR favoured 'respect for the family, work and religion', as against only 35 per cent of those who voted for the FN.[1]

This resistance of catholicism is residual. In a dynamic perspective one must above all remember that the Catholic crisis was, quite as much as the destruction of the working class, one of the necessary conditions for the development of the FN. Before the war the Church was capable of completely fixing the extreme Right opinions of the electorate. Today she no longer has the strength to do so.

ABSTENTIONISM

The Left, like the Right, is stricken with a process of disintegration. The normal form of the 'anomy of the Left' appears to be abstention rather than radicalization. At the time of the 1984 European elections, many political analysts underlined the enormous increase of the rate of abstention in certain zones where the Communist Party had collapsed. More generally, the geography of abstention in France during the Eighties has shown up certain consistent situations indicating, like the FN vote, the existence of ideological anomy in certain regions.

In May 1984, the map of high abstention coincides more or less with that of the FN. Many of the zones of strength are common – the Paris region, the east Paris basin, Lorraine, Alsace, the vast Rhône–Alpes–Jura region and Bouches-du-Rhône. There are, however, two important differences. On the Mediterranean rim, excluding Marseille, abstention is not, in relation to the national average, as strong as the vote for the FN. In the West, on the contrary, between Calvados and Gironde, the rate of abstention is relatively higher than you might think from the strength of the FN vote.

So abstention is frequent in the regions of the East, where disintegration of the working class is a particularly important phenomenon. A very simple set of hypotheses allows one to explain the links and the differences between the extreme right vote and abstentionism. In the regions where foreign immigration is high, or the disintegration of the traditional working class very advanced, the FN vote represents a right-wing anomy, while an excessive abstentionism represents a left-wing anomy.

On the Mediterranean rim, a high point of social disintegration, the relative weakness of abstentionism in relation to the FN vote, which is very high, is due to the fact that in that region, and that region only, the FN simultaneously bites into the local right- and left-wing parties and unites the disarray of both. In the West the high rate of abstentionism reveals ideological dithering in a region where part of the electorate, between 1967 and 1981, moved from right to left, and where the absence of immigrants made a radicalization of the FN type rather difficult.

The FN vote and abstentionism are geographically related, as indeed they are in the opinion polls. A SOFRES analysis shows that the rise of abstentionism was particularly clear amongst workers between the municipal elections of 1977 and 1983.[2]

So it was a simultaneous disintegration of the Right and Left of the French political system that we witnessed between 1981 and 1984, rather than a worsening of the conflict between Right and Left. The traditional

Map 46
Abstention in 1984

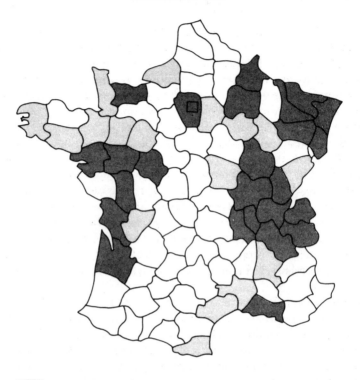

◼ Over 44 per cent of registered voters
▢ Between 42 and 44 per cent

As for map 45.

mythology is no longer adequate. The dissolution of the working class and catholicism destroyed the fundamental dualisms which traditionally structured the French nation. The rise of abstentionism on the left and the electoral strength of the extreme Right are two parallel movements, resulting from the same cause.

THE BRITISH PRECEDENT, A TRANSITION PHENOMENON

The result of temporary social disintegration, the FN is probably a transition phenomenon. It is backed by social groups which are in the process of disappearing, and in a way it is a final ideological spasm. Its influence over the national elites is practically nil. The FN, much more than the Communist Party or the Socialist Party, is cut off from the cultural, administrative and economic elites of the country. All the opinion polls show that its impact is particularly weak on the upper rungs of the civil service, the senior executives and the teachers. Its absence at the level of the national elites in itself defines the FN as a void, *a black hole*, rather than an ideological force. It radically distinguishes it from other extreme right movements, such as German Nazism or Italian Fascism, which succeeded in seducing the highest cultural sectors of their respective societies.

The FN has no future, because it *does not really exist*, or not in the same way as the Socialist Party, the Communist Party, the UDF or the RPR. It is not grafted on to any anthropological areas or particular systemic values. Moreover, it lacks a coherent ideology.

This optimistic forecast, founded on an analysis at a given moment, has not yet been completely verified by an electoral development. The parliamentary elections of 1986 and 1988 showed a certain resistance to the FN. They also underlined the stability of its geographical distribution. An analysis of the English social and political evolution of the seventies makes it possible to define in advance the development cycle of this type of movement, and to reinforce the prophecy that the FN will disappear relatively soon.

The disintegration process of the English working class was both more massive and earlier in date than that of its French counterpart. Large in numbers to start with, the English working classes shrank as early as the sixties. The National Front appeared at the beginning of the seventies, a Fascist and xenophobic movement, as surprising in the country of fundamental liberties as is the FN in the country of civil liberties.

The National Front programme was as meagre and empty as that of the FN. Its geographical implantation was similar, but less regular. The National Front did well during the 1974 municipal elections in the working-class areas affected by West Indian or Pakistani immigration. It obtained astonishing scores in certain constituencies. However, immediately after, at the 1974 general election it collapsed.

The history of the National Front is typical of a transitory anomy, a phenomenon of ideological disarray, linked to a process of social and cultural disintegration. It would be really astonishing if the fate of the FN were to be very different.

Conclusion – 1988

The fundamental problem of French political society is no longer the excessive violence of partisan conflicts. The electorate no longer identifies with the insurmountable antagonisms which in the past divided communism, socialism, the classic Right and Gaullism. Neither the split between the Right and the Left, nor the internal divisions within these tendencies, give the citizen that feeling of security which results from belonging to a camp or group. Today France suffers from the opposite ill. The absence of ideological identification has everywhere produced a feeling of unrest, and the impression that the system does not work, even when there is no threat of a serious crisis.

The disappearance of Right–Left dualism is the most obvious aspect of the disintegration of the old system. The politicians themselves, whose social function is to act out and dramatize political life, are no longer able to disguise the insignificance of the notion of Right and Left in the actual management of the country's affairs. Cohabitation did not result primarily from François Mitterrand's skill, Jacques Chirac's goodwill, or even from the hidden subtlety of the Fifth Republic's institutions, but from the immense desire of the French people to lessen the conflict between Left and Right. As early as 1986, more than 70 per cent of the French were in favour of cohabitation. The fact that the experiment failed in practice does not mean that the old struggle is about to be reanimated. It merely reveals that France cannot avoid the normal laws of human organization, and consequently cannot be led by two people at the same time.

In foreign policy the new consensus has been able to express itself fully and, one has to admit, in a positive fashion. In this department the party leaders do not feel a need to feign non-existent ideological antagonisms.

All the differences between Right and Left have not, however, disappeared. Manual workers, a social group that has less and less impact on French society, continue in the majority to vote for the Left. Practising Catholics – a species in the process of extinction – continue to vote mostly for the Right. But certain inversion phenomena already spotlight the changes in the nature of Right and Left. Most characteristic has been the move to the right on the part of the young in 1986, certainly for the first time in contemporary French history. In that year 50 per cent of those in the eighteen–twenty-four age-bracket voted for the Right. In 1978 62 per cent of the young had voted for the Left.[1] This astonishing change in behaviour (a left-wing orientation of youth was a constant of European and not merely French political life) must be interpreted with caution. The move to the right of the eighteen–twenty-four age-group does not mean that it was the nature of youth which had changed, but the nature of the Left. The desire for change, typical of youth everywhere and at all times, has departed from the Left. Formerly two alternative definitions of the Left were possible: in nineteenth-century France, in particular, the Left was either the party of the oppressed, or the party of change. Today a single definition remains valid – to belong to the Left is still perhaps to identify with the oppressed, i.e. the unemployed, the workers, the immigrants, the Neo-Caledonian natives – but it no longer represents a desire for change, i.e., in today's context, a necessary reorganization of the French productive system.

All this seems perfectly normal if one analyses the sociological and cultural mechanisms leading to the growth of the PS between 1967 and 1981. The new 'socialism' is in fact not motivated by the emergence of new forces. On the contrary, it feeds on the disintegration of other ideological forms – in this case catholicism and communism. As the result of an ideological collapse, the Socialist Party has very logically become the great French conservative party, with moreover a moderate form of conservatism. The Socialist Party does not wish the French productive system to transform itself too rapidly, which would be too painful for the social groups which have been dislocated by the economic events. The Fabius government, however, demonstrated that the new Socialist Party was ready to accept a slow rebuilding of the industrial system.

THE LEFT WITHOUT SOCIALISM

One must, in fact, say that the PS is not now socialist. It no longer expresses firm and clear aspirations towards economic intervention. The old Socialist Party, anchored in its strongholds of the South-West and the North, in authoritarian stem family regions, had a natural, spontaneous respect for the authority of the state. The new PS, which draws its electoral strength from the entire national territory, no longer depends exclusively on the concept and tradition of state control prevalent in the South-West and the North. Powerful in the heart of the Paris basin, which it shares, as it does all regions, with the new Right, it also now depends, perhaps above all, on the national liberal and egalitarian tradition, which is instinctively hostile to the authority of the state.

While it maintains its position in the peripheral regions, the PS should handle authoritarian values with care. It should in practice navigate between the contradictory aspirations of the various regional electorates. The same thing, however, can be said of the Right. Like the Socialist Party, the new Right is simultaneously situated in liberal and authoritarian zones, egalitarian nuclear family regions and others held by the stem family. In fact, the penetration of the Right into socialist Occitania, which was inaccessible to traditional Gaullism, silently reinforces the authoritarian state control component of the Right. That is why an exaggeratedly liberal policy of the Thatcher type puts the balance of the French Right in danger. The absence of hostility to denationalization, clear in the opinion polls, must not create illusions. Many of the difficulties of the Chirac government in 1987 came from the fear felt by a large section of its exaggerated militant and ideological rather than technical liberalism. Liberal dogmatism will never please the middle classes of the Midi, who veer towards the right, but for whom dependence on the state as provider of schools, *lycées*, jobs in the aeronautical industry and the Post Office is a secular tradition and a way of life. Generally speaking, the opinion polls show that acceptance of denationalization does not imply that the confidence which the French have in their great state administration has been shattered. The image of liberalism progresses without really affecting attachment to the state. The Bourse crisis of 1987 will no doubt not increase the love of the French for uncontrolled capitalism. The Right, like the Left, will in future have to steer a course between a social security system which is untouchable and an industrial system which can slowly be denationalized. Dominated at its centre by liberal values France on its periphery includes too many regions with a tradition of authoritarian ideology.

This continued impact of ideological values rooted in regional family traditions prevents a headlong rush of interventionism by the PS or of liberalism by the Right. It also makes it possible to explain the emergence in 1986 of an anti-racist Right, which is absolutely hostile to *Front National* ideas.

THE RIGHT WITHOUT RACISM

The model of interpretation which this book sets out makes a distinct difference between systemic values, rooted in the regional family systems – liberal or authoritarian, egalitarian or non-egalitarian – and the opposition between the Left and the Right, a secondary dualism characteristic of all political systems. This conceptual distinction enables us to understand why the French Right was unable, and did not wish, to question the universalist principles inherited from the French Revolution. The ideal which predominates in France, that all men are equal, is in fact linked neither to the Right nor to the Left. It takes its place in the anthropological structures which dominate the centre of the country, the Paris basin, with its family ideal of absolute equality between brothers. This fundamental idea of equality asserts itself both on the right and on the left. It prevents any racist deviation of the national system.

Immediately after the 1986 elections, the arrival of the Front National in the Chambre des Députés and the move to the right of the young, gave a momentary impression of a complete disintegration of the French political tradition. However, as early as December 1986, French youth, which was no longer left-wing, put a stop to the action of the government in the matter of a reform of the Nationality Code. The strike of university and secondary school students in the winter of 1986 became after the death of Malik Oussekine a demonstration of anti-racist beliefs, in the great republican tradition.

The disintegration of the party system, consequently, does not imply that national ideological traditions have been abolished. The Left–Right oscillations will continue, more and more rapidly, and more and more lacking in real significance. France, however, will never deviate towards excessive state interventionism, uncontrolled liberalism or racism. She will continue to be herself.

Postscript – 1990

Since this book was first published, just before the Presidential elections of 1988, the disintegration of the traditional French political system has proceeded on an even broader scale. The dissolution of the Catholic, communist, Gaullist and socialist ideologies and electorates appears clearly as an irreversible phenomenon, characteristic of the post-industrial age. The raising of the cultural level, the collapse of religious practice, the retreat of the working class indicate structural changes that are going to last. The France of the nineties will be more and more clearly dominated by salaried middle classes that dispense with strong religious beliefs and are incapable of deep ideological loyalties.

Since 1965–70, the crumbling of these ideologies has encouraged new political phenomena, often strange and sometimes alarming. Three main phases can be distinguished.

First of all, the Socialist Party has been the great beneficiary of this disintegration. Between 1967and 1978, its growth occurred at the expense of the Catholic Right. Between 1978 and 1981, it began to pick up the remains of the Communist Party.

The arrival in power of François Mitterrand opened up a second era. The failure of the Mauroy government halted the development of the Socialist Party and allowed Jacques Chirac to return briefly to power. These ups-and-downs of political life did not, however, stem the inexorable process of decomposition in the traditional electorates – Catholic, communist, Gaullist and socialist. And because electors freed of their ancient beliefs must go somewhere, the Front National appeared in 1984 to pick up individuals and groups thrown on the loose by the disintegration of traditional ideologies. The Presidential elections of 1988 marked the culminating point of this second phase. The Front National, having taken voters from Gaullism in the Paris region, and from communism on the Mediterranean coast, won 14.4 per cent of all votes cast, by penetrating Catholic and working-class circles in the east of France – or the ex-Catholic and ex-working-class circles, to be more exact.

During the third period, which began with the return of the Socialist Party to power in 1988, the new force in the political system was abstentionism. Opinion polls, however, revealed the existence of two forms of abstentionism, one of *consensus*, another of *alienation*. The consensual abstentionist no longer believes in the fundamental importance of the conflict between Left and Right. Considering the candidates of both tendencies to be reasonable and acceptable, and thereby finding some difficulty in choosing, he ends up by abstaining. An elector of this kind cannot be suspected of hostility to the democratic process. He merely carries the game of appeasement to its extreme limits. He takes advantage in his own way of the end of the ideological hatreds of the years 1945–65 which, by separating communists, Catholics, Gaullists and socialists, had made of French political life a series of autisms. The consensual abstentionist is satisfied with the world as it is. He belongs to the new, easy-going salaried middle classes. He will go and vote if he has time and, above all, if the electoral theme of the moment interests him.

The alienated abstentionist comes from another world, both social and moral. He belongs to the strata of society that are menaced and exasperated by the speed of the post-industrial transformations – small businesses, the independent artisan, the proletariat that is falling apart. His refusal to vote expresses a rejection of the world of today, a conscious hostility to modernity. If he hesitates, it is not between a gentle Left and a civilized Right, but between abstentionism and Lepenism.

The weakening of the Socialist Party is one of the characteristic features of this third phase, with abstentionism arising out of disintegration. The socialists certainly did not succeed in winning the loyalty of its new, originally Catholic, communist or Gaullist electorates. The European elections of 1989 confirmed these recent tendencies – rate of abstention 51 per cent, socialists stagnant at 23.4 per cent, Front National at 11.7 per cent, breakthrough by the ecologists who reached 10.6 per cent. The emergence of the Green electorate revealed the instability of the socialist electorate of Catholic origin. The map of the ecologist vote with its bastions in the east, the west and to the south-east of the Massif Central in fact reproduced fairly exactly the old map of religious practice – a sign of a permanent Catholic element within the central Left, in spite of the disappearance of religious practice. The Dreux by-election in November–December 1989, which resulted in the election of a Front National candidate, demonstrated the fragility of the socialist electorate with communist or Gaullist origins in the heart of the Paris basin, an old dechristianized region.

My original text of *La nouvelle France*, which I have left untouched, contained an exact description – prophetic, as it turns out – of this overall mechanism of decomposition. The evaluation of the Front National as a transitional phenomenon and a temporary result of ideological disintegration will, however, have seemed excessively optimistic today. Five to six years of life, 10–15 per cent of total votes cast, this shows roots of a kind, even if Lepenism, a minor ideology associated with post-industrial transition, appears more and more like a hot-headed form of abstentionism. On the Mediterranean coast, in the suburbs of Paris, in Alsace, the FN boasts of a few strongholds, with local electorates able to exceed 20 per cent of total votes cast. The relative under-estimation of the anti-foreigner problem resulted from under-estimation of the disarray caused in certain sectors by the transition to a post-industrial society.

The development of secondary education – which must be said to be a good thing – has extended the social stratification of the country. As a counterpart to the new qualified (both those with high-powered and more modest diplomas), there has grown up a corresponding category of non-qualified, whose economic future is very uncertain, and who may not gain access to the peaceful and cushy jobs of the tertiary sector. The cultural movement polarizes the social structure, creating in its lower echelons lasting feelings of resentment, of non-participation in the new world – in a word, of alienation.

This polarization of the social structure has been aggravated by the collapse of the two Churches – Catholic and communist – which played a role as support for the popular classes. The withdrawal of the Church and the PCF has got rid of an ideological rivalry, but has also led to a weakening of fundamental social bonds. These two institutions, equally universalist, also had the common task of assuring stable personal relations between different social strata. It was quite clear in the case of the Church, which wanted explicitly to cut across classes and associate in the same Faith workers, peasants and bourgeois. But communism, in spite of its doctrine of the class struggle, was in practice hardly less cross-class. It certainly attracted the workers, but in the Paris region, along the Mediterranean and on the north-west border of the Massif Central, it also appealed to certain peasants and a section of the middle classes. At the time of its greatest power, the PCF was in fact better installed among intellectuals and teachers than among the proletariat. The end of the Church and the PCF, therefore, signals the disappearance of those vertical lines between classes, which strengthened rather than weakened social cohesion, even if their most obvious effect was to produce two rival societies rather than a single one. French society in the years 1980–90, if more homogeneous than yesterday's on the material plane, with its workers and peasants owning motor-cars, television sets and refrigerators, has become much more stratified on the spiritual plane. More than formerly, French society is made up of a simple juxtaposition of socio-professional strata – separate worlds that do not communicate. At the top of the social ladder the élites believe in Europe and the world scale, while down below the workers are panicked by the acceleration of economic movement and sink into the most primitive racism. The duet of popular racism and the internationalism of élites epitomizes the new polarization of the social structure on the level of values.

The emergence between 1984 and 1990 of new political behaviour alien to traditional French culture has indeed been greatly facilitated by the break in the vertical links between élites and the less educated section of society. The anti-foreigner vote is one of the symptoms of this social malaise, which is particularly acute among the unqualified workers emerging from the disintegrating proletariat. But one can easily find non-political indications of this disarray. The rise in the suicide rate (+46 per cent between 1970 and 1984) and the spread of drug-taking are two particularly obvious symptoms.

It would be a serious mistake to regard the immigrant as the only, or even the main, determinant of the anti-foreigner vote. The presence of strangers is a necessary catalyst but not sufficient in itself to explain the harmful political features of the years 1984–90. The immigrant in France plays the sad role of scapegoat in a society that is for the moment sick from its transformations and ravaged by its own peculiar anxieties. The feelings of emptiness, isolation and frustration, which result from economic, religious and ideological change are not simply brought on by the immigration phenomenon.

Notes

PART I THE HIDDEN FORCES

1. The full title is *An Inquiry into the Nature and Causes of the Wealth of Nations.*

CHAPTER 1 SOUTH AND NORTH: TWO SYSTEMS

1. On Waldensian attitudes towards the Scriptures, see Tourn, G. 1980: *Les Vaudois*. Turin and Tournon: Réveil-Claudiana, 11–14, 55.

2. On Catharism and literacy, see Borst, A. 1984: *Les Cathares*. Paris: Payot, 120.

3. On the Reformation in Strasbourg, see Dickens, A. G. 1974: *The German Nation and Martin Luther*. London: Edward Arnold. On Protestantism in the north of France, see Deyon, S. and Lottin, A. 1981: *Les Casseurs de l'été 1566. L'iconoclasme dans le Nord de la France*. Paris: Hachette. For a cartographical approach to the survival of protestantism in the North, see Mours, S. 1966: *Essai sommaire de géographie du protestantisme réformé française au XVIIe siècle*. Paris: Librairie protestante, appendix 2 (map).

4. The *family system* is a system of values defining the affective relations between individuals. The *household* is a group of people sharing a dwelling and financial resources.

5. de Brandt, A. 1901: *Droit et Coutumes des populations rurales de la France en matière successorale*. Paris.

6. Borst 1984: 107–8.

CHAPTER 2 THE INFLUENCE OF EUROPE

1. Shipbuilding, in recession at the time, contributed little to this overall figure.

2. On English social history and individualism in the family, see Macfarlane, A. 1978: *The Origins of English Individualism*. Oxford: Basil Blackwell.

CHAPTER 3 THE CHURCH AND THE REVOLUTION

1. 1947: *Catéchisme à l'usage des diocèses de France*. Bourges: Tardy.
2. On this point, see T. Tackett's essential *La Révolution, l'Église, la France. Le serment de 1791*. Paris: Le Cerf, 1986.
3. Langlois, C. 1974: Les effectifs des congrégations féminines au XIXe siècle. De l'enquête statistique à l'histoire quantitative. *Revue d'histoire de l'Église de France*, January–June, 39–64.
4. Potel, J. 1977: *Les Prêtres séculiers en France. Évolution de 1965 à 1975*. Paris: Le Centurion. See especially the table on pp. 132–4.
5. Calvin, J. 1541: *Institution de la religion chrétienne*. Paris: Les Belles Lettres, 1961, III, 62.
6. Calvin 1541 (1961): III, 23.
7. In *Les Grands Écrits réformateurs*, Paris: Aubier-Montaigne, 1948, 255.

CHAPTER 4 THE PEASANTS

1. This is why few documents touch on farms in the South. The family farm did not, like the great estate, produce much in the way of documents to be stored in archives.
2. The area covered by the ninety French *départements* is too small to allow satisfactory statistical verification from the point of view of probability theory. In a forthcoming work on Europe there will be a statistically satisfactory verification of the link between rural proletariat and dechristianization.
3. Hence the name 'authoritarian family' (= stem family) which I have adopted in *The Explanation of Ideology. Family structures and social systems*, Oxford, Basil Blackwell, 1985.
4. Cf. de Brandt, A. 1901: *Droit et Coutumes des populations rurales de la France en matière successorale*. Paris, 186–9.
5. In this analysis of heredity customs in the West, I do not follow Jean Yver's *Essai de géographie coutumière*, even though this was a pioneer analysis of regional differences in France. The collections of customs analysed (dating from the sixteenth century) often apply their formal rules to areas that are too extensive for an anthropologist. The definition area for heredity customs is not the province, but a geographical zone that can be either greater or smaller. No one would think nowadays of describing family systems in nineteenth-century France with the aid of no other source than the Code Civil, which is egalitarian in conception but masks the inegalitarian systems of the South. It is just as unreasonable to use the customary law of sixteenth-century Brittany to give a complete picture of Breton heredity customs. De Brandt's method, which for a later date descends to a more restricted level (the *arrondissement*), is more reliable. It invalidates the general egalitarian view put forward by Yver by stressing the absence of division in kind in the West. It enables us also to identify inegalitarian customs and the stem family in most of Breton-speaking Brittany, thus confirming the analysis of households drawn from the 1975 census. De Brandt

also locates pockets of strict egalitarianism, and even communal sharing, in Côtes-du-Nord, which is a very interesting exception because this *département* has been the only one in the West to show an overall swing to the left (cf. Brandt 1901: 184–5).

The data provided by Jean Yver therefore seem more trustworthy when they cover a narrow area. For example, one can accept without difficulty primogeniture in the regions of Caux, Ponthieu and the Boulonnais. One can also accept the existence of *coutumes préciputaires* (i.e. allowing the favouring of one child) between Amiens, Lille and Cambrai. In all these cases the analysis is focused at the necessary sub-provincial level. (Yver, J. 1966: *Égalité entre héritiers et Exclusion des enfants dotés. Essai de géographie coutumière.* Paris: Sirey.)

6. The concept of share-cropping is a perversion of the ideal of equality. The landowner and the peasant divide up, fifty-fifty, the product of the harvest. This absurd vertical matching conceals a mechanism of exploitation that is particularly harsh.

7. Le Play, F. 1879 (2nd edn): *Les Ouvriers européens.* Tours: Mame, V, 6, 255–322.

8. 1901: 42.

9. Dussourd, H. 1980 (new edn): *Au même pot et au même feu. Études sur les communautés familiales du Centre de la France.* Paris: Maisonneuve et Larose.

10. 1901: 252–61.

CHAPTER 5 FAMILY AND IDEOLOGY

1. For a world-wide formulation of this hypothesis, see Todd, E. 1985: *The Explanation of Ideology. Family structures and social systems.* Oxford: Basil Blackwell.

2. Rousseau, J.-J.: *Du contrat social.* Paris: Le Seuil, 'Points Politique', 1977, 172–3.

3. New edn 1980: *Tableau politique de la France de l'Ouest.* Paris: Slatkine, 413–24.

4. Siegfried, 1980: 397.

5. Todd, E. 1976: *Seven Peasant Communities in Pre-Industrial Europe.* Unpublished University of Cambridge thesis, 71–2.

6. Freud, S. 1962: *The Future of an Illusion.* London: Hogarth Press.

7. Calvin, J. 1541: *Institution de la religion chrétienne.* Paris: Les Belles Lettres, 1961, III, 67–8.

CHAPTER 6 THE CATHOLIC RIGHT

1. New edn 1980. Paris: Slatkine.

2. 1970. Paris: Armand Colin.

CHAPTER 7 SOCIALISM

1. Rials, S. 1983: *Le Légitimisme*. Paris: PUF, 28.
2. For a detailed account of the debates within the SFIO and the ensuing splits, see Sternhell, Z. 1983: *Ni droite, ni gauche*. Paris: Seuil.
3. Indeed, in Spanish Guipuzcoa all Basques are considered noblemen.
4. Pyrénées-Atlantiques includes the French Basque country and Béarn. The Basque country is more strongly right-wing than Béarn.
5. Agulhon, M. 1970: *La République au village*. Paris: Plon, 377.
6. See Henry, L. 1972: Fécondité des mariages dans le quart sud-ouest de la France de 1720 à 1829. *Annales ESC*, May–June and July–October, especially 915 and 1001.

CHAPTER 8 GAULLISM

1. In particular at the time of the 1851 plebiscite. See Bluche, F. 1980: *Le Bonapartisme*. Paris: NEL, map p. 275.
2. New edn 1982: Paris: Aubier, 322–33.
3. Seiler, D. 1980: *Partis et familles politiques*. Paris: PUF, 206 and 352.
4. See Bernstein, S. 1980: *Histoire du Parti radical*. Paris: Presses de la Fondation nationale des sciences politiques, I, map p. 303.

CHAPTER 10 THE TRADITIONAL FRENCH POLITICAL SYSTEM

1. During the 1920s the Parti Radical, very powerful at the time, was dominant simultaneously in the South-west, which was to turn socialist, and at the heart of the Paris basin, which was to swing to Gaullism (Bernstein, S. 1980: *Histoire du Parti radical*. Paris: Presses de la Fondation nationale des sciences politiques, I, map p. 303).

CHAPTER 11 THE END OF THE MANUAL WORKERS

1. Marsh, D. C. 1965: *The Changing Social Structure of England and Wales, 1871–1961*. London: Routledge and Kegan Paul, 202.

CHAPTER 14 THE THIRD CRISIS OF CATHOLICISM

1. The proportion of women taking the pill only reached 20 per cent around 1976. The proportion of women using the coil only reached 10 per cent around 1980. On these points see Léridon, H. (ed.) 1987: *La Deuxième Révolution contraceptive*. Paris: PUF, 'Cahier de l'INED', 117, especially p. 72.

CHAPTER 16 THE REVENGE AND DISINTEGRATION OF THE RIGHT

1. SOFRES opinion poll in *L'Extrême Droite en France*, 'Dossiers et documents du *Monde*', 111, p. 3.
2. SOFRES: *Opinion publique 1984*, 129 (towns of more than 30,000 inhabitants).

CONCLUSION – 1988

1. SOFRES 1987: *L'État de l'opinion. Clés pour 1987*. Paris: Le Seuil, 230.

Index